**Praise for Zoe FitzG**

Imperfect En
*A Daughter's Story of Love, L*

"I could quote from the book all day . . . but instead I'll just recommend that those intrigued by the subject spend a little time with the ailing but ferocious Margaret and her daughters. A decision to die can sound romantic or it can sound repugnant. Carter shows us what it was like in reality."

—Paula Span, *The New York Times*

"Carter's memoir about her terminally ill mother's decision to end her own life becomes a bittersweet tale of how Carter and her sisters coped with their mother's botched efforts, their own sibling rivalries, the ongoing controversy over assisted suicide, and the hard, final task of acceptance."

—*Elle*

"A poignant memoir of a daughter's struggle to accept her mother's death."

—*Kirkus Reviews*

"Carter tackles a depressing subject with dark humor and heart."

—*Booklist*

"Zoe FitzGerald Carter delivers a moving and darkly funny account of this elusive and often grim topic."

—LiteraryMama.com

"*Imperfect Endings* raises difficult questions about love and loyalty, but it is written with such style and sympathy that it is difficult to put down."

—Frances Dinkelspiel, "City Brights," SFGate.com

"In her wise and moving memoir, journalist Zoe Carter tackles a difficult subject—her mother's decision to end her own life after years of severe illness. Many of us will find ourselves facing this kind of dilemma as our parents move toward death, and I cannot imagine a better guide than this thoughtful, compassionate book."

—Julie Metz, author of *Perfection: A Memoir of Betrayal and Renewal*

"A beautifully written story of pain and loss, spiked with subtle humor and gentle wisdom."

—Judy Bachrach, TheCheckoutLine.org, and author of
*Tina and Harry Come to America: Tina Brown, Harry Evans, and the Price of Power*

"Zoe Carter is a luminous writer with a dramatic story to tell. With wisdom, poetry and dark humor, Zoe describes her ailing mother's courageous decision to end her life. In years to come, plenty of sons and daughters will face the same moral and practical dilemmas as Zoe's family; *Imperfect Endings,* with its wit and love, will provide an invaluable resource, as well as remain a fascinating, fabulously compelling read."

—Jennifer Finney Boylan, author of *She's Not There* and *I'm Looking Through You*

"I love this book! Zoe Carter has taken what could be a very sad story and turned it into something beautiful and incredibly insightful. Her portrayal of her mother is wonderful, and reveals in moving and illuminating detail a slice of Washington life."

—Kate Lehrer, author of *Confessions of a Bigamist: A Novel*

# imperfect
# endings

*a daughter's story of love, loss, and letting go*

## Zoe FitzGerald Carter

SIMON & SCHUSTER PAPERBACKS

NEW YORK   LONDON   TORONTO   SYDNEY

Simon & Schuster Paperbacks
A Division of Simon & Schuster, Inc.
1230 Avenue of the Americas
New York, NY 10020

First Simon & Schuster trade paperback edition March 2011

SIMON & SCHUSTER and colophon are registered
trademarks of Simon & Schuster, Inc.

For information about special discounts for bulk purchases,
please contact Simon & Schuster Special Sales at
1-866-506-1949 or business@simonandschuster.com.

The Simon & Schuster Speakers Bureau can bring authors
to your live event. For more information or to book an event,
contact the Simon & Schuster Speakers Bureau at
1-866-248-3049 or visit our website at www.simonspeakers.com.

*Designed by Kyoko Watanabe*

Manufactured in the United States of America

1   3   5   7   9   10   8   6   4   2

The Library of Congress has cataloged the hardcover edition as follows:

Carter, Zoe FitzGerald.
Imperfect endings / Zoe Fitzgerald Carter
p. cm.
1. Carter, Zoe FitzGerald—Family. 2. Hemlock Society U.S.A. 3. Suicide—
United States. 4. Terminally ill—United States. 5. Parents—United States—Death.
6. Right to die—United States. 7. Mothers and daughters—United States.
8. Authors, American—California—Biography.
R726.C35 2010
616.85'8445—dc22          2009022245

ISBN 978-1-4391-4824-2
ISBN 978-1-4391-4831-0 (pbk)
ISBN 978-1-4391-5421-2 (ebook)

*For Anna and Mira*

# Note to the Reader

Everyone in this book has been given a pseudonym, with the exception of a few public figures and myself. In some cases, distinguishing details about these individuals have been changed as well. Furthermore, while I have made a good-faith effort to convey the truth or essence of everything that I recount, certain events and scenes have been compressed in order to better meet the needs of the story. Finally, as is the case in all memoirs, dialogue is by necessity an approximation, especially in scenes from the distant past.

imperfect
endings

*Don't leave me alone in the twilight*
*Twilight is the loneliest time of day*

—THE BAND

# View

I don't have to answer the phone. On my knees in the bathroom, daughters just settled into the tub, I have the perfect excuse to ignore it. Let the machine pick it up instead. But I push off my knees and head for the door, my brain several steps behind my body as it usually is by this time of day.

Only then do I pause, reluctant to leave the steamy warmth of the bathroom, the giddiness of my naked children who are lolling at one end of the tub, pouring water on each other. At four and eight, Lane and Clara are hardly at risk for drowning, but I remind them to be careful—keep the water in the tub, hold off on the shampoo— and step out into the bedroom.

Shading my eyes from the blinding late-day sun, I cross the room, glancing out at the glimmering strip of the San Francisco Bay and, just beyond it, the hazy outline of the Golden Gate. Four years on the West Coast and this view of water and sky still thrills me.

I pick up the phone, annoyed with myself for answering it, sure it's someone calling to either sell or beg something from me.

"Oh, there you are! Have I caught you at a bad time?" It's my mother. Her voice sounds cheerful and a little excited, as if she has good news. "I was just looking at my calendar and wondering if you could come to D.C. the first weekend of February."

"I'm not sure. I'll have to check. What's up?" I drop onto the bed, heart beginning to clamor. I know what's up.

"Well gosh, honey, I've been trying to find a good time to *end things* as you know, and I was hoping that weekend might work for you. I haven't called your sisters yet, but of course I want them here too. And your girls if you can bring them. I'm still working out the details, but—"

"Jesus, Momma," I hiss, cupping my hand over my mouth so Clara and Lane can't hear me. "You make it sound like a family reunion!"

"Well, there's no reason to get huffy, Zoe," she says. "I can't plan anything unless I know you girls are available. Can you just take a quick peek at your calendar?"

"No, I can't! I'm in the middle of giving my kids a bath, I don't have my calendar, and I can't think about this right now."

"Fine." Her irritation is palpable and for a moment there is silence. "So when can you call me back?"

I want to say *never*. I will never call her back if she insists on talking about killing herself. But I think of her lying alone in her big empty bed, of her dying alone because her daughters weren't willing to show up, and my petulance turns to shame.

"I'll call you tomorrow."

"Okay, sweetie." Her voice is cheerful again. "That would be great. Talk to you then!"

I stand up and look out the window, the sounds of splashing and laughter faint in the background, as if my daughters—or, for that matter, my entire life—had just receded into the distance. I watch the last burning rays of sunlight disappear behind Mount Tamalpais, the vast, glorious landscape slowly turning from gold to gray.

# Arrival

Despite my assurances that I'm perfectly happy to take a cab from Dulles Airport, my mother insists on hiring a car to pick me up. The driver is a slim, good-looking man in a dark suit, so sleek and well groomed that I'm immediately conscious of my wrinkled Gap capris and unbrushed hair.

"Any bags?" he asks, voice as smooth and carefully modulated as his appearance. He glances around the baggage claim, now teeming with fellow passengers from California, most of them as casually dressed and disheveled as I am. Funny how they'd seemed perfectly presentable at the boarding gate in San Francisco, but here at Dulles, under that self-important wave of ceiling, we've all turned to bumpkins.

I indicate my scuffed leather tote overflowing with spare clothes, books, and a large box of See's assorted nut chocolates—a gift for my mother—and to my embarrassment, he takes it from me. Together we make our way out of the terminal.

Sliding into the back of his gleaming black Town Car, I collapse against the thickly cushioned leather seats and close my eyes. Maybe this car service thing was a good idea after all.

"So, how's Mrs. Draper?" the driver asks, turning to look at me. "We haven't heard from her for quite a while."

"My mother?" I sit up, blinking my eyes, which are blurred and sticky from my contact lenses. "Uh, about the same, I'd say. Just staying a little closer to home these days."

"Hmm." He seems to consider my response and I wonder if he thinks I'm holding something back, which of course I am. But I can't exactly say, "Oh well, you know, my mother's pretty focused on dying right now. She just can't quite figure out how to do it. In the meantime, she's taken to her bed."

The fact is, none of us had taken her very seriously last summer when she first started talking about ending her life. Diagnosed with Parkinson's in her mid-fifties—almost twenty years ago—she was tired of the endless drug cycles, the constant revving up and slowing down, the inability to stay in one state long enough to just *forget* the damn disease. But kill herself? It seemed unlikely. My two sisters and I chalked it up to a mild depression and near-pathological need to be in control.

But then she joined the Hemlock Society and began proposing actual "death dates," the most recent being May first. (The previous two were abandoned due to the lack of a "good, solid plan.") And this weekend she's arranged to have a volunteer from the Hemlock Society's "Caring Friends" program fly in from Oklahoma to discuss how they might help her do the deed. He's due in tomorrow morning.

"Well, I'm real glad to hear she's all right," the driver continues, thoughtfully. "We were talking about her just before she rang yesterday, wondering if she was okay. We used to pick her up two, three times a month. Take her out to Baltimore to see her aunt. She's a special lady, your mom."

I'm touched that the driver—his name is Derrick—has asked

about my mother and called her "special," although I realize Capitol Car and Limo may have been merely wondering whether to close the file on her. On the other hand, I've seen her inspire this kind of interest and affection from strangers my whole life.

My mother has a doe-eyed, romantic quality that people find irresistible: Men want to protect her, women want to be her friend, and everyone agrees she's stylish and beautiful. With her dark eyes and hair, her prominent cheekbones and chin, she looks like Jackie Kennedy, only a taller, rangier version, not so coiffed and demurely feminine. Even now, with her spine buckled from osteoporosis, her face gaunt and shuttered from illness, she projects an appealing Victorian fragility.

What's funny is that this image of her couldn't be further from the truth. My mother's shy and vulnerable demeanor belies a stubborn, unsentimental nature. Although quick to admire people whose intellectual or artistic accomplishments she deems worthy, she can be casually brutal in her assessments of friends and strangers alike. My entire life I've heard her describe people as "terribly angry" or "not very bright," and she once remarked about her own goddaughter that she hadn't amounted to a hill of beans. Yet somehow this quality is never apparent to people outside our family. Even her closest friends seem to view her as a frail and exotic flower permanently in need of their care.

The conversation tapers off as we speed up the long, unlit parkway that runs beside the Potomac River, and I'm grateful for these last few moments of darkness and quiet. My oldest sister, Katherine, will be at my mother's house by now—she flew in from Rhode Island earlier today—and I'm glad she's here but also nervous about seeing her. Relations between us have never been easy and they've become especially fraught since my father's death seven years ago.

Closing my eyes against the onslaught of passing headlights, I can't help wishing it was my other sister, Hannah, meeting me here.

"I can't do it," Hannah said when I called to ask. "Dan has to travel to Toronto for a music festival, Fiona has a school play, and I'd have to take Evie with me. And, frankly, flying with Evie is a nightmare." Hannah's two-year-old was famous for throwing up on planes. "Besides, if Momma sticks to her current plan of killing herself on May first, I'll be down there soon enough."

"But what about the Hemlock guy?" I asked her.

"Death's little helper?"

I laughed. "Actually, I think they're called exit guides. But whatever he's called, Momma wants us there when he comes."

"I'm sorry, Zoe. You're going to have to deal with this one by yourself."

I wanted to remind her that I'd been to D.C. for ten days in February while she hadn't been since Christmas, but I couldn't bear for there to be any friction between us right now. Just fifteen months older than me, Hannah has always been my closest ally in the family, but since my mother started this death and dying kick, we've become like two halves of the same brain. A cross-continental support network of two. "Maybe I'll see if Katherine can come," I said finally, trying not to sound reproachful.

"Don't hold your breath. I doubt Katherine's going to show up for Momma's death any more than she did for Poppa's. Why ask her?"

But I did ask her, and to my amazement, Katherine agreed to come.

My stomach lurches as the car swings onto Key Bridge and heads toward the glowing lights and cobblestone streets of Georgetown. I focus on the sound of the tires, the cool touch of glass against my forehead. A dread, so familiar that it's almost comforting, fills me as we make the ascent up Wisconsin Avenue, past the soaring, lit façade of the National Cathedral, and then onto Ordway Street.

I peer up at my mother's enormous gray stucco house, looming like a dilapidated ocean liner over the street below. The front door swings open and Katherine steps out under the bright porch light. Her hair, fair like mine, reaches almost to her waist. She stands, eyes shaded, looking down the wide slate stairs at the overgrown ivy bank spilling onto the sidewalk. Her posture is tense and watchful, as if she's been waiting for someone to come and take her away. To rescue her from what lies inside.

# Prescription

"You made it," my mother says in a small, happy voice as I walk into her bedroom. After giving me an awkward hug in the hall, Katherine had headed back toward the kitchen. "How was your flight?"

"Fine. No major delays. Just the usual run-of-the-mill annoyances," I say, going over to the bed to kiss her. Her sheepdog, Bruno, leaps up, barking ferociously at my approach, and then, recognizing me, wags his tail and flops back down on the bed. My mother reaches up and grabs my shoulders. Her grip is tight and surprisingly strong, although I can feel the deep tremors running through her arms.

Releasing me, she sinks back onto her pillow. I pull the thick blue and white quilt back around her shoulders and adjust the cord to the oxygen tank next to her bed. Despite her strong features, her still-lovely cheekbones, she looks oddly childlike with the pink ruffle of her flannel nightgown framing her face. Her once dark and luxurious hair lies flat against her head and I notice that the gray has crept almost to her ears. After forty years of meticulously coloring her hair, my mother is finally going natural.

"How're you feeling?"

She wrinkles her nose. "Well, I was trying to make this darn list all day for that Hemlock fellow who's coming tomorrow and now my arm and shoulder are killing me."

"What list?" I ask, instantly wary.

"They ask you to give a summary of all your medical conditions. So they can evaluate you."

"You mean, decide if you're sick enough to die?"

I say it lightly but deliberately, wanting to hurt her. I realize I've been half-expecting her to chicken out, cancel the appointment, and am angry that she hasn't. I could be at home right now enjoying a quiet Friday night with my husband, Jack, and my children, instead of back in D.C., embroiled in my mother's suicide plans.

But she only laughs. "Yes, exactly. They don't want you killing yourself if you've only got a hangnail."

I smile, concede. I haven't seen my mother this chipper for weeks. "Well, I hope you came up with a worthy document."

"My problems are actually pretty impressive, you know."

It's true. My mother has congestive heart failure, asthma, chronic pulmonary disease, osteoporosis, arthritis, and low blood pressure, which causes her to occasionally and unexpectedly pass out. But Parkinson's is still the biggie and there's no question it's getting worse. She's had several episodes of aphasia—basically a Parkinson's-induced brain logjam that renders you incapable of speech—and has recently begun experiencing bouts of uncontrolled writhing, or dyskinesia, that indicate her Parkinson's meds are beginning to fail.

She also suffers from the occasional memory glitch or crossed wire. In one particularly disturbing episode last summer, she insisted I was born on New Year's Eve because she remembered "all the nurses were having a party and couldn't be bothered with me." I was, in fact, born in late March. Dementia is a common side effect of Parkinson's and these moments frighten and mortify her.

"I do know. It's amazing you're still around."

"Right. Well, of course, that's the problem."

Out of both wit and energy now, she shuts her eyes. Her features instantly retract, giving her a blank, stern expression like the statues of the dead saints in the underground vaults of the National Cathedral, where my friends and I used to wander after school. It's an expression I'm familiar with from watching her sleep (so unlike the lax softness of my children's sleeping faces), and I realize that our conversation has been exhausting for her.

Glancing over at her bookshelves, I skim across the familiar titles: *Who Dies?*, *The Good Death*, *The Tibetan Book of Living and Dying*, and, of course, *Final Exit* by Hemlock Society founder Derek Humphry. There are even multiple copies of her favorites so she can hand them out to friends. My husband calls it the Library of Death, which is more appropriate than he realizes. Hidden behind those books, on a shelf just below eye level, are sixty tablets of Seconal, a potent sleeping aid. More than enough to cause permanent sleep.

It was last June when my mother and I went to see Dr. Harmon, a local psychiatrist and prominent member of the Hemlock Society. My mother had just joined the society, and someone in their Texas headquarters had suggested she approach Dr. Harmon to see if she was a good candidate for "self-deliverance," as Humphry calls it, and, if so, to request a prescription for Seconal.

I agreed to go with her, although the idea of my mother committing suicide was pretty theoretical back then, kind of like our yearly disaster drills in Northern California meant to prepare us for the "Big One." Still, I was impressed that she'd found this death-friendly doctor and made an appointment with him.

Driving to Dr. Harmon's office on a tree-lined residential street near Dupont Circle, my mother kept looking over the notes she'd scrawled on the back page of her weekly planner and I could see that she was nervous. She hates public speaking and likes to prepare herself before meetings and even phone calls. I had more than once found cryptic comments like "ask why angry" next to my initials or one of my sisters' initials, on her calendar.

"Don't worry, he's going to love you," I whispered as we walked up the path to Dr. Harmon's pretty, white-shingled house. "Just be your normal, charming self."

"Thanks," she said drily, clutching my arm. "If it was only that easy."

We were almost at the top of the stairs when a woman in somber, nondescript clothes and an old-fashioned bouffant hairdo came through the door. I pegged her as a retired government secretary or administrator from one of the drab apartment buildings on nearby Connecticut Avenue. She hurried by without looking at us, leaving a palpable cloud of melancholy in her wake.

A tall, white-haired man appeared and waved us into a large, comfortable room with sofas and bookshelves. He was relaxed and gracious—not what I'd expected at all. I wondered why this attractive, likable man was so deeply involved in the world of sickness and death. A traumatic experience with a parent or spouse? A patient? Or perhaps he was anticipating a difficult death himself, although he looked healthy enough, youthful and fit despite the white hair.

"So," he said, smiling at both of us. "Why don't you tell me why you're here?"

My mother's jeans-covered knees did a little dance at the edge of the sofa, where she had perched looking precarious and uncomfortable. It took several throat clearings before she said, "I wanted to talk to you about ending my life. Or at least having the option to end it."

"I understand." He gave her a kind smile. "Can you tell me why you might want that option?"

My mother glanced over at me and I nodded encouragingly. "I'm seventy-five. I've had Parkinson's since my fifties and, as I'm sure you know, it's a degenerative disease. Things have gotten much harder for me in the last year—even walking is getting difficult. And it's only going to get worse."

Once again she paused, pushing down on her knees with her elbows to keep them still. She looked small and hunched, her still-abundant dark hair overwhelming her pale, sharply boned face. I hated seeing her so vulnerable and added, "My mother has some other medical conditions she wanted to mention."

She smiled gratefully and went through her list of ailments—the heart problems, the asthma. When she finished, we both looked over at Dr. Harmon, who sat, fingers laced and resting against his chin, clearly waiting for her to continue.

"I don't . . . ," she began, then stopped.

"Go on, please."

"I don't know when I'll be ready to end my life, but I feel like there's going to be a time when I don't want to go any further. I can see what lies ahead."

"Can you tell me what that is?" Dr. Harmon said softly.

"Well, I've belonged to a Parkinson's support group for years. Several of the people in my group have died. Friends of mine. They were in very bad shape at the end. Completely helpless really. I don't want to go through that."

I'd known about the support group, but this was the first I'd heard about any of its members dying. I felt an unexpected surge of tenderness.

"Let me ask you something, Mrs. Draper," Dr. Harmon said, leaning forward and giving her a serious look. "Would you say you're depressed?"

"No." My mother gave a little toss of her head, as if to demonstrate her point. "I do feel lonely sometimes. My husband died a few years ago and my children live in other cities. But I have friends and I don't believe I'm depressed."

Dr. Harmon turned to me. "How about you? Do you think your mother is depressed?"

I wanted to say, yes, of course she's depressed. Why else would she be talking to you about ending her life? But I simply said, "No,

I guess not. I would say my mother's unhappiness is pretty reasonable given her situation."

"Okay." Dr. Harmon placed both his hands on his knees with a brisk slap, as if getting ready to rise. "You've come to get a prescription for Seconal. Am I right?"

"Yes," my mother said, the word exploding out of her as if she'd been holding her breath. "That's exactly right."

"Good. I'll write it for you and you can get it filled today if you wish. Wait a couple of months and then get it refilled. Your third refill should be two months after that. We don't want to alarm the pharmacist. In the end, you'll have sixty pills, plenty to cause death. If you have any other questions, I'm happy to answer them."

My mother looked over at me, clearly pleased, but I felt a strong urge to argue with the charming doctor. I was still reeling from the abrupt interjection of Seconal into the conversation, the bald mention of death. Was there really nothing more to discuss before he ran off for his prescription pad?

"Um, well, I have a question," I said, avoiding my mother's gaze. "I'm not exactly clear how you make the decision to give—or not give—someone a prescription for Seconal."

"That's an excellent question," he said, sitting back in his chair and giving me his crinkly-eyed smile. "I don't give prescriptions to everyone, but your mother is dealing with a very serious disease that, as she knows, is going to worsen over time. And I don't believe she should have to live any longer or suffer any more than she herself wants to."

I nodded, still wary.

"I don't believe she's in a state of acute stress or depression," he continued, "and you've confirmed that for me. She also seems mentally competent and fit. If I had any question about this, I wouldn't give it to her. The woman you passed on your way in, for example, came for the same thing and I said no."

I pictured the drab woman who'd passed us without speaking and couldn't help asking, "Why did she want it?"

Not expecting him to answer, I was surprised when he said, "She was recently diagnosed with a degenerative eye condition that will eventually lead to blindness. Understandably, she was upset. But I didn't think it was the right time for her to make such an important decision."

"But you do think it is the right time for my mother?" I persisted, still amazed that he could be so certain.

"Yes. I do."

"Momma?" I say softly, coming closer to the bed and letting my hand fall on her arm. "I'm going to go get something to eat. With Katherine. I'll come back and check on you in a little while."

"That would be nice, Zoe. Thank you. You can leave the light on. And Zoe?"

"Yes?"

"I'm glad you're here . . . Katherine too."

"Hmm." I lean over and kiss her forehead. "See you soon."

But I don't leave. I stand, watching her sleep, thinking of all the conversations we've had about various ways to die since that meeting with Dr. Harmon. Overdose on Seconal or morphine? Get someone from the Hemlock Society to help her, or do it on her own?

The strange thing is that, as a child, I was obsessed with exactly these sorts of questions. I drove my family crazy asking: *Would you rather be shot or burned? Drowned or hung? Dropped from an airplane or left in the desert with no water?* The grotesque nature of these questions was as lost on me then as it is lost on my mother today.

I reach over and smooth my mother's hair, taken by a sudden fear that she's going to die tonight and I'll be left with all my doubts and grievances, my unbecoming anger.

# Silver Dagger

SPRING 1967

We were playing Riding School with three large wooden sawhorses in the backyard when my mother came around the house looking cross.

"Girls! I just got a call from someone down on Newark Street. They've got Puppy and Bowser. They found them knocking over garbage cans. Which one of you let them out?"

We turned and looked at the gate that led out to Ordway Street. It was standing wide open. The three of us had been in and out of it numerous times to pick cherries off the tree that grew on the bank outside the yard.

"Katherine? Hannah? C'mon now. Whoever let them out has to go get them—now! I have the address right here."

I had no idea when the dogs left, but I remembered seeing Hannah's dog, Bowser, sniffing something down by the front sidewalk. Had I let them out?

But my mother wasn't looking at me. They were not my dogs.

I couldn't get a dog until next year when I turned eight. It wasn't my fault.

"Hannah, you know you let them out," Katherine said in her bored, it's-all-the-same-to-me voice. "So you better run and get them."

"Oh God, Katherine, you're such a liar!" Hannah yelled, turning to glare at her. "If anyone let them out, it was you. Besides, Bowser wouldn't run away if Puppy didn't go first. *You* go get them." Hannah's dark curly hair was plastered to her pale face and there was dirt and cherry juice on her chin. We'd been playing for several hours and, for once, Hannah and Katherine had been getting along.

Katherine just looked at Hannah, her eyes half-closed, smiling her bored smile and tossing one of her long blond braids behind her shoulder.

My mother watched this, looking deeply annoyed.

"Zoe?" she said, turning to me, her voice less angry. "You tell me. Which one of them let the dogs out?"

My face felt stiff and hot and I could sense both my sisters staring at me. I hated it when my mother did that, made me tell her what happened after they got in a fight or broke something or let the dogs out. But I was the one she trusted, the good one. The one who told the truth.

Except she was wrong, I wasn't good—or truthful. I wanted to tell her this, but I knew she'd be disappointed. So I pretended I *was* good so she would love me the best and think I was special.

"Um, I th-think it was Hannah," I said, looking at the ground, bracing myself for Hannah's wails. "But I'll go help you get them," I added quickly, looking over at Hannah, hoping she would understand. Telling on Katherine was out of the question.

"Good girl, Zoe." My mother was pleased with me. "That's very nice of you."

I watched Hannah stalk out of the yard. I wanted to run after her, tell her I was sorry, but I didn't.

"So you want to play some more?" Katherine asked. She was also pleased with me.

"No thanks," I replied. I didn't feel like playing.

"Suit yourself." Katherine disappeared around the side of the house after my mother, and I was left all alone.

I lay down on the grass and looked up at the sky. I felt small and flat under its wide, empty glare. Underneath me, the earth began to spin. I didn't move. If I did, I might fall off and be lost up there forever.


The air was full of dust and mothballs and the smell of dog. It got in my nose and made my eyes water. Katherine's dog, Puppy, lay pressed against my legs at the end of my sleeping bag, gently snoring. I wondered if Katherine was mad that Puppy was on the floor with me and not with her up on the bed, but I didn't ask.

I was the favorite sister. Katherine liked to pick a favorite sister to sleep in her room and it was pretty much always me. She and I would listen to records after the lights were out, after my mother told us to go to sleep. My favorite record was by Joan Baez. I always imagined that I was her, singing:

> Don't sing love songs, you'll wake my mother
> She's sleeping here right by my side
> And in her right hand, a silver dagger
> She says that I can't be your bride

We also listened to the Lovin' Spoonful and Bob Dylan, but Joan Baez was my favorite singer and "Silver Dagger" was my favorite song. I liked to imagine my mother with a silver dagger, ready to jump out from behind the bed and protect me.

Katherine's room was big and dark. It sat by itself off the large second-floor landing. On both sides of the landing, separated by a door, were two sets of adjoining bedrooms with a bathroom be-tween them. Hannah and I slept in one set of bedrooms, and my parents slept in the other; their second bedroom was my mother's "study." I felt sorry for Katherine because she was all by herself in the middle, with only the empty landing and all those closed doors to keep her company.

Our house was big and ugly. On the outside it looked like a gray box. Inside, the walls were shiny and white and there wasn't much furniture. The year before my parents had built a big room where our back porch used to be. It had high ceilings and large, triangular windows. We called it the Big Room. My mother said it was mod-ern. She said that flowery pillows and big couches were fussy and old-fashioned. They reminded her of her grandparents' house. But I thought maybe I'd like a house like that, where I could curl up and read without worrying about all that empty space at the top of the walls.

Katherine's room had high ceilings, too, but I felt safe in here. Having Katherine near made me feel brave. I didn't have to worry about robbers and ghosts the way I did in my own room. Katherine wasn't afraid of anything.

Sometimes I felt bad about leaving Hannah by herself, next to my empty room. Katherine liked to say mean things about Hannah when I was in her room, and soon I said them too. We talked about how vain Hannah was, how she always looked in the mirror and tried on my mother's clothes and was such a goody-goody.

Lying there talking, Joan Baez singing on the record player, I felt daring and grown-up and wise. Katherine was eleven, four years older than me, and I knew I must be special to be her favorite.

But sometimes she said things that shocked me, like the night she told me she hated our father.

"You do not," I said, feeling a little less tough and happy. "I mean, you might get mad at him, but you don't hate him."

"Yes, I do," she said curtly. "I hate him. He's a jerk. He always acts like such a hotshot when we have parties, making everyone tell him how great his cooking is and showing off on his stupid guitar."

I thought about the way my parents' friends clapped and nodded and sometimes danced when my father brought out his guitar or put on the latest recordings of him playing drums with his jazz band. Did they really think he was showing off?

"Well, I don't think he's so bad," I said, finally. I was willing to bad-mouth Hannah, who was my best friend, but I was not ready to criticize my father, who terrified me.

"Oh, you're just scared of him," Katherine said, and I could hear her disgust in the dark.

"Uh-uh," I said. "That's stupid."

But it was true. I was also scared of her. But I could never say this out loud. To anyone. Not even Hannah or my mother.

# Big Sister

I find Katherine at the kitchen table reading the newspaper while Rosa, my mother's Chilean caregiver, carries platters of food to the table. Katherine looks very much as she did at eighteen: hair parted in the middle; long, pretty face free of makeup; and the kind of clothes—wrinkled khakis and running shoes—that reveal her complete disdain for anything associated with fashion.

It was always so. While my middle sister, Hannah, and I fell headfirst into every major style trend of the last twenty-five years—spiked hair, too much eye makeup, shoulder pads and cargos—Katherine watched from the sidelines in her baggy T-shirts and outlet store jeans. In a way, I admired her lack of vanity, but I also felt it was a message to the rest of us, especially my mother, that she stood apart, unwilling to engage in the family's petty concern with appearance.

She barely looks up as I come in and give Rosa a kiss on the cheek, nearly weeping with happiness at the sight of the perfectly roasted chicken, foil-wrapped baked potatoes and salad laid out on the table. My mother has remembered to provide food, and even arranged for Rosa to cook my favorite meal! This makes me extraordinarily happy: in some small but vital way, my mother is still taking care of me.

Opening the fridge, I spy white wine and beer and the sparkling cider that Katherine likes to drink. I think of all the times I've arrived here with my daughters, all of us exhausted, frazzled and hungry, only to watch my mother vaguely pull cans of chicken broth from the cupboard. Had all my stern lectures about the trials of traveling across country, especially with young children, finally sunk in?

I ask Katherine if she'd like cider and, glancing up from her paper, she says, "Sure. That works for me." Filling up her glass, I have an urge to tell her she should appreciate this food and drink, that it's hardly standard protocol. But then I have a terrible thought: What if my mother did all this—the chicken, the cider—because *Katherine* is here, and it has nothing to do with me at all? What if she had no idea this was my favorite meal and did it to please Katherine? Even though my sister has visited my mother *maybe once* in the last year, while I've come repeatedly.

The total unfairness of this makes me jerk the cider bottle upright, releasing a spray of yellow bubbles across Katherine's paper.

"Whoa, watch it," she says, pulling the paper away as if I might decide to spill more cider.

"I didn't mean to," I say, sullen despite myself. "Get it yourself the next time."

She laughs. "Well, aren't we in a good mood."

Rosa hurries over with a dishrag and stands between us wiping the table. "So, girls," she says. "Everyone ready to eat? You both hungry, no?"

"Starving," I say, smiling down at her. Despite her big bosom and brightly dyed red hair, Rosa is a tiny woman, barely five feet tall, and I'm amazed she can get my mother to the portable commode by herself. Although she's lost three or four inches of height, my mother is still a tall woman, at least five foot seven.

Rosa watches while Katherine and I help ourselves to generous amounts of food. "I'll go check on your mother, okay? See if she wants anything to eat."

"Okay, Rosa," I say. "Thanks. How's she been recently?"

"Well, she's sleeping a lot more. Still eating pretty good. I just wish . . ." She pauses, then rushes on. "I just wish she didn't talk about dying so much. All those books she has—death this, death that. Everything death. I love your mother, as you know. Like she was my own. I never want to say anything bad about her, but—"

"Don't worry, Rosa," Katherine says, rolling her eyes as she spears a large piece of potato and puts it in her mouth. "It's never stopped us." I shake my head at her. I'm not above complaining about my mother, but sharing a laugh with Rosa at my mother's expense is pointless. Rosa adores my mother. Since moving in to take care of her, she's turned her own husband down when he wanted to visit from Chile and, despite my mother's recently hiring a young Jamaican woman to relieve her during the day, it's been difficult to persuade Rosa to take time off.

"I just don't think it's healthy, that's all. I tell her, Mrs. Draper, you shouldn't think about dying all the time. You have so much good in your life. Your friends. Your daughters. Your beautiful grandchildren. Why you want to die? Why?"

Katherine and I both stop eating. This is the exact question I've been posing to my mother for weeks, with no satisfactory reply. I'm strangely hopeful that I will, at long last, get an answer. "So what did she say?"

"She says she doesn't want to live like this. In bed. Sick all the time. That she has nothing to look forward to except getting worse. That it's no way to live."

I nod, disappointed. I've heard all this before. The trouble is, these reasons don't add up for me. I understand why she's afraid—the Parkinson's endgame isn't pretty—and I'm sympathetic to that fear. But my mother's life is not without its pleasures: she has a small group of smart, interesting friends who telephone and come visit; she enjoys her food; she reads *The Washington Post* every day and watches the nightly news on PBS. And, as Rosa pointed out, she has three daughters and six grandchildren. Why not enjoy what she has instead of relentlessly plotting the end?

"It makes me worried," Rosa continues, tugging at the dish-cloth. "I think sometimes she might be . . . planning something."

Instinctively, I avoid looking at Katherine, afraid she might say something flip or, worse yet, confirm Rosa's suspicions. To prevent her from speaking, I say, "I wouldn't worry, Rosa. I think she's just a little anxious. All those books and talk are just a way of making her feel more in control."

"Yeah, she's big on control," Katherine says.

Rosa looks worriedly at Katherine, but I give her a reassuring smile and, after a moment, she leaves the room.

"Guess she doesn't know about Mr. Death coming tomorrow," Katherine says, scooping up another mouthful of food.

"Momma told her it was Poppa's cousin coming to visit," I say, assuming she will think this is funny. Her response surprises me.

"Oh, that is so typical," she says, dropping her fork with a clang. "Asking us to lie for her—*and* pretend to Rosa. That's just sick, Zoe. If she's going to plan her suicide with this guy, then she's going to have to deal with people knowing about it and that includes Rosa."

"Jesus, Katherine, you don't have to be the big defender of truth and justice. I think it should be Momma's decision how much she tells Rosa. And as you can see, Rosa's not going to be happy about it."

"Listen, Zoe." She narrows her eyes at me. "You may be willing to play along with her little games, but I'm not. I agreed to come down here this weekend, but you can't control what I do now that I'm here."

"Whoa, slow down a minute. Rosa is Catholic. If she knew how serious Momma was about killing herself, she might quit. And that would make our lives, especially my life, a lot harder. It took us a long time to find her."

Katherine stares at me. I force myself to hold her gaze, something that's not easy for me. After all these years, I still find my sister intimidating.

"It's just Poppa and his affairs all over again," she says finally, but her tone is detached, as if she's lost interest.

Ready to fight, I'm thrown by this unexpected shift and, before I can stop myself, say, "Yeah, well, your telling Momma about those didn't exactly solve their marital problems. She obsessed about them for years after he died."

Katherine smiles and takes a sip of cider. "Zoe, Zoe. Always trying to protect the guilty. Even if it means lying your head off and keeping everyone's dirty little secrets."

"Fuck you."

Katherine laughs. "Gosh, it's like old times around here."

Furious, I get up to clear my plate with half the food still on it. I know I'm being childish, but I doubt Katherine ever intended to tell Rosa about my mother's plans; she just wanted to remind me that she was still in the game, that nothing had been conceded despite her physical absence.

"You know, Zoe," she says, calmly, as if nothing's happened, "I do think Momma has the right to die if she wants to."

"I do too," I say, wondering if this is true. "But it's not just a question of rights. It's about whether or not it makes sense."

I stop. It made perfect sense to my mother, so who am I talking about? Myself, obviously. And the reason it doesn't make sense to me is that I don't want her to die. More important, I don't want her to *want* to die. Her willingness to consider it makes me feel inconsequential, like I'm not worth sticking around for. But I can't admit this to Katherine; it's not the kind of thing we say to each other.

"I just don't think she's that badly off," I finish, lamely.

"Well, it's not up to you—or me—to decide that. Why not keep an open mind, see what the man has to say? If Momma's serious about ending her life, we should respect that."

She's right, but standing at the sink, rinsing the food off my plate, I can't think of a single example of Katherine expressing a desire to respect our mother's wishes. And yet, I know that this distance she maintains with our mother—her reluctance to visit or call—arises from some serious old hurt. Conflicts between Katherine and our parents were a constant when we were growing up, and one of the tenets of Katherine's identity is that her childhood was a misery. Our parents didn't understand her; they didn't realize how unhappy she was in school; they made her feel stupid when she was, in fact, extremely bright but dyslexic—the list goes on. While she's never said it explicitly, I assume it's why she's stayed out of the caretaking rotation with our mother all these months, and why she stayed away when our father was dying.

Was it a reasonable response? Perhaps. Our father was no walk in the park for any of us, but especially for her. And yet I can't help feeling that, flawed as he was, she could have tried a little harder. Death was a once-in-a-lifetime event, after all. Didn't we have an obligation to salvage what we could before the door slammed shut forever?

But I bite my tongue, aware that these observations will be met with resistance, if not outright hostility. I may be forty years old, but I'm still her little sister.

And so instead I fill the kettle. Ask if she wants tea. Mr. Death is coming tomorrow and I want to pretend that we're in this together, at least for one more night.

# Dinner

My father had cooked spaghetti carbonara. I loved the rich, sloppy blend of egg, cheese and bacon mixed into the long strands of pasta. But as the words between my parents and Katherine got louder and my father's forehead turned red and sweaty under the bright kitchen lights, I found it difficult to eat.

My parents and Katherine were fighting about her schoolwork. Her sixth-grade report card had been "terribly disappointing," and my mother said she needed to work harder. Katherine said she *did* work hard but her teacher stank and she hated her. She also hated my parents.

"Stop fighting," Hannah suddenly yelled, from her chair next to mine. "It's not fair to make Zoe and me listen to you three fight every night!"

I couldn't believe she'd said that. She was either very brave or very stupid. I didn't look at her but just sat, staring at my plate. The food looked weird and ugly now, like throw-up.

"Shut up, Hannah," my father said, turning to her. "This has nothing to do with you."

"Why don't you and Zoe clear your plates and go upstairs?" my mother said to us, not looking at my father.

"Then I'm going upstairs too," Katherine screamed, standing up and grabbing her plate.

"No you aren't," my father said, jumping out of his chair and making a grab for her plate. "Put that down right now."

"Fine."

I watched, halfway out of my seat, as she lifted the plate and threw it down on the table, shattering it. The pieces of plate were stuck under the gluey strands of spaghetti so they didn't go very far, but the sound was like someone's head cracking.

We all stood there, waiting for the next thing to happen. My father moved first. He reached out and slapped Katherine, hard, right across the face. She turned and darted behind him. She grabbed the fire poker hanging next to the fireplace and swung it at him. She was off-balance and the poker was heavy. My father easily grabbed it away from her. She turned and ran out the back door. I started to cry.

Later my mother came up to tuck us in and I asked her, "Why did Poppa get so mad?"

"Oh, he was just a little cross with Katherine tonight," she said, giving me a firm kiss on the forehead and standing up to go. "It's fine now, don't worry. All families fight sometimes."

But not like our family, I thought, feeling sick again as I imagined the splattered spaghetti and my father reaching out to slap Katherine across the face. I held my stuffed lion tight and listened to her say the same thing to Hannah in the room next door.

As soon as she left, I went into Hannah's room and got into bed with her and we played with our stuffed animals in the dark. Her pig told my lion we were moving to France. I wondered how we'd get there, but she told me not to worry. She would figure it out.

# Mr. Death

The morning after I arrive in D.C., I wake in my old bedroom and spend several minutes mentally returning the walls to their original egg-yolk yellow, and restoring my teenage posters and wall hangings.

While my sisters' bedrooms languish under peeling paint and stacks of books and clothes, my mother has cleared out all my old belongings, repainted the walls white and installed a matching dark blue quilt and rug, making it the official guest room. A bookshelf of my books—*Little House on the Prairie*, *The Wizard of Oz*, *The Autobiography of Malcolm X*—and a faded poster for *Waiting for Godot* are all that's left of the eighteen years I lived here.

Squinting at my watch, I see it's already ten—seven my time—which feels much too early for a Saturday morning but puts me hours behind the rest of the household, especially Katherine, who's probably been up for ages. Pulling on a sweatshirt and a pair of jeans, I start downstairs but then return to my room and change into a fitted black shirt and a pair of high-heeled boots. I finish the job by twisting my hair into a bun and applying my darkest, reddest lipstick.

I cross the hall to inspect myself in my parents' full-length mirror, turning sideways to admire my nipped-in waist and pointy heels.

Mr. Death better not mess with me, I think, or he's going to be one unhappy little exit guide.

Down in the kitchen, Katherine is sitting at the table and I note with surprise that she's also more dressed up than usual. She has on a deep maroon peasant blouse instead of her usual T-shirt and her waist-length hair is pulled back in two barrettes. She's talking with Rosa about Vioxx, one of the drugs my mother takes to control the pain in her arthritic shoulders. Katherine suggests that my mother should see an acupuncturist instead.

"A what?" Rosa asks, looking puzzled. "What you call it?"

"Ack-you-punk-chur-ist," Katherine says, employing the firm, cheerful voice she used with her children, Peter and Shannon, when they were toddlers. Despite her own fraught childhood, Katherine is a remarkably good mother: loving, patient and adventuresome. At twelve and eight, Peter and Shannon have traveled more than I have, and they are plucky, sweet-natured children. Travel is, in fact, the family business. Katherine and her husband, Brian, a mild-mannered man in his early fifties, run a mail-order company called The Traveler's Mail Box, which offers things like organic bug repellent and walking sticks made from salvaged wood.

Rosa keeps saying, "yes-yes," and making little acquiescing movements with her head as Katherine mimes putting a needle in her arm. I know Rosa's trying to catch my eye, but I move carefully around them, pouring myself coffee and making toast.

I'm the one who thinks my mother's general practitioner, Dr. Fielding, should keep giving her Vioxx, despite the drug's known side effects. Having recently witnessed my mother in the grip of dyskinesia, I'm vividly aware of what uncontrolled arm movements can do to the uncushioned bones in her shoulders.

Lifting a plate down from the cupboard, I recall my nightmarish visit last month. Clara and Lane were with me and both children were excited to see "Nana," expecting to find her as she'd been at Christmas six weeks earlier, weak but still ambulatory, happy to sit and listen to them talk about soccer and school. Instead, we found her lying on her bed, moaning, unable to speak, her torso twisting and turning against the pillows. After hurrying my children to bed, I'd spent the night massaging her back and arms, applying warm and cold compresses and finally, physically, restraining her shoulders by lying next to her and hugging her.

The morning brought no relief and after repeated calls to her neurologist, each more frustrating and unhelpful than the last, a nurse told me Dr. Cowan thought my mother was overmedicated—they had recently increased her main Parkinson's medication, Sinemet—and we should return to the original dose. I pointed out that she'd been having writhing episodes before the increase of Sinemet; the writhing was in fact the *reason* for the increase. What made her think reducing the dose was going to help? The nurse merely repeated the doctor's orders. When I told her that it was not an acceptable answer, she suggested I write a letter of complaint. When I asked her what kind of heartless, piece-of-shit neurologist would make it this hard for her own patients to get help, patients who probably didn't have a daughter to dial the phone for them, she hung up on me.

And so I took matters into my own hands. I knew that protein interferes with the efficacy of Sinemet, temporarily canceling it out. Once my mother's damaged neurotransmitters were left to their own devices, she would temporarily shut down, entering a state akin to a waking coma, with little or no ability to move. My mother had avoided protein for years, except for small amounts very late in the day. If she consumed it earlier, she would freeze up. But surely freezing was better than rolling around in uncontrolled pain.

So I had Rosa fry up a pan of bacon, a food my mother loves, and I fed it to her, strip after greasy strip. And the writhing stopped, for a while. Long enough for my children to tiptoe in and talk to her, even if all she could do was smile vaguely in their direction.

Since then, the writhing has returned only very intermittently and for shorter periods (which indicates she *was* overmedicated), but its arbitrariness still terrifies her. This is why she takes Vioxx and why there's always bacon in the house. They are her insurance against the pain, and more important, her fear of the pain.

What the neurologist thinks of the Vioxx (or the bacon) I'll never know, because my mother has decided to stop seeing her. In fact, she says she's done seeing doctors altogether, done with the endless prodding, poking and assessing. It's physically and emotionally draining, and what's the point? Her exact physical status will be irrelevant soon enough, she says. In the meantime, Rosa and I continue to get her regular prescriptions filled and we get in touch with her G.P., Dr. Fielding, whenever there is a change in her condition.

I glance over at Katherine, who is still talking to Rosa. I know I should tell her all this and perhaps I will, but for now it's easier to let her believe she can show up and straighten us all out. Besides, it's almost ten-thirty, and the man from Hemlock is due in half an hour. I want to see my mother first.

"I'm going in to see Momma," I say, interrupting her. "Do you want to come with me?" Katherine gives me a funny look, as if I've asked her a trick question. I wave my coffee cup in the direction of my mother's room. "C'mon. We have a visitor coming soon, remember?"

We both look up at the clock and, after a moment, Rosa does as well.

"She told me your father's cousin is coming to see her this morning," Rosa says, brightly. "That's so nice. I understand it's been a while since you've seen him, and now he gets to see all three of you together."

"Actually, Katherine and I have never met him," I say quickly, before Katherine can say anything. I move toward the door and Katherine follows me. "You can show him in when he gets here,

Rosa." My words sound overly formal, peremptory—lady of the house. I give her a smile by way of apology.

"Okay," she says pleasantly, but I hear, or imagine I hear, a faint coolness. Rosa and I are usually the ones in cahoots, plotting against the doctors, whispering our thoughts about my mother, working out the details of her care. But now I'm keeping a secret from her and I wonder if she senses this. Perhaps Katherine is right and this deception is a mistake.

My mother is sitting up in bed when we enter the room and I see Rosa has helped her put on lipstick and powder. Like mother, like daughter, I think, leaning over to press my own red lips against her cheek. Katherine goes over and sits on the dark blue couch in the corner, where I usually settle.

The room was once my father's art studio and its plain white walls and floor-to-ceiling windows have the same austere, modern feel as the rest of the house. Other than the small blue couch five or six feet from the foot of her bed, the only furniture is a flat-topped wooden desk my mother uses as a bedside table, a couple of straight-backed chairs for visitors, and a floor-to-ceiling bookshelf filled with books and photographs and knickknacks.

The room's size and starkness are somewhat softened by the homey blue patchwork quilt covering my mother's queen-size hospital bed, the sunlight blazing in from the overhead skylight.

"How did everyone sleep?" she asks brightly.

"Good," I say, grabbing one of the wooden chairs. "How about you?"

She raises her eyebrows and gives a little moue of distaste. "Pretty well. Until I got stomach cramps at four in the morning. Poor Rosa had to help me to the commode the rest of the night. She must be exhausted."

"Stomach cramps?" My own stomach feels suddenly queasy and

I put down my coffee cup. It could be the Vioxx: Abdominal bleeding is one of the drug's side effects. *Damn.* I'd better call Dr. Fielding.

"Can we talk about what we're doing here this morning?" Katherine asks briskly, as if we've been nattering on about nothing. "What exactly is our agenda?"

"Well, I'm glad you asked, Katherine," my mother says, beaming at her as if she'd just offered to move in and be her personal nurse. But I can see she's nervous. Her head and torso quiver and her legs kick spastically under the heavy blue quilt. "That's just what we need to discuss. Thank you!"

I try not to roll my eyes and focus instead on the picture window over my mother's bed that overlooks the yard. Thin stalks of green bamboo poke up along the back fence, although the lawn looks weedy and brown and there's only the vague remnant of a flower garden along one side. Washington's magnificent spring is well under way, but no one has planted anything in our yard for years.

"Why don't you begin by telling us what you hope to accomplish?" Katherine continues, as if calling a board meeting to order. "And why you want Zoe and me here."

Uncertainty crosses my mother's face, but when she speaks, her voice is strong. "I want the two of you—Hannah too, of course—to understand what it is I'm planning to do. This seemed like the best way to accomplish that. I also thought it was important for you to know about the Hemlock Society and—"

"Momma, we know about the Hemlock Society," I interrupt her. "You've sent us each a copy of *Final Exit*. I helped you get a lethal dose of Seconal. We know you want to end your life. What we don't know—what *I* don't know—is why you want to involve a total stranger."

"Well, there's no mystery about that, Zoe." My mother gives me an annoyed look. "Sometimes it doesn't work. You take the pills and you don't die. The exit guides are there to make sure that doesn't happen."

"So what, they put a pillow over your face?" I ask.

"Well, I don't know exactly," she says in an offended voice. "That's why we're having this meeting. To find out."

There's a quiet knock at the door.

"Rosa?" my mother calls, nerves or exhaustion making her voice crack. "Is that you?"

Rosa's bright red hair appears like a flame at the edge of the door. "Your cousin is here, Mrs. Draper!" she says. "Shall I show him in?"

For a moment my mother says nothing, but her limbs betray her, bucking and then stiffening as she attempts to control them. Her face tightens into a grimace, as if invisible hands have pulled her skin toward her ears.

"Yes, Rosa," she says through flattened lips. "That would be nice."

I reach over and take her hand as Rosa opens the door.


A stout man in a black suit takes a cautious step into my mother's room, hesitates for a moment, then walks quickly toward her bed.

"It's a great pleasure to meet you," he says, bowing and offering her a pudgy hand, which my mother immediately takes, dropping my own. For a moment I think he's going to kiss it, but then he does a kind of bowing, shaking thing, and without acknowledging Katherine or me, stands clasping her hand, staring intently down at her.

Observing him from the side, I interpret his expression as a mix of intense sympathy and grim determination. His face is large and mottled and he breathes heavily, making that loud, whistling noise peculiar to overweight men. He exudes such an aura of evangelical zeal I half-expect him to start praying for the salvation of my mother's soul. I have a strong urge to kick him. At least then he'll have to acknowledge me. So far, he's been oblivious to both Katherine and me, as if his business is with my mother and my mother alone.

She looks flushed and girlish. "Very nice to meet *you*," she says, stumbling over her words. "Thank you so much for coming. Oh, and these are my daughters, Katherine and Zoe." She makes a gracious, sweeping gesture with her free hand, which trembles and jerks through the air.

She tries to free her other hand, but he doesn't let it go. He does, however, turn and give Katherine and me a small, courtly bow. "Honored to meet you both," he says. "I'm hoping we'll all get along just fine."

*Git along juss fahn.*

It seems Mr. Death is a good old boy. He's even wearing one of those hokey Western string ties with his cheap-looking black suit and I imagine a faint whiff of stale sweat, as if he's been wearing the same shirt for several days.

"I'm Zoe." I thrust my hand at him, forcing him to let go of my mother's and shake. "What did you say your name was?"

"My name's Hank Smerler, ma'am, but everyone calls me Bud. You can call me either one, but mos'ly people back in Tulsa just call me Bud."

Without even looking at her, I sense the expression of fixed politeness settle on my mother's face. It's a look I'm deeply familiar with. My spirits rise. "Bud" Smerler may have something she wants, but he also has a serious social handicap. My mother is a solid Washington Democrat, a liberal even, but she's also a cultural and intellectual snob, and this man is definitely not a member of the tribe.

"Bud it is," I say. "Glad to meet you. Can we get you anything to eat or drink before we get started?"

He looks surprised; I imagine he's used to people running him off their property on these little death jaunts, not offering him lunch.

"Thank you, ma'am. I'm jus' fine for now."

"Okay. Well, why don't you sit here?" I pull my chair several feet back from the bed and firmly guide him into it. "I'll sit over here with my sister." I perch next to Katherine on the couch. "So, I guess we should get started."

"Well, now, Mizz Draper—" He addresses my mother, inching his chair closer to her bed.

"You can call me Margaret . . . Mr. Smerler."

"*Bud,* Margaret. Call me Bud."

"Bud," my mother says, amused but playing along.

"Tha's right. Now I don't want to jump in here too quickly and make anyone uncomfortable, Mizz—Margaret—so I want to hear from you, and a'course your lovely daughters here, what y'all want. But first I want to make it clear that I am here for you, Margaret. *You're* the one who's a member of this organization, and *you're* the one makin' this important decision to end your life."

"Thank you," my mother says. She sounds really happy and grateful, like he just canceled some terrible thing that she'd been dreading except, of course, the terrible thing is continuing to live. My upbeat mood deflates a little.

"Excuse me, but I'm not sure she's decided that." I break in before he can continue. "I believe she's just looking for some information, so she can, you know, *make* that decision."

Bud and my mother both look at me as if I've said something completely dim-witted. Clearly I've overreached.

"Margaret?" Bud looks over at her. "You wanna answer that?"

"Certainly," my mother says, giving him another thankful look. "I've told you, Zoe, I don't want to live like this. I'm stuck in bed. I can't really read or write anymore. It's getting harder to breathe and, if you recall, I was in excruciating pain for close to a week in February—pain that still comes back sometimes, and could get worse. I have nothing but greater indignities ahead. My body is falling apart and, I'm sure you and Katherine would agree, my mind as well."

As she talks, I think again about that terrible night during my visit last month when she begged me to bring her the vials of Seconal from the bookshelf. She couldn't take another minute of the pain, she told me. She wanted to die. "No, Momma," I said, almost crying. "We'll get through this, I promise. It'll get better. You can do it then if you still want to. But not now. Not when you're desperate and in pain. Please. I need you to wait."

"Okay," I say quietly, settling back on the couch. "Let's hear it. What exactly are you proposing?"

"Shall I?" Bud looks inquiringly at my mother, who nods. I notice her shaking is better, but she looks exhausted. "Okay. You see, Zoe, what we offer people like your mother is help with a capital H. Once they've made up their minds to die, they don't want to go halfway and end up a vegetable in some hospital with a buncha tubes stuck in 'em. And that's where we come in. We offer a safe, easy way to help your mother end her life with no unforeseen consequences."

He reaches into a bag I hadn't noticed and pulls out a piece of tubing, a plastic bag and a small canister with a valve on top. "Now y'all probably heard of helium, right? You have any grandchildren, Margaret?"

"I do," she says, taking several minutes to recount all their names and ages while he nods and smiles. Katherine shifts violently on the couch behind me and I assume she finds this parody of a normal conversation as horrifying as I do. Rage unfurls inside me like toxic smoke, although I'm not sure which one of them deserves it most.

"So you must be familiar with helium balloons, right?" he asks, still addressing my mother. "Birthdays and special occasions? Maybe you even tried a little once and your voice got all high and squeaky?"

"For God's sake, we're all familiar with helium!" Katherine's voice leaps out from behind me, making me jump. "What, exactly, is your point?"

"Katherine—" my mother says reprovingly.

"No, no, she's right, Margaret. I can definitely chew on a thing too long. My own wife would tell you that. She tells *me* all the time." He laughs comfortably, until he catches a glimpse of Katherine's face and stops. I feel a surge of affection for my big sister. With her on my side, maybe we can put a stop to Bud.

"Well, what you don't know about helium—Katherine, is it?" he asks, turning to her again. "Is that helium is one of the deadliest gases around. If you inhale pure helium, you lose consciousness in less than three minutes—and you're dead in five."

He picks up the tubing and the bag and what looks like a cheap terrycloth headband. "Now, what we recommend is that the person ending their life puts this bag over their head, puts this tubing in their mouth, then reaches down and turns the valve on the helium tank. Oh, and they can put this thing around their neck, too, just to speed things up." He holds up the grungy white headband. "Then they settle back, relax, and they're dead within a few short minutes."

*Would you rather inhale helium or take sleeping pills? Die with a plastic bag over your head or while trying not to vomit up Seconal?*

There's a silence in the room. Katherine speaks first. Her voice is surprisingly calm. "Where does she get the helium?"

I give her a dirty look, which she ignores. Her eyes are fixed on Bud.

"Well now, Katherine," he says, looking pleased but a little nervous, "this is what we do. We find a date when one or both of y'all can be here and no one else is in the house. Then me and another volunteer from the society come back with a small tank of helium, the tubing and everythin'. Margaret here puts the bag over her head and turns on the gas.

"We stay with her until we're sure she's dead, take the tank and everythin' and leave. Y'all call the coroner's office to let 'em know there's been a death. They show up, either that night or the next morning, dependin' on how busy they are. Then once they write up the death certificate, the funeral home can come fetch her."

"So you mean someone from the coroner's office comes here and examines her?" I ask.

"That's right," he says.

"So what if they notice she's just been suffocated? Or has helium in her system?"

"Well, I can tell you, in my experience, that's never happened." Bud takes out a crumpled white handkerchief and mops at his face. "Listen, I know this sounds pretty terrible to some people. And I hope no one here is mad at me or nothin'." He gives the two of us a beseeching look. "I jus' want you folks to know I don't get paid to do this job. I do it 'cause I believe in it. And I hope when my time comes, someone is willin' to do the same for me."

He looks back at my mother. "That's pretty much it, Margaret. Now you jus' need to decide what you want to do. If you go ahead, you need to pick a couple dates, call the office and ask them to schedule it. Dependin' on my availability, we can do it the beginning of May like you want, or later in the month. But things may get harder over the summer 'cause my wife and I are plannin' some trips. Jus' remember when you pick that date, you need a family member here to let us in and out and no one else can be in the house."

"Wait, what about Rosa?" I ask my mother. "How are you going to deal with her? It'll seem a bit suspicious if we send her home the one night you happen to die."

"We can tell her you're helping me, Zoe, and we want her to take a night off."

"But, Momma, think about it," Katherine says, impatiently. "You can't die the first and only night Zoe takes care of you. It's going to look like she killed you or you killed yourself with her help."

"Exactly," I say. "And what if Rosa decides to report her suspicions to the home-care agency or the police? They figure out she's just been gassed, and I'm under arrest for murder. Assisted suicide isn't legal, remember? Unless you live in Oregon."

My mother looks a little bug-eyed at this but then says, vaguely, "Actually, I was hoping all three of you could be here."

"Okay, so all *three* of us will be facing murder charges," Katherine bellows. "You aren't addressing the *issue*. It's fine with me if you want to kill yourself, but I can tell you right now that none of us, not even Zoe, is going to put herself in legal jeopardy to help you do it."

I glance toward the door and notice my mother doing the same. "Katherine, keep your voice down," she says stiffly. "I don't see why you and Zoe are talking about murder. *I'm* the one taking my life."

"Well, Margaret, I think what your daughters are saying is, helpin' *you* is puttin' *them* at risk. And I unnerstand why that concerns them. I take that risk ever' time I help someone. But that's where we may differ, if you'll beg my pardon, girls. You see, I believe your mom needs some help. We all heard her—she doesn't want to live like an invalid. In pain and with no chance of gettin' better. And frankly, if I was in her shoes, I wouldn't either."

"But what about us?" I ask, jumping up off the couch. "What about her children and grandchildren, who want her around?"

"Sit down, Zoe," my mother says, sharply.

"No. I won't," I say, turning to face her. "Is this the way you want to die? With a plastic bag over your face and a couple of complete strangers watching you suffocate? I'm sorry, Momma, but I think that sucks."

"Zoe—"

"Well now, miss, I think if we all take a deep—"

"She's right."

About to leave the room, I stop. It's Katherine.

"What?"

"I said, I think you're right. Dying like that *would* suck. It would totally suck. I mean, is that really your idea of 'death with dignity,' Momma? It certainly wouldn't be mine. But maybe we should discuss it after Mr. Smerler leaves."

"Margaret?" His voice is pleading, uncertain.

"Mr. Smerler, maybe you could give me a moment alone with my daughters. I'm sure Rosa can find you something to eat or drink. We'll just be a few minutes. I'm sorry to be so rude."

"No, ma'am. Don't apologize. Families often have a hard time unnerstandin' this thing. Just take your time. Don't worry about me."

The man stands, bows deeply to my mother, and leaves the room.

"Oh my God!" Katherine lets out a derisive snort. "Is that guy for real? What were you thinking, Momma? Do you really want Gomer Pyle performing your last rites?"

Although I feel the tiniest bit sorry for him, the sheer relief of having Bud out of the room makes me giddy, and I start to laugh. Pretty soon, Katherine joins me and I have to wipe my eyes, which have started to stream. I haven't had this much fun with my sister in years.

My mother stares angrily at us. But then her head drops back on the pillow and she smiles ruefully. "Well, girls, the truth is, Bud may not be the last person I want to see on earth."

"Thank the Lord!" I flop down on her bed and kick my boots onto the floor. I feel like kicking my legs up in the air as well but settle for stretching out on the bed.

"But what am I going to do?" she asks, plaintively. "We have to figure something else out. Make another plan."

Although this is addressed to me, Katherine jumps up and says, "How about we throw a big party and give you all the balloons?"

My mother groans. "Very funny."

She turns back to me. Her hand vibrates lightly, then more insistently, on my arm. "What about it, Zoe?" I hear the dread in her voice, the panic that we will leave her trapped and helpless in her imploding body. "Will you help me?"

"With a capital *H*," I say, smiling up at her.

But I don't mean it. I love my mother and I don't want her to die.

# Midnight

It was New Year's Eve and Sharon Reynolds and I had been playing in her stuffy attic for hours. All day, we'd been boasting about staying up until midnight, but neither of us cared much anymore. We were worn out from our sleepover the night before and from ice-skating that afternoon. It felt like days since we'd wobbled around the rink, clutching each other's hands and trying not to fall.

Sharon was my best friend. She lived next door to me in a big white house. She was twelve, a year older than me, and had an older sister and two teenage brothers. Her mother worked on political campaigns and had a voice like a man's.

"I'm bored," she said, tossing aside the Barbies we'd been playing with. "Let's go eat."

I immediately jumped up to follow her. Mrs. Reynolds loved to cook and they kept things like bittersweet chocolate, a treat my mother didn't allow, in their house. Mrs. Reynolds and my father liked to argue about dishes and recipes and compete over who was a better cook. I could tell she'd been impressed when my father had cooked an entire pig for our Christmas party this year. It had an apple in its mouth and everything.

When we got downstairs, the Reynoldses' house was full of women in long dresses and men in suits. I went to look for Tess, our cleaning lady, who'd come over to help with the party. She was in the kitchen putting together plates of food. I wanted to talk to her, but there were too many grown-ups in there.

Sharon grabbed a crab pastry, but I liked the powdery Christmas cookies Mrs. Reynolds bought at Anderson's Bakery on Wisconsin Avenue. I wrapped up a bunch in a napkin and went looking for Hannah and my mother. (Katherine was babysitting at the Cattralls' house that night.) I could hear my father singing and playing guitar in the Reynoldses' den.

I found Hannah in the living room, sitting next to the tall, spindly Christmas tree, playing cards with two older girls I didn't know. She was wearing a light purple dress with an oversize collar that had belonged to my mother when my parents lived in Paris. It was way too big for her, but she'd pinned up the collar with a giant brooch from my mother's jewelry box. My father had whistled when she came downstairs and told her she looked eighteen. She was only twelve, a little over a year older than me, and I thought she looked ridiculous.

I waved at her but she ignored me, so I went to find my mother. She was sitting on a wicker couch on the Reynoldses' sunporch. She wore dangly gold earrings and a dark blue dress that dipped in the back and showed off her shoulders. She was talking to Mr. Brown. The Browns lived on the other side of the Reynoldses, and Mr. Brown had bushy eyebrows that moved up and down whenever he talked. He was perched on the arm of the couch, leaning down and putting his face next to my mother's. I watched to see if his eyebrows touched her face.

She tried to speak to me, but Mr. Brown kept talking. She gave me an apologetic look and I went back into the kitchen for more cookies. Tess asked me if I was having a good time and I said, "Not really."

She laughed. "Only twenty more minutes till midnight, honey. Then you can go home."

Sharon came into the kitchen looking perky and important. Her mother had asked her to get out the pots and pans. I felt excited myself. This was only the second year I'd been up until midnight on New Year's Eve. All around me, people were shrieking and asking what time it was and pulling on their coats. Someone had thrown open the large glass doors that led to the Reynoldses' front porch and everyone was spilling outside, smoking cigarettes and laughing. Sharon and I each had a frying pan and a spatula, and we danced along the edge of the porch, where we could see everything.

"Five minutes to midnight," Mrs. Reynolds bellowed. She stood by the open doors making come-on-out gestures with both arms. She had black, shiny hair and a black fur coat and looked like a bear, only tall and skinny.

I saw my mother come out. She was also wearing fur and Mr. Brown was holding her arm. I heard someone yell, "Coming through, coming through," and my father appeared in the doorway with Hannah on his back, his arms around her legs. She was laughing and kicking her feet and telling him to put her down.

"Can't let my daughter miss the festivities, now can I?" he asked loudly. "Gotta ring in the new year! Nineteen hundred and seventy-two!"

He shrugged Hannah higher up on his shoulders but then staggered backward with a look of surprise on his face. There was a loud, shivering crack as he and Hannah crashed through one of the glass doors. Mrs. Reynolds screamed. Someone behind me shouted, "Midnight!" And there was a deafening clatter of pots and pans banging and horns blowing and shouts of "Happy New Year!"

Loud jazzy music started playing and I saw Sharon's older

brother Daniel and his friend Malcolm laughing up on the balcony over the porch. People were kissing each other and beginning to dance. I pushed my way past them, trying to get inside. Sharon yelled after me and I looked back and saw her dancing like a go-go girl, hair whipping across her face.

I got to the open door just as a bright light came on inside. My father sat on the floor surrounded by broken glass. He was holding his eyeglasses and wiping his face with a white handkerchief. Hannah sat next to him crying. Mrs. Reynolds had an arm around her. My mother rushed past me.

She stepped over my father's outstretched legs and went to Hannah, who was holding her wrist. When she pulled her hand away, I could see blood. Some of it had dripped onto her purple dress. My mother crouched down and took her hand. She and Mrs. Reynolds were talking, but I couldn't hear them over all the noise.

Broken glass crunched under my party shoes as I stepped into the room. No one said anything to me and I stopped, uncertain what to do. Behind me, people were still blowing horns and shouting "Happy New Year," and I wished I was still outside dancing with Sharon. But I had to stay here. This was my family.

"Should I call an ambulance, Margaret?" Mrs. Reynolds asked my mother.

"No, but I think I'd better take her to Emergency. She might need stitches."

"Hey, what about me?" my father asked. "Don't I get any stitches? Doesn't anyone care about me?" My father had put his glasses back on, but his face looked fuzzy and out of focus. I wondered if he'd hit his head.

"Oh, for God's sake, Jonathan, hush," Mrs. Reynolds said in her raspy voice. "You're perfectly fine. You're just damn lucky you didn't kill yourself, or . . . worse." She turned back to my sister, who was making little hiccupy sobs but looked okay.

"Well, I don't see how you can call a guy who's just fallen through a glass door lucky, but I'm sorry about the mess, Joan. I must have slipped on something. Could have happened to anyone."

My mother stood up and, without saying anything, reached out to help my father off the floor. He got to his feet but then pitched toward her. "Whoops-a-daisy!" he said with a giggle. I could see blood on his white collar.

"I think you're bleeding, Poppa," I said, but he didn't hear me. He was bending over with his hands on his knees looking at Hannah. She winced when he reached out and touched her shoulder. "You okay, honey pie? We sure took a tumble."

Mrs. Reynolds rolled her eyes and gave my mother a little smile. "You better go lie down, Jonathan. You hit your head pretty hard."

"That's okay. I've got the hardest head in Washington, D.C. Just ask my wife."

We turned to look at my mother, but she'd left the room.

"Hey. Where'd she go?"

"She went to fetch her purse. She's taking your daughter to the emergency room."

"Oh, for God's sake!" My father looked annoyed. "I'll never hear the end of that. I can take her—*if* it's even necessary."

Mrs. Reynolds stood up. She was almost as tall as my father, and her usual isn't-life-funny? look was gone. "No you can't, Jonathan. You're in no condition to drive. Now back off like a good boy or I really am going to get mad at you. You already owe me a new glass door."

My father stared at her for a moment and I thought he was going to yell, but then he sighed and shook his head. He fumbled in his pocket for a cigarette and turned away to strike a match.

I didn't want my mother to leave and I didn't want to go home with my father. I thought about going to the hospital with Hannah and my mother but decided to stay at Sharon's house instead. Mrs. Reynolds wouldn't mind. She always said I practically lived with them anyway.

In fact, I wondered if maybe I *could* live with them.

There was an extra bed in Sharon's room and every night before bed we could go up to the third floor and play Ping-Pong with her older brothers, Steven and Daniel. Then, in the morning, Mr. Reynolds could make us pancakes and take us sailing on the Chesapeake Bay in their thirty-two-foot schooner. Afterward, we could pile into their car and go for ice cream with our heads stuck out the window, singing. In the summer I'd go on vacation with them to a dude ranch, where Daniel and I could get lost and spend the night together in the woods.

For months, I lay in bed imagining some new and exciting chapter of my life with the Reynoldses. Even after my sister's stitches were healed and you could barely see the scar.

# Walking with the King

*Oh, I'm gonna walk, I'm gonna walk*
*Oh, I'm gonna talk, I'm gonna talk*
*I'm gonna sing, I'm gonna sing*
*Of the heavenly king, of the heavenly king.*

—ANONYMOUS

After Bud leaves, I go for a run down to the National Zoo, and then Momma, Katherine and I eat plates of leftover chicken in my mother's bedroom and watch a *Nova* program on AIDS. Almost immediately after it ends, Katherine disappears into her room upstairs and I can hear her talking on the phone. I think about calling Jack and the girls, or maybe Hannah, but can't muster the strength. Instead, I grab a blanket and a glass of wine and curl up on the couch, where I often sit to talk with my mother or read the paper while she dozes.

Rosa gets my mother ready for bed and she immediately falls asleep, the switch from conscious to unconscious invisibly thrown. She lies with her long, pale fingers folded across her narrow chest, unmoving and soundless in the middle of her bed. The room is dark except for the small reading lamp next to me.

Glancing across at my mother's bookshelf, I can just make out the large photograph of my parents angled toward my mother's bed. It was taken on a trip to Egypt sometime after the three of us left home. My mother is wearing a bandanna on her head and she and my father have on sporty, earth-colored anoraks. They look at each other with attentive, happy expressions that reflect the companionableness that seemed to blossom between them toward the end of my father's life. I can see why my mother loves this image.

It reminds me of the story my parents used to tell about how they met, a story as distilled and idealized as this photograph. In fact, I sometimes suspected the two of them had cooked it up together, choosing which details to keep, which ones to lose, and which ones to embellish in order to keep the world—and especially their children—from perceiving a more complex truth about who they were.

The story always began with the chicken cacciatore.

The setting was my mother's friend Mitzy's apartment in the West Village. The year was 1948. My father was twenty-three, a student at Columbia Law School and my mother, who was two years older, was at Columbia, getting her M.A. in clinical psychology.

The party was in full swing when my mother walked in, caught the enticing scent of tomato and herbs, and—"following her nose"—went into Mitzy's kitchen and found my father leaning over a simmering pot.

"I thought how marvelous it was to meet a man who could cook," she would say at this point, while my father looked pleased with himself. "And I thought here was a woman who had that certain *je ne sais quoi*," he'd reply, making an exaggeratedly Gallic expression, even kissing his fingertips.

Shaped, edited and performed in tandem, the story pleased me enormously; I loved its promise of nurturance (the chicken) and romance (the *je ne sais quoi*). It was only later that I came to understand how much more they must have seen and understood about each other during that fateful encounter in Mitzy's kitchen.

Here was my father, a middle-class, midwestern boy, new to New York City, face-to-face with my glamorous, aristocratic-looking mother. Not only gorgeous—and I assume for him there was a strong physical attraction—but with the finishing school posture, tasteful clothing and style of speech that would have signaled her membership in a world he was determined to join: a world of culture and sophistication and casual prosperity arising, at least in part, from a backdrop of "family money."

This was not my father's background. His own father was a farm boy from Illinois who had attended the University of Illinois on a scholarship. My grandfather's first job was in the mail room of a machinery company in Chicago that made industrial cranes. Quickly moving through the ranks, he ended up as president of the company. It was a real pull-yourself-up-by-your-bootstraps, American success story that included a second home on the shores of Lake Michigan and a son at fancy East Coast private schools.

In the end, my father did exactly what his father had done: re-create himself and move up the social ladder. It was a story familiar to the point of mythology, the plot to half the great American novels. And yet it would be unfair to say that my father married my mother merely for her money or her social standing. I believe that the *je ne sais quoi* he saw in her included more than her pedigree. She was, like him, a misfit, determined to escape the restrictive boundaries of her upper-crust social world. Which brings up the question of what my mother saw in my father when she walked into that small, fragrant kitchen.

One thing is certain: Despite his height and dark-rimmed glasses, my father was nothing like my mother's previous beau, the patrician Elliot Richardson, who would later distinguish himself as a hero in the Watergate scandal. Nor was he anything like the rich, indolent boys from Virginia my mother was used to dating, including her second cousin Conrad, an avid fox hunter to whom she was briefly engaged in college.

Brash and charming, and a bit rakish in his loose tweed coat, my father would certainly have had a drink in one hand and a cigarette in the other, somehow managing also to stir the pot. Offering her a taste of broth, he would bring the wooden spoon to her lips in a gesture both practiced and daring: *a man who could cook.* Somehow one could not imagine Elliot Richardson chopping vegetables or playing guitar at parties or sitting in on drums at Greenwich Village jazz clubs.

In short, my father was not entirely the right sort, as my mother's very proper Aunt Marianne would have said, which probably worked in his favor. He was a daring step outside her usual milieu, yet not so far afield as to be ruled out entirely. He was, after all, a Yale graduate studying to be a lawyer and would go on to have a perfectly respectable career as an associate in a law firm in Paris (where Hannah and I were born), a stint in the State Department, his own law firm in D.C. and, for the few years before he retired, a senior position at the International Satellite Corporation.

There is no question in my mind that he loved my mother and that she loved him, despite the ways he would go on to disappoint her. As for me, loving my father wasn't so easy, although his dying certainly helped.

My father was a big man, over six feet tall with broad shoulders and narrow hips. Not handsome exactly—he wore thick, black-framed glasses, and his features were heavy and somewhat coarse—but physically commanding. Loud and animated in social situations, he demanded attention from the people around him. It was only with us, his family, that he was remote and secretive.

For years, he hid how much alcohol he consumed, tossing down drinks while he cooked and then drinking "only wine" with dinner.

And more than once he claimed to have successfully quit smoking while continuing to smoke at work and in his car. Somehow, it was always one of us, not my mother, who caught him.

It was the same with his affairs. I still wince remembering the night my mother called to ask me why Hannah, Katherine and I had never told her about Rebecca, a woman he'd had an affair with back when I was in college. I was in my late twenties by then, living with my fiancé, Jack, in Brooklyn, and I can recall looking out at the dim confines of our backyard, the so-called garden that went with our garden apartment, and cursing my father.

The truth was, the three of us had known all along. My father had told Hannah about Rebecca during Hannah's freshman year in college, ostensibly to console her after a bad breakup with her boyfriend, and Hannah had immediately passed the information on to Katherine and me.

I remember being stunned, not only by the fact that my father was having an affair but by the extent of what he'd revealed: Hannah knew Rebecca's profession (professor at Georgetown), sexual history (she liked women as well as men), and family status (divorced, one teenage son). Hannah had even *met* the woman at one of my father's jazz gigs, an entirely safe venue at this point because my mother had stopped attending his musical performances years before, claiming that she got too sleepy and the smoke bothered her.

"So what was she like?" I asked Hannah, feeling, as I often did, that despite the small difference in our ages, she was way ahead of me. I mean, there she was calmly talking about my father's sex life while I sat there like an idiot.

"Beautiful. Smart. *Nice.* She followed me into the club's bathroom and told me she wasn't interested in marrying Poppa or breaking up his marriage. Also something about how he still really loved Momma."

"Oh. Well. That was big of her."

We sat smoking cigarettes on the back porch and discussing the matter. Earlier we'd shared a joint—my parents were out—and I have a hazy memory of our deciding it was impossible for two people to be everything to one another anyway. Disturbed as I was by Hannah's revelations, I remember thinking there was something appropriate about having this kind of adult conversation just as I was preparing to leave home.

But listening to the sadness and hurt in my mother's voice that night in Brooklyn almost ten years later, I felt only guilt and anger that my father had implicated us in his betrayal. And then the thud of inevitability as my mother told me of another affair—an affair she *had* known about, back when we were little—with the much younger cousin of one of our neighbors. Apparently, my father had confessed to my mother in the middle of D.C.'s famous Black and White Ball, a glamorous charity event for which my mother had commissioned her seamstress to concoct a slinky, ankle-length dress covered with black and white sequins, a dress that currently hangs in my closet in California.

"God, Momma, that was shitty of him. Why didn't you leave him?"

"I did. I left for a week."

"You did? But where were we?" My voice rose childishly as I imagined my sisters and me, three small, defenseless girls, willfully thrust into this chaotic adult situation.

"I took you with me. We stayed with my cousin Maeve in New York. Maeve's two children were also young and she had a very good nanny." My mother laughed darkly. "Maeve took me shopping and to lunches at fancy restaurants all week, apparently to cheer me up. It was so exhausting after a while, I had to come home."

"That was it? You just . . . got over it?"

"No." The word hung between us, small and forlorn, and I wondered if my mother was going to cry. I hoped not. She hated crying in front of anyone. She continued, voice strong, "I told him he had to break it off and of course he agreed. Although frankly, knowing what I do now, I doubt he did. I also told him if he ever had another affair, I would leave him. For good."

I was torn between wanting to praise my mother for taking such a strong stand and fearing what was going to happen next. Was Rebecca going to be the end of my parents' marriage? And how had my mother found out about her anyway? Given my mother's earlier threat, I doubted my father had volunteered the information.

"What are you going to do?"

"I don't know, sweetheart. Strangle him maybe."

I sank to the floor, forcing the black coils of the phone cord to stretch to their full length, the tension draining from my body. *She wasn't going to leave him.*

"But you never answered my question, Zoe. How long have you girls known about this?"

"Well . . . I'm not sure exactly," I said, wanting to protect her, and myself, and not sure how to do either. "Not that long."

"Zoe—"

"Look, I'm really not sure. How'd you know we knew anyway?"

"Katherine." She sighed again. "For some unfathomable reason, your father told Katherine about Rebecca when he was up in Boston on business last fall. God knows why. He hasn't been involved with her for ages. Showing off perhaps. Katherine wasn't amused and decided to spill the beans when we went to visit her. I must say I was impressed."

I was too. My father was notorious for flying into rages and, depending on how much he'd had to drink, was not above making a scene. She'd taken a risk, but it didn't surprise me; Katherine was tough and she'd never gotten along with my father. And while she'd been willing to keep Hannah's secret, she wasn't willing to keep his. How could he have miscalculated so badly? He'd essentially handed her a loaded gun and asked her not to use it.

Lying next to Jack that night, a pillow over my head to blot out the sounds of the neighborhood cats outside the window, I wondered why my father had never told *me* about his affairs, while apparently having discussed them with both my sisters. Did my strong alliance with my mother make me too dangerous, or did my father feel I wouldn't—or couldn't—understand these complicated private matters? It would be years before I realized that these questions weren't relevant, that asking them assumed the existence of a discerning, sober intelligence that had largely ceased to exist.

Six months before he died, my father drove off the side of the road on his way to a Christmas party because of a sudden bout of double vision. The doctors checked him into the hospital and ran the usual tests—CAT scans, MRIs, blood work—but couldn't explain it. He seemed to have stabilized when, out of the blue, his blood pressure soared and he began to shake and sweat. The doctors told my mother he was suffering from DTs—delirium tremens—brought on by alcohol withdrawal. It was the first time she believed he was an alcoholic.

"Are you serious, Momma?" I asked her. "The three of us have been telling you that for years."

But when I thought about it, I realized that, while she'd never agreed with the point, she'd never argued it either. Nor had she expressed any particular shock or dismay.

"What you don't realize is that everyone used to drink a lot," she said. "And he always held it so well. I guess I thought that meant he wasn't a true alcoholic."

"But he didn't hold it well," I snapped. "He blew up over nothing. He repeated himself. He never let people get a word in edgewise. God, there are so many ways his drinking affected him!"

I wanted to bring up his affairs, and the leering, inappropriate way he had with women when he'd been drinking, but I stopped myself. Surely she knew all that. Besides, my father was in the middle of a health crisis, one that would eventually lead to a diagnosis of non-Hodgkins lymphoma, and my mother wasn't well herself.

"You're right, I suppose. Actually, a lot of things make more sense to me now."

"They do? Like what?"

"Oh, small things." She paused as if uncertain whether to continue. "Actually, I was thinking about how he used to insist on going down to the bar or restaurant ahead of me when we were traveling. It would make me mad because he'd never wait for me to finish getting dressed and go down with me. I finally realized it was so he could get a couple of drinks in before I arrived." She gave a half laugh. "As if somehow those drinks wouldn't count if I wasn't there."

I could tell it pained her to reveal even this small deception. My mother had always been a staunch believer in a united front and would never criticize my father to us, even when we'd go to her in tears after one of his rages. When my parents did argue in front of us, it was in French so we couldn't understand. But perhaps my father's hotel charade was emblematic of all the bigger ways he'd dissembled and deceived her—and the ways she'd chosen to remain oblivious to them.

Although I felt a degree of pity as I listened to her that day, there was also a certain mean satisfaction. My sisters and I had paid a price for my mother's obliquity all those years, for believing the "script" instead of the evidence, and it was hard to forgive her for normalizing my father's volatility and neglect. All that whitewashing of the marriage and my father's behavior had left the three of us profoundly alone with the experience, each in our own way trying to cope: Katherine by disdaining him, Hannah by becoming the pliant daughter he could show off at gigs and parties and I . . . well, I never really figured out what to do, but chaotically borrowed from both strategies.

And so I responded unsympathetically. "I don't know why he bothered to hide it from you. It's not like you ever asked him to cut back or not drink so much."

"I did once or twice, you know. When we were younger. It made him absolutely furious. I guess I just didn't think it was something I could control."

"So you decided he wasn't really an alcoholic."

"No. I really didn't think he was an alcoholic."

"Until now."

"Until now."

Too tired to go up to bed by this point, I curl up on the couch and close my eyes, comforted by the familiar late-night hum of the house, the diffuse vibration of distant machines (the heater, the dishwasher), the sound of Rosa preparing for bed in the room next door. Back when it was our dining room, there was an enormous rough-hewn wooden table in there big enough to seat twenty people. It was where my father used to throw elaborate parties and lead his guests in a rousing *grand cri d'enthousiasme* for the excellent food and wine.

When he was dying, it became his bedroom, the massive table moved out to the Big Room to make way for a rented hospital bed. I can still perfectly recall the strange day seven years ago when he took to that bed for the last time.

Katherine and I had arrived at different times that morning, just as we had last night, pulling up in separate airport cabs. It was late May, six months after his diagnosis, and Hannah and I had been to see him many times. Katherine had come just once, but my father had apparently been waiting for the three of us to arrive before beginning what I came to think of as his Final Descent.

He was perfectly fine when he came into the kitchen for breakfast, according to my mother, decked out in his usual baggy sweater and jeans. As fine as anyone could be with lymphoma-related tumors invading his brain. But as soon as he sat down at the table, his mental circuitry seemed to shut down. By the time I arrived, he'd been sitting there for over an hour, utterly immobile, not talking, eating, or moving, just staring blankly into space the way people do when they're preoccupied or thinking deeply. Except it looked to me like he was watching something, his own collapsing infrastructure perhaps, his expression shifting between blankness and surprise.

I gave him a hug and asked him what was wrong, but he just sat there staring across the table, his wide shoulders slumped, an intent look on his face. Then, just before Katherine arrived, he took a long, deep breath and said, "Something strange. I don't know." And that was it. When my sister arrived minutes later and made her cheery hellos, he didn't respond, at least in any recognizable way.

Instead, he began to sing. Or, more specifically, to produce drawn-out, wordless exhalations: a melding of consonants and vowels in one sustained, low-pitched note. When he ran out of air, he would pause for several moments, take a harsh, tremulous breath, then begin again on a different note, a new constellation of sounds. This went on for several hours, during which the three of us wandered in and out of the room and my mother made repeated phone calls to the doctor and sat next to my father, rubbing his back.

When I think about it now, it seems odd that no one called 911, though I remember that even then my mother was adamant about people dying at home and not getting "carted off to hospitals." (She'd recently insisted Rosa Scotch-tape handwritten signs under every phone in the house exhorting, "Do Not Call 911!!!") But given my father's alarming behavior that terrible day, it seems amazing no one suggested it.

By midafternoon, he'd collapsed onto the table, his hands alternately scrabbling across the wood and lying motionless, no longer singing or responding to us in any way. After trying numerous times to help him walk to the dining room, Hannah, Katherine and I simply dragged him there, still sitting in his chair, and somehow managed to lift him onto his bed.

He broke his silence only twice before he died five weeks later.

Both times it was to chime in with music we had playing on a tape deck in the corner of his room. His voice sounded cheery and surprisingly robust. The songs he chose to sing reassured and buoyed us: a Dixieland jazz version of the old gospel tune "Walking with the King," and Willie Nelson's "Don't Get Around Much Anymore." It was a message; my father knew he was on his way out, but he wasn't that upset about it.

No one expected him to die. It was the one thing that was said over and over at his funeral. He was a force of nature, an original, a man of so many talents and so much vitality, it seemed he would live forever. His friends were hurt and confused by his dying, as if men like my father—brash, amusing men with big personalities, big ideas—were meant to live longer, fuller lives than more ordinary people. People like them.

During the ceremony, modeled loosely on a Quaker funeral, a small, pre-selected group of speakers, including Hannah, stood up and spoke and then the floor was opened to the guests. One by one they rose, and with humor and eloquence reminisced about my father. I found myself responding to their words, liking and even loving this crazy, madcap man who trimmed the lawn with nail scissors and made bouillabaisse at four in the morning. I began to wonder what was wrong with this charming man's daughters. Not to mention his wife. Why didn't we have funny stories to tell, tender moments to share?

Oh, there were a few, I suppose. After all, I too cooked with my father once at four in the morning. Not bouillabaisse, only tuna fish salad, but we made the mayonnaise from scratch, which was pretty amusing since my friend Suzanne and I were high as kites and even beating egg yolks can be hilarious under the influence of drugs.

We were juniors in high school, arriving home from a party just as my father drove up, drunk but mellow, after playing with his jazz band at a club in Virginia. We converged in the kitchen and soon my father had Suzanne and me cranking away on the old-fashioned eggbeater, laughing like maniacs, while he toasted bread and chopped celery and onion, and poured us glasses of wine. Everything tasted amazing.

It was nice. A nice moment with my dad. He was still a pretty decent drunk back then. He hadn't started repeating himself or getting angry or blacking out and making passes at my friends, as he did later. And it was true what they said about him. He was a man of many talents, many passions—cooking, fly-fishing, playing drums, reading—all of which he pursued with single-minded intensity. Oh yes, reading. I think my father's happiest moments were sitting at the kitchen table with a book, a pack of cigarettes and a drink while something fragrant and oily bubbled away on the stove.

True, he read mostly mysteries, but also Shakespeare and, every few years, *Ulysses.* The man's brain was as supersized as the rest of him. Even crippled by radiation, his brain was bigger than most people's, according to his doctor, which might have been flattery but probably wasn't.

Actually, I needed to believe it wasn't, because it was during this time, the precious few months after radiation and rehab and before the tumors returned, that I finally had the father I'd always wanted. And so I had to believe I was accessing the essence of my father, not just the manifestation of a right-brain injury.

My father's entire being was transformed by illness—illness and the cessation of alcohol. Almost as if the doctors had lasered away the great, blustering edifice of his personality along with the brain tumors, leaving a sweet and gentle man I barely recognized but immediately loved: the father of my dreams.

I shaved the hair that clung in wisps to his enormous scalp, held his arm on our short walks down the block, lifted his feet onto the bed when he went to sleep at night. I fed him small mouthfuls of cereal and ice cream and helped his Ghanaian caretaker, Dalia, who called my father Chief, massage his hands and feet. Not only did I feel comfortable with this physical contact, I reveled in it. It was the first time physical exchanges with my father had ever been simple or easy. Our conversations were also effortless and direct.

"It seems I'm dying," he told me once, sitting on the edge of the bed.

"Yes," I responded, startled. "It seems you are. Are you scared?"

"A little bit," he said, smiling. "Mostly just surprised. It's funny how you never think it's going to happen to you. And then it does."

By that time the tumors had returned, stronger this time, ready to finish the job. Even the Great Brain couldn't withstand the assault and began sending us odd, scrambled messages like cryptic haiku. "In Rain Don't Saw." "He Came Fellow Down." My mother and I would nod and smile. We didn't want to hurt his feelings.

Then came the day at the kitchen table followed by the long days watching him die. The false alarms in the middle of the night when his breathing grew loud and ragged, and we clutched his hands and told him he could go; the inward-turning hands; and, at the end, the slow creep of blue that started at his feet and gradually encased him, spreading like cool ash across his skin.

Through it all, my mother remained stoic and uncomplaining, crumbling only when friends expressed sympathy, or showed their own emotions, and I could tell she wished they wouldn't. She'd always been good in a crisis, good at rising to the occasion, and it was important that she maintain that façade.

On the night he died, my mother, Jack, our one-year-old daughter, Clara, and I had just eaten Chinese takeout on various chairs and couches set up around his bed. By this point, being in the room—and even eating a meal at my dying father's bedside—was a normal, even cozy event. We spoke freely and laughed when Clara pushed away my plate and insisted on nursing.

Relaxed and full, I went up to take a bath. I'd just slipped into the water when Jack knocked on the door. "I think you'd better come down," he said. "Your father just stopped breathing."

*Stopped breathing?* Stupidly, I wondered if that meant he was dead and, if so, why had he died right after I left the room? After all the time I'd spent with him, all those late nights when we'd dramatically gathered to "see him off," it would have been nice to be there when it happened. Still, feeling more curious than upset, I toweled off, dressed and went downstairs. Clara staggered happily toward me, unaware of what had just transpired, and we all stood around the bed looking down at him. "Go give your mother a hug," Jack whispered, taking Clara from me.

Of course, I thought, moving around the bed to embrace her, he's right. I should acknowledge her loss. Stiff and bony in my arms—these last weeks had been hard on her—my mother smiled at the gesture. But neither of us cried. We were ready for him to go. It didn't feel sad. It felt right.

Even before I called my sisters, I phoned Dalia. She said she'd known he was going to die that night, and would be right over. Together, the two of us dressed him. We tossed away his ugly blue hospital gown and put on blue jeans and a plaid shirt. It was awkward getting his arms into his sleeves, his pants up around his hips. Moving him this way and that, we kept jostling his head and his eyes kept sliding open. Either Dalia or I would reach over and close them again.

For weeks, I had disturbing dreams about my father's eyes. He would be talking and walking around as if he was still alive, but then I'd look him in the eyes and see that strange, blank stare. Sometimes I'd try to explain to him that he was dead. That he should really go back where he belonged. But usually I pretended not to notice. I still didn't want to hurt his feelings.

# Departure

Monday morning, the alarm goes off. My first thought: I'm leaving my mother.

The day rushes toward me in a series of vivid, exhausting images—car, airplane, car, family, home—and I can practically smell the stale, exhaust-tinged air, feel my knees go numb against the airplane seat in front of me as the going-home malaise settles darkly around me.

Somehow this journey between old and new homes feels unbearable. I sink deeper into my bed, imagining for one wild moment that I can will it away. Dial my life forward a day and wake in my own bed.

There's a soft knock on the door, and Kendra, who comes in on weekdays to give Rosa a break, sticks her head in and says, "Hey, Zoe. Your mom wanted me to make sure you were awake."

"Kendra. Thanks. You didn't need to do that."

"It's okay. I'll make you some coffee."

"Great. Make it strong. I can barely move."

She laughs and heads down the stairs as I stumble into the bathroom. Kendra is in her twenties, a small, soft-featured Jamaican woman who wears tight jeans and brightly colored wigs and nails. My mother says Kendra is moody, but my daughters are both madly in love with her. Whenever they come here, she takes them to the park and the movies, plays catch with them in the yard, and makes them snacks; all the things I find impossible to do when I'm here.

Down in the kitchen, Kendra hands me a cup of coffee and tells me to sit, then brings over a plate with a toasted muffin, jam and butter. During the week, my mother has an older Hispanic woman, Sonia, who comes in to cook and clean, but Kendra and Rosa do all the physical care and fix many of my mother's meals.

"Kendra! You're spoiling me."

"Hey, I don't mind. You've got a long day ahead of you. You gonna bring my girls next time you come?"

"I think so." Actually, I have no idea. With Bud out of the way, I'm not sure whether May first is happening or not and, if it is, whether I will bring Clara and Lane with me. My mind recoils at the idea. Although Clara was at my father's bedside when he died, she was just a baby. Now she's eight, observant and sensitive. What will it mean for her—or Lane—to see my mother talking and acting normal one day, and dead the next?

"Well, you tell them I love them and I miss them." Kendra says this softly, standing at the sink rinsing some dishes. My eyes blur with tears and I have to put my coffee down and wipe them quickly on my sleeve. "Thanks, Kendra, I will," I say, coughing to cover the break in my voice. "I'll tell them."

I knock on my mother's door and she immediately calls, "Come in!" I know that she's been waiting for me and that she's dreading my leaving. She was determinedly cheerful when Katherine left yesterday but fell asleep for hours as soon as she left. At dinner last night—she in bed, I on the couch—she'd seemed tired and depressed, repeatedly mentioning that she wished we all lived closer.

"Does Kendra have my breakfast yet?" She sounds annoyed and, with her quilt pulled up to her chin, looks like an angry child. "I've been up for over an hour and she hasn't brought me anything."

"She's making oatmeal. I'm sure she'll be in soon."

"I just don't feel like I can depend on her. Last week when I asked her to get something for me at the drugstore, she was gone for *two hours*."

"She probably had some of her own errands to run. It must be hard having a young son and working here every day."

My mother looks unconvinced. I'm impatient with her complaints and criticisms. Kendra has told me repeatedly how much she loves working for my mother and how she worries about her on her days off. But I don't mention this. I don't want to argue with my mother right before I go.

"When are you leaving?" She fiddles with the edge of her quilt, not looking at me.

"The car will be here in fifteen minutes."

Her fingers are shaking and the edge of the quilt trembles in her grasp.

"I hate having you go." Again, that petulant tone.

"I know. Me too." Actually, at this point I'm dying to go. What I hate are these good-byes.

"I can't stand living like this. With no one here to take care of me."

"What do you mean no one to take care of you?" Irritation saves me from more difficult emotions. Doesn't she realize how good she has it? Unlike so many older people, my mother has enough money to stay in her home *and* have round-the-clock care. She should appreciate it. "You have Rosa and Kendra and Sonia, Momma. Isn't that enough?"

"No, it's *not* enough, Zoe. I need a parent. Not people who are hired to take care of me."

"A parent? What are you talking about?" My mother's parents

were glamorous, neglectful people who both died when my mother was young. "Your parents never took care of you. Ever."

"Well, that's true." Oddly, she seems to brighten at this thought and even smiles. "But that's what I need. Parents. No one else can really give me what I need."

"Oh, Momma. Is it really that bad? You have friends that come by—Joan Reynolds, Judy Brown, Marilyn Fletcher. Katherine was just here. Hannah and I come when we can. And next time I'll bring the girls. They love it here."

"I know, Zoe. You've all been wonderful. I just feel all alone and stuck in my bed with nothing to do."

I'm afraid she's going to mention May first and I don't think I can stand it. "Well, I'm sorry, Momma. I'm sorry that I have to go, sorry that you don't feel more positive about your life. Just try to remember all the good things you have. And we can keep talking about the . . . other stuff."

"I don't know if we should have dismissed Bud so quickly."

"Momma. *Please.*"

There's a tap on the door. "I have your breakfast, Mrs. Draper." Kendra pushes open the door. "Your car is outside, Zoe."

My heart aches as I go over to hug my mother good-bye. For a long moment, we hold each other, unable to talk. I turn to walk away, still speechless, but not before I catch sight of her face, reddened and crumpled, and covered with tears.

# Coming Home

Arriving is the worst. Emerging into the long hallways of the San Francisco airport, I feel as blank and gray as the fog the city is famous for. I recognize Jack by his tall, lanky frame and blond hair but can muster only a vague stirring of affection. I put my arms around his neck, feel the warmth of his lips on my travel-parched mouth, but remain numb, untouched.

With my children, Clara and Lane, there is, happily, no need to pretend. Their shy, rapturous joy at my return elicits the normal rush of maternal feeling. But with Jack, the man I've loved for fourteen years, I'm forced to mimic emotions that are temporarily absent. It reminds me of a game I play with Clara who, at age eight, is still into full-time make-believe. When the fog hides our view of the San Francisco Bay, we peer out the window and point to the things we know are there but can't actually see.

"There's the water, Mommy. Right there. Do you see it? It's blue and green with little waves. And there's the bridge and Albany Hill. Can you see all the houses on it, Mommy?"

She's so intent on my "seeing" that she's unaware I'm only pretending to see. My husband, on the other hand, is a sensitive man, acutely tuned to the nuances of rejection, and he sees right through my little performance. He's been kind enough to blame it on the "situation"—deteriorating mother, dutiful daughter—but his generosity is wearing thin and we've grown fractured and unfriendly. Only sex redeems us, but sex is getting harder for me to accomplish. At this point, I cannot bear to be opened up any more than I already am.

But somehow, on the night of my return, we manage it, and I'm determined to enjoy the postcoital payoff—affection, or at least the absence of Jack's resentment—while it lasts. To that end, I've shared only vague details about the weekend with Bud. Jack is a lawyer with a doctorate in biochemistry; he works for one of the Bay Area's top biotech companies. He's rational, analytical and cautious. My little story of helium and plastic bags and people disappearing in the night will strike him as dangerous if not completely insane.

Next to me, he begins to snore. His arm drops away, and the cool air hits my bare skin. Our bedroom is large and drafty and on cold nights, it feels like sleeping in a tree house.

"Jack." I prod him with my elbow.

"Sorry." He snuggles against me, breathing heavily in my face. "Did I miss something?" He gathers a handful of my hair, long again like when I was a teenager, and gives it a gentle tug.

"You haven't told me about the weekend," I say, pulling the covers up, releasing a puff of warm air into the room. "How'd everything go with the kids?"

He doesn't respond right away and immediately I'm on guard. Is there something he hasn't told me? Images of Clara wandering lost and frightened, Lane crying inconsolably, race through my brain. And then—instantly—I'm furious. So furious I can barely breathe. Can't I leave the kids for *three goddamn days* without something happening to them? Do I have to take care of *everybody*?

"It was great." Jack's voice is sleepy and warm with remembered pleasure. "I mean it's weird when you're gone, but it's pretty fun being the only parent. I took them to the park, let them sleep in here a couple of nights. I made pancakes . . ."

I close my eyes as the adrenaline recedes, grateful that I didn't betray myself. I am, in fact, moved by this image of my motherless family curled up together at night, and touched that Jack thought to turn my absence into a mini holiday-with-Dad.

"They were kinda expecting you to call though," he adds, voice neutral.

I'm instantly contrite. "I know, I know. I blew it."

"Hey, at least you managed to have sex with me." Jack kisses the top of my head. "As for the kids, they miss you, but they'll be okay. This isn't going to last forever."

As much as I want to ignore the message-within-a-message, I can't. "You mean they miss me when I'm gone? When I'm at my mother's?"

"Mmm." He hesitates and then adds, as I know he will, "And when you're home. Look, Zoe, you're exhausted, you're distracted. Clara says you're late picking her up at school half the time. You disappear into your room every time Hannah or your mother calls. And you left for three days and didn't call. You don't think they notice?"

"Shit, Jack, I'm doing what I can, including asking my mother to try to call when they're not home. But give me a break. These trips are a burnout—the whole situation is a burnout. You'd be stressed too if your mother was dying."

"Your mother isn't dying, she's *talking* about dying, or killing herself, or getting someone else to kill her, or whatever it is this week. And she's got you in a state over it, which means we're all on hold. You, me, the kids, your writing. All of it. How long is she going to keep this up? Calling everyone to announce some new plan every five minutes. And how long are you going to run to her every time she calls?"

I turn away, pull my legs toward my chest. I know Jack is right.

My mother is putting too great a demand on me and I'm letting her, but I'm shocked at the unfairness, the vehemence, of his accusations. Jack never used to get angry. It was one of the things I found continually surprising about him. Anger was the main currency in my household growing up, the place we met and acknowledged each other most fully, and the absence of anger in a person is disconcerting to me.

Perversely, I used to think it signified a general lack of feeling in Jack, a deficit, even as a small piece of myself hurtled toward him, desperate to be loved by such a man. But now it seems I have conjured the beast and there is no getting rid of him. I'm a corrupter, an emotional virus that, once transmitted, can never be contained. And yet, like in one of those TV commercials where comically rendered vermin invade your sink or your tongue or your toenails with diabolical glee, I feel a small tingle of satisfaction along with my dismay: his anger has made us more equal.

*How long are you going to run to her every time she calls?*

I can't answer that question. No, I *can* answer that question, but it's better not to so I pretend to go to sleep. Closing my eyes, I imagine my mother lying in her bed, lonely and afraid. Not of death but of the long, ugly road leading to death. And because I'm her daughter, both by birth and by design, I'm trapped on that road with her until one of us, or perhaps both of us, can engineer her release. Which means that, despite my husband's anger and my children's unhappiness, the answer is: *Always. I will always run to her when she calls.*

I telephone Hannah as soon as Jack leaves for work, dropping the kids off at school on his way. I feel so relieved when they go that I hate myself. I've always needed large stretches of solitude, but I used to also enjoy noise, parties, intense one-on-one conversations, friendships and flirtations. Now I just want to be left alone.

Hannah doesn't pick up, so I leave a message on her machine and fetch my laptop along with a second cup of Peet's Holiday Blend. It's mid-March, so I'm not sure what holiday we're celebrating, but the coffee is wonderful: hot, fragrant, and so dense that the whiteness of the cream is almost entirely negated.

Despite a near-paralytic inertia, I settle on the couch and turn on my iBook. For months now, my novel has languished in the slim casings of my laptop like an abandoned pet, unfed and unloved. When people ask what I do, I tell them I'm writing a novel, but the truth is I talk about writing a novel, I don't actually write it.

This brings up a slew of uncomfortable truths: that my husband thinks I'm still writing a novel, that I'm financially dependent on my husband, that my promising career as a journalist back in New York City has evaporated, and that no matter how hard I spin it, I'm a housewife—a housewife with artistic pretensions and a death-obsessed mother.

The novel—a murder mystery—is about a young woman struggling with the psychological and emotional dislocation of becoming a mother. I began writing it the year after Clara was born in an attempt to make sense of what the hell had just happened to my life. The writing of the book has become a story of interruptions as well, first by the sickness and death of my father, then by the move across country, the birth of my second daughter, and now the demands of my mother.

My family history is rife with failed writers. The grandmother whose poetry was so bad even my ten-year-old father was embarrassed by it. The grandfather—my mother's father—who published a couple of novels, a handful of short stories and a screenplay before retiring at the age of thirty-five to drink and drug himself to death in the family's country house. And my mother, who's worked on the same autobiographical novel for over twenty years, with no end in sight except, of course, her own.

It's not discipline she lacks. I can't remember a time when she didn't spend most of her day locked up in her study working. Nor is it writer's block: she's produced thousands of pages. It's a willful resistance to finishing. Every time she comes close, she finds a way to start over. For months after my father died, I worked on her book, helping her edit and shape it and, just when I thought it was done, she hired another editor and took off in a new direction.

How many times have I heard her say, "It'll be done by summer," or "In the fall," or "Certainly by Christmas"? I fear it will be that way with death as well. She has already set and changed her final "deadline" twice, once in early February and again in early March, and now May first may go by the wayside as well. I don't want to go through a process of mental and emotional preparation—final conversations, attempts at acceptance—only to have it not happen.

Finishing my coffee, I click on the folder icon entitled "Mystery," open chapter one and begin to read. But it's too late. The invisible wire that connects me to my mother has hummed to life and I'm instantly transported to the stark white walls, the blue square of bed, where she lies planning for death. I make this journey so reflexively, so completely, I can practically smell the Nivea cream she uses on her skin, the musty scent of her clothes. I stop reading. Close my eyes. A terrible calculation unrolls in my head.

If she does kill herself on May first, I could theoretically get back to writing sometime in late May. But then the kids get out of school in June and the disorganized jumble of half-day summer camps and the yearly family vacation in Vermont begins. It will be months before I have any real time to write. Perhaps it's best that I don't try. It's simply too painful. Like finding myself at the bottom of the same ditch over and over again. Every time I claw my way back up to the road and start to move forward, there's another huge gap in time and I find myself back at the bottom of the ditch.

I click Save and Close and sit staring across the room, wondering how much more I'll have to give up before this is over.

# "You're Nobody Till Somebody Loves You"

## AUGUST 1972

A few days before we had to pack up and drive home from Vermont, the whole family went to a dance at the Mountain View Country Club.

Hannah spent all afternoon changing her clothes and sneaking into my parents' room to try on my mother's jewelry. I snuck into their room, too, when my mother was out swimming, to scoop a handful of change off my father's desk. I did this every few days so I'd have money for candy bars when I took the boat into town. I always ate them on the way home. If my mother found the wrappers, she got mad. She said I needed to watch my weight.

I only had one dress, so it didn't take me long to get ready. I went downstairs and found my father reading a paperback at the kitchen table. He was smoking a cigarette and having a drink, his hair slicked back like he'd just come out of the shower. He was wearing a light blue shirt and white pants and a navy blue blazer hung on the back of his chair. He was playing drums at the dance that night with some other musicians from around the lake.

"Hi," he said, looking up briefly. "All ready?"

"Yep," I said, and then just stood there. I didn't want to sit down and talk to him, but it felt funny just to walk away. He started to read again, so I called the three dogs out from under the table and went outside and sat on the deck overlooking the lake. I let my dog, Leo, a small Lhasa Apso I'd gotten on my eighth birthday, climb into my lap. I'd have dog hair all over my dress, but I didn't care.

"There you are." My mother stepped outside. She had on a green sleeveless dress and brown sandals. Her perfume smelled sticky and sweet in the fresh outdoor air and I wondered why women liked to smell like that. Probably because men liked it, I thought, although I couldn't think why.

"Don't you want to put your hair up?" she asked. "I hate seeing it in your face like that."

"No. It's okay, Momma. I like it this way."

The screen door opened behind her and my father came out. "Jesus, Margaret. Where the hell is everyone? We're going to be late."

Hannah appeared in the doorway behind him. She was wearing a short flowered skirt and white tank top with the outline of her bra visible beneath it. She also had on green eye shadow and red lipstick. My father took a step backward and pretended to wipe his brow.

"My, oh my. Where did this gorgeous woman come from?"

Hannah stepped out on the deck and did a little pirouette.

"Is that my lipstick you're wearing?" my mother asked, sounding cross.

"Yes," Hannah said, smiling, putting her head to one side. "I had to use yours. I don't have any, remember? You won't let me buy any."

My mother started to say something, but my father laughed and threw his arm around Hannah. "She's got you there, Meggens.

Now let's take Cinderella here to the ball before she turns back into a pumpkin."

"Where's Katherine?" I asked, starting toward the side of the house.

My mother shooed the dogs inside and called to Katherine, who quickly scuttled out across the porch. I thought I saw smudges of eye shadow on her eyelids too, but I couldn't tell for sure because she had her head down and her hair over her face. I'd never seen her wear makeup. She said it was dumb. I kept trying to see, but she spent the entire ride staring out the window, turned away from me. Normally, Hannah and I would have giggled and made faces at each other about her, but Hannah didn't seem to notice.

The parking lot at the Mountain View was filled with cars, and the clubhouse, a large wooden building with a long front porch, was brightly lit and filled with people. I wished I could sit in the car and wait until it was over, but my mother said, "Honestly, sweetie, it's not a funeral. You'll have fun. But get that dog hair off your dress first, okay? You're covered with it."

Inside, the music started and my father began to sing. "You're nobody till somebody loves you. You're nobody till somebody caaaares . . ." He made an exaggerated, croony face when he sang and I was relieved when he went back to just playing the drums. He always looked happy and relaxed when he played drums, like there was nothing he'd rather be doing. He nodded and smiled at the other musicians when they took solos, and sometimes hit an extra hard beat.

Couples streamed in through the doorway and started to dance. My mother leaned against a table talking to a small blond woman in a red dress that didn't cover her knees. I couldn't find either of my sisters, so I went over to the punch table and got some crackers and cheese.

The band started "Bésame Mucho," and the woman in the red dress climbed onto the stage and played the violin. She played really well and when she was done everyone clapped and cheered and my father stood up and pretended to sweep his hat toward the floor. On the next song, he and the violin lady stepped off the stage and danced together. They laughed as they twirled across the dance floor and the other couples moved back and made room for them.

The band played a few more songs and I was about to wander outside when Hannah showed up, shouting to be heard over the music. "C'mon, Zoe. Let's dance!"

"No, you go ahead," I shouted back at her.

Just then a man with thick, dark hair, wearing a button-down blue shirt and khakis, came over and grabbed Hannah by the hand and pulled her onto the dance floor. I recognized him from other dances. His name was Tom Jackson, and he sometimes played trombone with the band. He was pretty old but not as old as our parents. I wondered if he knew that Hannah was only thirteen.

I watched him twirl Hannah across the floor, her bare legs flying under her short skirt, and then went and sat on the porch.

On the way home, my mother said she would have appreciated it if my father had danced with her more.

"Don't be ridiculous, Margaret! I was playing. What did you expect?"

"You had time to dance with Meryl Stone."

I thought of the violin lady in the short skirt. I'd seen them dancing several times during the evening.

"Meryl's a member of the band. I was just being polite."

My mother made an exasperated sound.

"You could've danced with Tom Jackson, Momma," Katherine said suddenly. She'd spent most of the evening out by the tennis courts with her friends but must have seen Hannah dancing. "But you would have had to peel him off Hannah first."

My father laughed and Hannah slapped at her playfully and said, "Shut up! I didn't see anyone asking you to dance."

"That *was* a little inappropriate, Jonathan. Tom's at least thirty-five."

"Oh, for God's sake, Margaret."

"I'm just saying—" But she stopped herself.

Looking out at the dark trees swirling past us, I was glad I didn't have to worry about getting along with a husband or dancing with anyone. Those things were clearly never going to happen to me.

# Hannah

I must have dozed off because I'm lying on my side with the computer jammed painfully into my hip when the phone rings. My mouth feels like cracked leather. I scrabble around on the couch until I find the portable phone.

"I'm losing it, Han," I tell my sister, making myself more coffee while I fill her in on the weekend with Bud. Back on the couch, I pull Clara's soccer jacket over my legs and clutch my mug against my chest. The morning fog from the bay hasn't burned off, and the house feels damp and cold. "Being in D.C. was insane—weirder than ever—but then I got home and I felt like I was sleepwalking. I still do."

"You're overloaded," Hannah says, kind but matter-of-fact. "You're shutting down. It's a trauma reaction."

Hannah runs a local arts council on Prince Edward Island, where she raises chickens and goats, and trains horses and dogs. She's married to a Canadian musician she met while studying maritime folklore in graduate school. She's enormously intelligent and I'm inclined to accept her interpretation of things, but not unquestioningly. Her diagnoses of people tend to go through phases—borderline personality disorder, passive aggression, sugar addiction—and I wonder if trauma is her current favorite.

Not that I don't find labels reassuring. Naming the pain means holding it away from you, labeled and contained, instead of allowing it to wreak its havoc inside you like some rogue strand of DNA, quietly lethal.

"I thought trauma was something that happened to victims of natural disasters or violent crime," I say, taking a sip of coffee. "Not privileged California housewives who don't even work for a living." Writing a novel hardly qualified, especially as I'd just given it up.

"Are you saying you don't think this insane death-and-dying drama Momma is putting us through is traumatic?" Hannah asks. There's a pause and I can hear her chewing something. We speak on the phone almost every day and will occasionally converse through entire meals. "I mean, what kind of mother asks her daughters to help plan her suicide and insists they be there when she does it?"

I think about Katherine saying, *I do think Momma has the right to die,* which was easy enough to say if you didn't plan on being there. I throw the jacket off my knees and go stand by the back door. A hummingbird zooms into view, hovers frantically for a second, then flits away.

"I just wish," I say, struggling to keep my voice even, "that she would ask us. Just once—*ask* us."

"You mean if we minded being there when she did it?"

"Well, that would be nice." I try for a humorous tone, but my voice sounds kind of squeezed. "Actually, I meant ask us how we felt about her dying."

"Oh, Zoe, I just don't think she can. She's never been good at talking about her feelings—and I'm not sure *our* feelings have much reality for her at this point. She's pretty focused on herself, on her own process. She always has been."

I look out at the garden, searching for the hummingbird, but am unable to locate him. I know what Hannah is saying is true: Our mother has always tended to focus more on how we appeared—put-together, successful, smart—than on how we felt. And God knows I've suffered the sting of her critical eye over the years. But I've also enjoyed a certain closeness with her that my sisters never had. And, as an adult, I've been able to access an earthy, subversively funny side of her that they always seem to miss. This can make talking about her difficult, even to Hannah.

I remember how excited I was about spending more time with my mother after my father died. Although her deteriorating health and my move out west would eventually make it impossible, she was a constant visitor in my Brooklyn apartment for the first few years after his death. We spent most of our time working on her book, but we also watched movies, went to Manhattan to shop, and once—memorably—had tea at the Plaza Hotel, a place her beaus used to take her during her twenties.

It started to snow while we were finishing our tea and by the time we emerged, the line for taxis stretched all the way down the block. Realizing we'd never get back to Brooklyn in time to pick up Clara at preschool, I panicked. There was no way I could drag my mother onto a subway—she was already too frail for that—and we were carrying the day's shopping. Just then, a limousine pulled up, a window rolled down, and the driver asked if we needed a ride. We looked at each other and, laughing, leapt inside, feeling very grand as we swept down Fifth Avenue, our Bloomingdale's bags at our feet.

Reflexively, I start to tell Hannah this story but stop. I want to hold on to it, let its sweetness comfort me instead of tossing it out for the usual dissection. So instead, I ask about her plans to come visit me in late May.

"I'm going to buy our plane tickets this week. The girls are totally excited. I'm just hoping we don't get blindsided. I wouldn't be at all surprised if Momma called an emergency death council in the middle of my trip."

I laugh. "She insists it's going to be all over by then."

"And do we believe her?"

"Not a chance."

After I hang up, I race upstairs and change into my running clothes. As usual, talking to Hannah has lifted my torpor, and given me a sense of things being bearable, if not exactly normal. It was always so.

In my earliest memories of Hannah, she is exuberant, loud. She tosses back her head and opens her mouth wide when she laughs so I can see down her throat and up her nostrils. Her skin is paler than mine, her hair darker and curlier. Only our eyes are the same, a murky gray-green flecked with brown.

We used to grab each other's noses and hold on tight, each trying to twist out of the other's grasp while keeping a firm grip, laughing and rolling around. My mother told us we were going to do permanent damage to our noses. We didn't believe her, but we stopped doing it anyway, in case she was right. Neither of us wanted to end up with a funny-looking nose.

Just over a year apart, we both liked to exaggerate the age difference between us. Hannah would carry me in her arms when we were playing in the lake in Vermont and call me her baby, even though I was practically as big as she was. And once when we were traveling, I pretended I was mentally retarded (something I did regularly at eight or nine) and held her hand all the way across the airport, dragging along behind her, pigeon-toed and blank-looking.

We never discussed this game, but I knew Hannah liked it too. After all, she'd been under Katherine's thumb since the day she was born, an event Katherine had essentially never forgiven her for. (Hannah's third birthday was famously ruined when Katherine snarled, "You may be three today, but you'll be two again tomorrow!") My willing submission to Hannah gave her the strength to stand up to Katherine and she in turn gave me safe harbor from Katherine's free-floating aggression. On nights when Katherine and my parents fought, Hannah and I retreated to her bedroom and did our homework or read together on her bed.

This happy arrangement ended when Hannah abruptly and dramatically went into puberty at the age of ten. Furious at her for changing so quickly and unexpectedly, for becoming something I couldn't understand and wasn't ready for, I pulled away. Her self-consciousness about her body made *me* self-conscious and our relaxed physicality disappeared.

Although Hannah has since confessed how unready she was for this change, how she felt prematurely ejected from childhood, at the time it seemed she embraced it with a vengeance. She adopted a sexy, older style of dressing, shaved her legs and wore makeup, and—by high school—was wearing vintage black dresses and heels. At fourteen, she could pass for twenty-five.

My sister's metamorphosis into a 1920s-style femme fatale threw us all into a tizzy. Envious of her sudden glamour and sex appeal, I secretly plotted how to be more like her. Katherine, on the other hand, expressed nothing but disdain, and her style grew ever more militantly plain.

But it is interesting that it was my mother who seemed to recoil the furthest. She grew critical of and distant from Hannah, blaming her when one of my father's guests, a delegate from an African country he worked for, lunged at my sister on her way to bed. After fighting him off, she told my mother. But instead of confronting the man, my mother told Hannah she should have worn a bra at dinner.

I imagine it wasn't just her precocious physical beauty that made my mother pull back. Hannah challenged her in other ways as well. Well read and articulate, she could talk circles around most people, including her teachers, but was almost expelled from our fancy private high school. She had a habit of turning papers in late, or not at all, and never seemed to care about grades.

Long after my sister outgrew these habits, my mother continued to question her judgment. While I earned enthusiastic approval for my choices—my husband (Jack), my home (New York), and my career (journalism)—my sister didn't fare so well. Her decision to live on Prince Edward Island, for example, was not just a choice, it was a bad choice, and on my mother's rare visits she would say things like "Gosh, people eat terribly around here. Are they as unhealthy as they look?" And "You wouldn't want Fiona to learn French *here*. The accent is awful." It went without saying that my mother didn't approve of Dan, a former Royal Canadian Mounted Policeman, who was responsible for taking her brilliant middle daughter to this godforsaken place.

At first I kind of liked it when my mother complained about Hannah. In fact, she criticized *both* my sisters, which made it seem as if I alone was above reproach. But by my early thirties, I began to feel the way I had as a little girl when my mother would demand I tell her what "really happened" after a fight or when something got broken. I was being forced into a role that I neither wanted nor deserved. And while I continued to let her complain to me about Katherine, I stopped letting her bad-mouth Hannah and would mock her snobbism about Canada and my sister's life there.

Of course, part of me was aware that my mother's negative spin on Hannah was as unwarranted as her positive view of me. It hadn't escaped my notice that my choices were eerily similar to her own. Like my mother, I was a writer, married to a lawyer, living in a large East Coast city. Which raised the question: Whose life was she really endorsing?

# Running

I forgo the stretching as I always do and take off running down the asphalt path that loops around Berkeley's Cesar Chavez Park. Waves from the San Francisco Bay crash against the rocks less than twenty feet from me, and the wind tangles my hair and makes my eyes tear. Looking out across the water, I can see the rusty red outline of the Golden Gate Bridge and, to the left, San Francisco, like a small mountain of children's blocks wrapped in a sparkling, misty gauze.

My upper back is stiff from the plane ride back from D.C. two days ago and I almost fall when a sudden rise in the path sends me lurching forward. At the top of the hill, the path turns sharply in-land and the wind drops away. In the sudden quiet, I can hear the slap-slap of my running shoes as I settle into my run. The waves barely swell on this side of the park, and by the time I take the next curve and head along the estuary that separates the park from I-80 and the Berkeley/Emeryville waterfront, the air is still and hot, and I'm sweating and breathing hard.

Exercise has become my routine, my distraction. I've even

signed myself up for a 10K in Sonoma on May thirtieth. There's something wonderfully linear and quantifiable about training for a race. You have $x$ number of weeks, you add $y$ number of miles per week, and there you are on race day, ready to perform. It's the perfect equation: predictable, finite and achievable. And even if I fail, the daily runs give me something to focus on. Something other than my mother.

With the helium off the table, and no new plan in its place, I've been afraid that my mother will push the May first date to the end of the month, forcing me to cancel my race and Hannah's end-of-May visit. But when I called my mother yesterday to remind her of my plans, she said, "Fine, fine. I'll be long gone. Don't worry." She sounded very certain and also a little sad and flat.

In the meantime, Rosa called last night to say my mother had suffered another bout of shoulder pain along with an upset stomach.

As I finish my first loop and head back out along the bay, I think about my phone call to Dr. Fielding this morning. I'd called to let him know about my mother's stomach complaints and to make sure it was okay for her to continue taking Vioxx. Amazingly, I'd been put through on the first try.

"Are her stools black?" he asked in his mild, slightly reserved way. My mother's G.P. is a tall, bearded man with a gentle, intelligent manner.

"I'm not sure. Why?"

"Well, that could indicate internal bleeding," he explained. "The diarrhea I wouldn't worry about. Any number of your mother's medications could be causing that. But check in with her about her stools."

"Um, okay. And what if they're black?"

"Well, that would concern me, quite frankly. Over time she could develop anemia or possibly an intestinal ulcer."

Over time? Over time is not really a relevant concept at this point, as Dr. Fielding well knows. Without mentioning her stash of Seconal, my mother and I had talked to him last fall about her wish to end her life. Doctor-assisted suicide was illegal, he said, looking over his bifocals at us, neither condoning nor judging my mother's wish to die. He could lose his license, and go to jail. "I'm sorry, Margaret, but I can't help you."

"And what about the shoulder pain, Zoe? Is the Vioxx helping?"

"I think so. Except when she's writhing. Actually, I was wondering if you might prescribe something stronger. All she has is the Tylenol with codeine that you gave her."

"I can give her a prescription for morphine, Zoe, but she has to promise to use it as prescribed."

"I understand. You've made your position clear."

"Yes, well . . ."

"It's okay. So you'll phone it in for her?"

"Of course. And give her my regards."

"I will."

Now, in that sweet spot between warm-up and fatigue, moving easily, just starting to puff, I wonder if the morphine was such a good idea. Between the Seconal and the morphine, my mother is amassing a pretty good arsenal of lethal drugs.

I finish the third loop—four and a half miles—and spend a few minutes stretching by the parking lot, letting the breeze cool me down. Looking across the bay to the open channel that leads to the Pacific Ocean beneath the bridge, I feel as I often have since moving here, small and precarious. A dot on the edge of a large continent.

Having lived on the East Coast for the first thirty-six years of my life, I find these vast expanses of water and sky a little unreal and frightening. Or perhaps it's the constant threat of destruction from below, the grinding underground plates that shift and strain beneath us, that gives this beauty its sinister edge.

The wind whips at my T-shirt, cooling the sweat on my skin and making me shiver. The gulls swoop and cry above me. The sound is wrenching, forlorn. She's leaving you, they say. *Leaving you, leaving you.* Something painful slices through my chest. I fall forward, literally unable to stay upright, my hands on my knees, sobbing. Grateful for the noisy wind, the gulls that soar and cry somewhere above me.

# Too Big

When my mother was little, her parents used to make her drink milk and take daily spoonfuls of cod liver oil because they thought she was too thin. In most of the pictures I've seen from her childhood, she is slender, almost spindly, her pale face hidden beneath a cap of unruly, curly hair.

But by her late teens, her hair had settled into sleek waves and her face was a study in dramatically sculpted planes. At five foot ten, slim and long-limbed, my mother had a vivid, equine beauty perfectly set off by her tailored clothes. There were the well-cut, custom-made dresses she wore when she and my father lived in Paris in the late fifties and early sixties, the modern white slacks and black tops she carried off with slim-hipped aplomb as a young mother in Washington, and the well-cut blue jeans and brightly colored cotton jackets she wore so youthfully in her fifties and sixties that made her look stylish and unique.

And yet she never considered herself the belle of the ball, never flirted or danced on the table or talked her way out of a speeding ticket. For all the insouciance she projected about her looks, she was always privately insecure and self-critical, perennially worried about getting fat or wearing the wrong thing. This grumbling discontent grew louder as she aged and osteoporosis and Parkinson's buckled her upper spine, forcing her neck and head downward and turning her once proud posture into a forward-tilting S.

One of the last times we went shopping together, my mother confronted her image in a department store mirror and, turning away in disgust, said, "Gosh, you go along, thinking you look pretty good . . ." Then, glancing at me, added, "*You* look good," in that begrudging tone she sometimes took when addressing my appearance, both blaming me and taking credit for my being pretty.

Having never sought out or expected admiration for her looks, she always assumed my sisters and I didn't need compliments either. Our appearance—especially our clothes and hair—was more often the object of criticism than of applause, usually because we'd transgressed her notion of appropriate dress in some way. A play at the Kennedy Center meant wearing a "nice" winter coat, not a down jacket, and lunch at her aunt Marianne's club in Baltimore inevitably called for a skirt or a dress. "Go change," she'd say angrily. "You can't wear *that*."

Of course, when we grew older, we stopped obeying these directives and, each in our own way, challenged her views of appropriate dress: Katherine by becoming aggressively unstylish and even unkempt; Hannah by turning herself into a bombshell; and I by following every fashion trend, flattering or not, and then moving to New York and wearing nothing but black.

But the real bone of contention between my mother and I wasn't my clothes, it was my body.

My mother had a friend, Mrs. Chancellor, a handsome, big-boned woman, well over six feet tall, who wore her hair in a sleek blond bun and had two tall, very pretty daughters of her own. When I was in seventh grade, Mrs. Chancellor took a sharp look at me and told my mother she better take me to an endocrinologist immediately to make sure I wasn't going to end up, as she put it, "too big."

When my mother told me we were going to go see a doctor in New York, I was sure that "too big" did not just refer to my height, although I'd always hovered at the very highest percentiles. (At twelve, I was already five foot eight and still growing.) I was sure it referred to the fact that I was, as our family doctor put it so kindly, *"un poco gordo"* (*a little fat* in Spanish).

Looking at pictures of myself at this time, I see a tall girl hiding her soft face under bangs and waist-length hair, a rounded but not obese, preadolescent tummy covered by a loose peasant blouse, legs long and slim. Certainly not the monster I felt myself to be. But my mother was obsessed with my weight. She encouraged me to exercise, discouraged me from eating, and, worst of all, insisted I weigh myself in front of her once a month.

I can still conjure the humiliation of walking into her bathroom, a white, high-ceilinged room, and stepping onto her creaky black scale. I quickly learned to put all my weight on one foot in order to snag the needle at a lower reading, and to avoid all food and liquids the day of my weigh-in. But any dieting in the previous month had usually occurred only in the previous few days and the number on the scale was always a disappointment to both of us.

But thanks to Mrs. Chancellor, being fat wasn't my only problem, I was also a giant. To her credit, my mother did attempt to soften the blow, billing the trip to New York as a sightseeing/shopping expedition with a quick stop at the doctor's on the side. Ruining the effect somewhat was the fact that I had to collect every drop of urine I produced over the three days leading up to the appointment—then carry it with me on the plane.

It's interesting that I remember very little of the appointment other than a dark X-ray room, a discussion about my bones, my relief at handing over all that pee, and the verdict that I would be under six feet, which fortunately meant I was spared a course of estrogen to kick-start my puberty and slow my growth.

But I remember our subsequent shopping trip at Bloomingdale's in hyperdetail: the glamorous, overbright lighting, the glass counters filled with jars and lipsticks, the shiny chrome handrails of the escalator and the static electricity snapping beneath my feet. Even the warmth of the dressing rooms, each one an enticing slice of pink and gold. I also remember what I bought: an expensive pantsuit in a gorgeous, tie-dyed blue, a kind of seventies hipster chick outfit that I loved to death even though I knew I'd probably never wear it.

It was the payoff, the consolation prize for being "too big," but I didn't care, because for one brief moment, as I looked at myself in the dressing room mirror in that crazy, gorgeous suit, I thought I looked good. Really good. And that one moment gave me hope that I would one day leave this disappointing, overlarge body behind and become, if not beautiful, at least normal.

# Phone Call

"Mommy, I love you," Lane says.

I'm lying on the couch with Lane on top of me, her small, sticky hands pressed against my cheeks. She peers intently into my eyes, her still babyish face as focused and dreamy as a lover's. I have a terrible urge to laugh—Lane is the undisputed master of the comic moment—but I've never liked parents who laugh at their children's unintentionally funny behavior, and I stifle the impulse.

"I love you too, sweetie," I say, my throat tightening as it so often does these days, going from neutral to tears in a single bound. A kind word from a store clerk, a poignant story on the radio, a sudden clear view of the bay can make me tear up and even sob. As if sensing this, Lane studies me closely. I smile at her and, after a moment, she gives a theatrical sigh of satisfaction and snuggles down against my chest. Wrapping my arms around her, I close my eyes and soak in the warmth of her soft little body.

Looking up, I see Clara staring at us with—what exactly? Hurt? Anger? Certainly something unhappy, if not downright murderous.

Clara has struggled valiantly with the intrusion of Lane into her life, but this flagrant display of devotion right in front of her is more than she can handle.

"Come join us?" I offer.

"No! Make her get off you, Mommy. She's always *on* you. It's revolting."

Again, I have to overcome the impulse to laugh. If only adults were so direct with one another, I think. But she's right. Lane, who nursed until she was almost three, is constantly in my lap or around my knees, demanding to be picked up. Of course, Clara was exactly the same until she was so rudely pushed aside. Watching her cope, I have real sympathy for Katherine, who was usurped twice—and in quick succession.

I reach over and grab hold of Clara's foot, but she scoots back, scowling at me. She's tall for her age, slender and willowy with full, rosy lips. As a toddler, she reminded me of Tweety Bird, all lips and wispy blond hair. At eight, she has the distinct promise of beauty, a fact that both frightens and thrills me.

"I'm going to get you," I sing teasingly, slipping out from under Lane and onto the floor. She giggles as I slither toward her, using my arms to pull myself forward. Behind me, Lane laughs and claps her hands. I get Clara's ankle in one hand and slide her easily toward me. Sitting up, I pull her onto my lap and wrap my arms around her. "Gotcha!"

"Tickle her!" Lane shrieks from the couch. "Tickle her, Mommy!"

"Tickle her?" I say. "Maybe I'll just tickle you instead." I bend my head, whisper in Clara's ear. "What do you think? Should we tickle your little sister?"

"Yes," she whispers back. "Hard."

"Hard? How hard?"

"*Really* hard."

"But not too hard, right?"

"Yes, too hard."

"Then I might have to tickle you first." I tickle her gently around the waist, and she squirms and flails in my arms.

"Yes, Mommy!" Lane claps her hands. "Tickle her! But tickle me too."

I turn and smile at her. "Okay. You asked for it." I whisper in Clara's ear again. "Are you ready?" She nods. "Are you sure?" She nods again. "Okay then. One, two, three . . ."

Together, we lunge toward the couch and fall on Lane, who flops onto her back in immediate surrender, wriggling and convulsing with laughter. I watch Clara closely, but she is surprisingly gentle, and after a moment she and Lane lie face-to-face, rubbing noses and giggling. I sit back, relieved.

Clara is now making silly faces and Lane is laughing her raucous, full-on laugh. Clara is laughing too, partly because eliciting this particular laugh from Lane is so satisfying. We all try, but Clara is by far the most successful. In fact, the first time Lane ever laughed, it was while watching Clara fling herself repeatedly onto a bed. She was sitting in my lap when this odd, explosive noise came out of her, and we all stopped and stared. She was four months old and we'd never heard her laugh before. Clara, of course, was thrilled and still takes pride in making her sister laugh.

The phone rings and I go into the kitchen to answer it, figuring it's Jack calling to say he's on his way home from work. "Oh, hi, Momma." *Damn! Why hadn't I let the machine get it?* "Is everything okay?"

"Everything's fine," she says, emphatically. "Dr. Fielding called. I guess you spoke to him and, well, I'm glad you did. Joan Reynolds stopped by yesterday and suggested I join the Friends Creek Hospice, and Dr. Fielding said he thought it was a good idea. He's going to write me a letter saying I have six months or less to live so I can enroll. That way it's covered by insurance. Apparently, they have hospice nurses that come to your house right after you die so—"

"Wait, Dr. Fielding says you have less than six months to live?"

I ask, slipping into the bathroom and shutting the door so the children can't hear. "Based on what?"

"Well, I told him I wasn't getting out of bed anymore and—"

"Okay, but that doesn't mean you're dying, Momma," I say, trying not to sound annoyed. "Did you tell him about your plans for May first?"

"No, I didn't. But listen for a moment." I can hear her start to wheeze, but whether from excitement or agitation I'm not sure. "Apparently the hospice will send one of their people over here after I die, which means *they* can examine me and we don't need to get the medical examiner. So the three of you can be here after all!"

She sounds pleased, but I feel weary and impatient. I don't want to be stuck in here whispering about death with my mother. I want to be back with my children, who now have the stereo playing and are galloping around the living room.

"So are you back to taking the Seconal?" I ask, sitting on the tub, watching myself in the mirror.

"Actually, I was talking to Katherine, and when I told her Dr. Fielding had prescribed me morphine, she told me her friend's aunt killed herself with an overdose of morphine." Again her voice has that underlying buzz of excitement. "Apparently it's quite easy to do. And it's unlikely anyone would notice since I'd be taking it for pain anyway. So I was thinking perhaps morphine is the way to go."

*Would you rather be killed by drowning or by fire? A single bullet or a firing squad? A rattlesnake bite or a poisonous mushroom?*

"Great," I say. "So we can all come home, have a big, happy family powwow, and then you can take morphine and die." It's strange being angry and watching myself be angry in the mirror. It feels like I'm acting, pretending to be mad.

"I don't know why you're saying that, Zoe! I'm actually quite pleased. But if May first is too soon for you, we can change the date—"

"I don't give a shit about the *date*," I say, my voice rising. "That's not the point. The point is I'm sick of talking about this all the time. It's *all* we ever talk about. And how do you think I feel when you call? Do you ever think for one second that I might be doing something? Like playing with my children, or working, or talking with a friend or—"

"Listen, I'm sorry if I've called you at a bad time," she says, sounding more annoyed than sorry. "I can call you back later. You should have told me."

"It's always a bad time, Momma!" I yell, thankful for the music in the next room. "Can't you see that? *I don't want you to die.* And I don't want to talk about your dying all the time, especially since we *don't* really talk about it. Not in any real way. You've never asked me how I feel about it, or talked about how you feel. You act like it doesn't mean anything. But it *does* means something. At least to me."

I feel a terrible grief push up inside me, but I fight it down. I close my eyes and imagine the cortisol churning through my adrenal glands. "Cortisol. Stress hormone. A real killer," my Chinese doctor always says, shaking his head as he feels my pulse or examines my tongue.

"Well, it won't be for very much longer," my mother says coldly, responding to my anger instead of my pain, and I wonder if she'll ever be ready to hear that part, or if we will spar and bicker right through the final death scene. My rage taps up a notch. Doesn't she have some responsibility to help me process this? Isn't that part of the message in all those books she reads, the Good Death creed she so ardently subscribes to?

"Don't try and make me feel sorry for you," I say. "Remember, you're not dying—you're *choosing* to die. And don't assume I'm going to be there just because it's morphine instead of Seconal, or a hospice nurse instead of a medical examiner. I have children to raise, Momma, and assisted suicide is illegal, just like Dr. Fielding said. You shouldn't even be asking me to do this! Have you even *considered* what might happen if—"

"What do you want me to do?" My mother cuts me off, her voice as angry as mine. "No matter what I suggest, you say you can't be there!"

"I don't know. I don't know, okay?" I'm screaming now, my voice bouncing off the tiles, anguish percolating wildly through my system. "But I can't talk about this anymore! Can you understand that?"

"Do you think I want to talk about this all the time?" Her voice is as hysterical as mine and the sound of it shocks and upsets me so much that I can no longer speak.

I hold the phone away from me, staring at it, then switch it off and yell "Fuck" several times at the mirror and start to cry. Tears of rage and frustration and then, finally, sorrow.

When I open the door a few moments later, Clara and Lane are huddled on the floor outside like frightened puppies. I sit and take them in my arms, tell them it's okay, don't worry. I'm not mad, not at them anyway. But even as I reassure them, I realize I can't protect them. Not from grief, or sibling rivalry. Certainly not from death. But I will try. At least I will try.

# Through the Glass

Grumpy and exhausted after spending the day on the plane, my daughters barely argued when I brought them up to bed even though it was way before their West Coast bedtime. We'd arrived at Dulles a few hours earlier and been escorted home by the debonair Derrick. After eating dinner with my mother in her room, I'd let the two of them take a long, noisy bath in her Jacuzzi tub while my mother and I talked and ate chocolates from the box of See's candies I'd bought at the San Francisco airport.

Snuggled between the two of them on Hannah's old bed, I work my way through a repertoire of Joni Mitchell tunes, continuing to sing even after both of them are asleep: "River," "Free Man in Paris," "All I Want." These songs take me back to my junior year in high school, when my best friend, Suzanne, and I were obsessed with the album *Blue* and spent hours singing together in her suburban bedroom. Suzanne is coming down from New York tomorrow to visit her parents in Bethesda but also to spend time with me and, as she put it, "see your mother before she pulls the plug."

I know my mother is expecting me to come back downstairs, but I swing into another verse of "A Case of You," my voice cracking softly on the octave-leaping notes of the chorus.

This trip to D.C. is supposedly the last one before the final one—the one on May first, when my mother actually kills herself—three weeks from now. She'd begged me to come "just to spend time together," and despite my disinclination to make another trip so soon, and Jack's irritation at my going, I'd agreed. I was the only one of the three of us she'd invited, and it was this as well as guilt over our recent argument on the phone that had convinced me.

Walking through the house earlier tonight, I'd felt tender and a little bruised. Running my hand up the dark wood banister, looking out the landing window at the shuttered swimming pool, the scrawny shoots of bamboo poking up along the back fence, I'd tried to imagine what it would be like to never come here again.

It's never been exactly cozy, this house. Even in its heyday, its high ceilings and minimalist furniture were better suited to hosting large parties than to playing games or curling up with a book. Once at the cutting edge of 1970s modernity, it's become something of a time capsule, a crumbling monolith, ridden with termites and decay. And yet it's the setting, backdrop and reference point for everything I've associated with the word *home* since I was a toddler.

"Alive, alive, I want to get up and jive," I sing as Lane begins to snore. "I want to wreck my stockings in some juke box dive."

Yeah, right, I think as I gently push my younger daughter's legs aside and roll off the bed. The days of dancing to Joni Mitchell—or anyone else—are so distant, it's as if they belong to somebody else. Ironic how shepherding someone toward death seems to speed you toward your own. Certainly my father's death hurried my mother down this road, and there are mornings when I'm sure I'll meet some worn and wrinkled hag in the bathroom mirror.

We're decaying at warp speed here, my mother and I. Like the house, with its rotting floorboards and leaky roof. Only my children are still vibrant and growing, their skin unblemished, their lives stretching abundantly before them.

"I was hoping you'd come down. Girls asleep?" My mother smiles, pleased that I've reappeared.

"They are. I think all that hot water knocked them out."

"Well, I'm glad someone's getting use out of that tub. I'm more or less limited to sponge baths at this point."

According to Rosa, my mother rarely walks more than a step or two, just far enough to get to the portable commode from the bed. I don't know if it's because she's weak from staying in bed or because her health has actually worsened, but the fact that she's also in diapers at night, something she's not yet shared with me, makes me think this new level of incapacity is here to stay.

And yet she looks well tonight, flushed and bright-eyed, excited about some new plan or idea. Ordinarily, this would make me tense, but not tonight. Tonight, I feel calm and oddly serene, my sense of impending loss wrapped in a gentle scrim of nostalgia. I have no wish to argue or cajole or talk her out of anything. I just want to be with her, soak up her voice, her physicality—and the physicality of the house that looms over us like a sad and weary giant.

Settled into my usual spot on the couch, I refill my glass from the bottle of wine I've brought in with me. Looking over at my mother, I feel only affection. Yes, there have been maternal lapses over the years, and yes, this death obsession makes me crazy, but there remains an innate sympathy between us, a bond that arises, I suspect, from the fact that, of the three of us, my nature—bookish, imaginative, sensitive—most closely resembles hers.

As a child, this often meant my being singled out for dispensation in the midst of sibling conflicts, but it also meant I could rely on my mother for a sympathetic hearing, for attentive listening when I described a book I was reading, or ideas I had about the world.

Is it any wonder that I became her main caretaker after my father died? Not only in the difficult first months, but in the years since: making sure she wasn't alone at Christmas, organizing her trips to Vermont every summer, spending my vacations with her, and— more recently—dealing with her doctors, counselors and home health workers. Not that my sisters have been entirely absent (Katherine has helped my mother with her finances, Hannah visits and calls), but I've been her emotional mainstay, the one she's turned to for sympathy and companionship. The good daughter.

As for the pressures that go with the job? Well, they've been pretty overwhelming, I can't pretend otherwise. But I don't want to think about them right now. Tonight I want to wallow in maudlin sentimentality, view my mother through the bottom of my glass, Joni Mitchell playing in the background.

"You'll have to meet Michael, my hospice nurse," she says. "He's been coming in to meditate with me every day this week. He even brought me a Tibetan bowl. You run a mallet around the edge and it makes a lovely singing noise. Also a CD of monks playing the bowls."

"That sounds nice."

"Oh, and he says he can provide morphine if I need it."

"I thought Dr. Fielding already prescribed it."

"Yes, well, the more the merrier."

In another mood, I might have bristled at this comment, but I just smile and raise my glass.

"You seem pretty merry yourself. What's going on?"

"Well, as I said on the phone, I think morphine might be the way to go."

"The way to go?"

She laughs delightedly. "Funny."

I want to say, *You do remember I haven't agreed to be here if you kill yourself with drugs?* But I stop myself. I can't go over this right now. And who knows? Maybe I can be here. Maybe she'll take the morphine and Rosa won't notice and the hospice worker will come, and no one will suspect it wasn't a natural death. Maybe. But I refuse to even think about it. I want to remain in this pleasant, half-stoned state as long as possible.

"So, do you think you'll be ready in three weeks?" I ask gently.

Her bright expression clouds slightly. "Three weeks? Is May first only three weeks away? Hmm. Well . . . I don't think I can be ready *that* soon."

"Really?" Something inside me slips sharply sideways—*kerchunk*—like a discordant note, but I skim past it, take another mouthful of wine.

"I still have some things I need to do."

"I see." The anger I expect to feel doesn't materialize. My mind is too loose and dreamy, and there's something about her behavior that's throwing me off.

"Don't worry." She laughs again, looking at me. "It won't be that much longer. I'm waiting to get copies of my novel made for the three of you. And then there's that children's story I told you about. Something I want to finish for all the grandchildren. Petra across the street knows an excellent illustrator, and she's going to meet with me this week. And I really should get an estimate on the termites. You three are going to need to take care of that before you sell the house."

"You don't exactly sound like a woman ready to die."

"No, no. That's not right. I am ready to die, Zoe. That's why I'm getting everything done."

And it's true, she does seem more organized and focused than usual. Clearly something has shifted. But then why the change of date?

"Momma, May first—I really thought that was it . . . I mean I brought the girls and everything thinking that . . ."

She looks sheepish. "I know, I know. I'm sorry. I shouldn't have made such a big deal out of it. And I realize I've changed my dates before. But, believe me, it's not going to be that much longer. Just have a little patience. I'm really glad you came."

I pour another glass of wine and stare up at the ceiling. I know exactly what Jack and Hannah will say but can conjure no outrage of my own. At least she's pushed the date back and not forward. At this rate, her body may give out on her before she manages to do herself in and the whole issue of dates and methods will be irrelevant. Which, at this point, feels like a happy outcome.

"Do you want to see the morphine?"

Startled, I watch her lean over, open the drawer of her bedside table and pull out a small brown bottle with a black-tipped stopper.

"That's it? I thought it would be some kind of powder."

"No, no. It comes in a liquid form. Very easy to swallow."

"Mmm." I watch her turn it in her hands and I realize that the unfamiliar emotion I am sensing in her is happiness. Happiness and relief.

But to me the bottle looks radioactive, evil, as if filled with some earth-destroying substance from a bad action movie. "Quick! Put it away!" I want to shout, but I watch silently as she tips the bottle upside down, making the light tremble and refract through the amber glass.


My mother's shockingly handsome "Boston Irish" father, a man whose short stint as a Hollywood writer allegedly included an affair with the actress Lillian Gish, was only twenty-eight when he fell into the clutches of an unscrupulous doctor who claimed he could cure his alcoholism. The "medicine" he prescribed was morphine. From that point until his death fifteen years later, my grandfather was a morphine addict *and* an alcoholic. He died, bloated and unrecognizable, refusing for reasons of vanity to see my mother, his only child.

Many years into his addiction, my mother spent a summer vacation with her father and stepmother at the family's country house in Effingham, New Hampshire. She arrived there from college only to have my grandfather make the rather odd request that she help him break his morphine habit, telling her that she was uniquely qualified for the job. His second wife, a timid woman who had followed him into alcoholism, was clearly not.

His plan was to give my mother all the drugs in his possession and then, over a period of weeks, have her mete out ever-smaller doses until—voilà—he'd be done. Cured. This worked until the night he came crashing into her room, cursing and threatening, and demanded she hand over the drugs, which she did. Perfectly pleasant and reasonable again the next morning, he let her know this wasn't a good time for him to quit after all.

Aware of this unfortunate aspect of my mother's history, I find it strange that she has embraced morphine so unreservedly as a means to end her life. But then, maybe there's something comforting about choosing a drug with such powerful familial associations.

"So how much do you have to take?" I ask, eyeing the bottle, which is now nestled against her chest.

"I'm not sure exactly." She holds it up again, gives it a small shake and then, to my relief, places it back in the bedside drawer. "Katherine said she would ask Raymond's cousin, the one whose mother killed herself this way, how much I need to take. But according to Sally Thursdale, whose husband is a doctor, a bottle this size would constitute a lethal overdose. At least for someone like me."

"Someone like you?"

"You know. Someone near death."

I look at her face, glowing in the soft bedside light. She looks awfully good for someone near death, but I don't say anything. I look up at the ceiling and drink some more wine. I notice the faint smudge of cobwebs hanging in wisps from the skylight over my mother's head. I wonder what it feels like to be high on morphine. I'll probably never know. My days of taking drugs are firmly behind me, except for the occasional overindulgence in alcohol. But there was a time when I wouldn't have hesitated to find out exactly how it felt.

Later, up in my old bedroom, I'm unable to sleep. A headache gathers itself behind my right eye and I wish I hadn't drunk so much. It doesn't take much to set off a headache these days—running too hard, staying up late, a couple of glasses of wine—and the pain can last for hours, even days, despite repeated doses of Advil.

My mind keeps bouncing from my mother holding the bottle of morphine to a scene in her "novel" about visiting her father in his hotel room in New York when she was about twenty and watching him tie a tourniquet around his arm and shoot up. And then I think about when I was twelve years old, away at sleepover camp, and made the mistake of bragging about smoking pot to Hannah in a phone call home. Scared about what it would do to my health, Hannah immediately told on me.

My parents, especially my mother, were understandably upset, although I wonder what they expected sending me to an ecology camp in Nevada in the early seventies. As I recall, my counselor's nickname was Weed.

"I just can't understand why you would choose not to be in your right mind," my mother said angrily when she picked me up at the airport.

"It's not that big a deal, Momma. It really didn't affect me that much."

But it wasn't true. I'd loved the dizzy, disconnected feeling it gave me, and how I'd suddenly noticed things, like the intricate patterns of veins in my hands, and the way the stars pulsated in the sky when we lay in the grass staring up at them. When I was high, I worried less about how other people saw me—we were, after all, equally impaired—and found myself firmly located in my body, senses alive, fully receptive to the lush world of colors and tastes around me.

But I didn't share any of this with my mother, who drove in a jerky, angry way and refused to look over at me as she talked.

"Well, I don't want you talking about it with anyone," she said. "And I don't want you doing it again. Can you promise me that?"

I did. But I knew it was a promise I'd never keep. Taking drugs had inducted me into a secret society, an alternate universe of empty attics and deserted parks, roach clips and wrinkled Baggies. And part of the pleasure for my friends and me was knowing that we were getting away with something, that we'd successfully slipped out from underneath our parents' supervision without them seeming to notice.

Fortunately, the love affair didn't last. I began to dislike the constant anxiety about getting caught—if not by my mother then by someone else's mother, or by the school or the police—and my best "highs" were often followed by debilitating lows: days of lethargy and depression, followed by insomnia and bad dreams. My brief foray into harder drugs further disenchanted me, and by the time I left for college I was, if not exactly a straight arrow, certainly a straighter one.

Although I would have denied it at the time, I was also anxious to reclaim my status as Momma's favorite, a position from which I'd been rather unceremoniously dumped just as adolescence hit, thanks to my weight and my flirtation with delinquency. I can remember following her around the house asking why she was angry at me, only to have her say, "I'm *not* angry," and walk away. Although my father took a much more liberal view of my activities, I didn't care; it was my mother's approval I craved.

The headache has crept around the back of my skull and I turn on the light and retrieve the Advil from my purse. Swallowing two tablets with some stale water, I think how my mother never even took aspirin when we were growing up, never drank more than half a glass of wine, and was always conscientious about her food and exercise. She was, in fact, something of a health nut. For years, she baked all our bread—heavy whole-wheat loaves that would harden into uncuttable lumps—and gave us oatmeal instead of boxed cereal, and refused to buy soda, candy, or potato chips.

How jealous I was of my school friends' suburban kitchens, where the Coke and Cap'n Crunch were there for the taking and Saturday mornings were orgies of sugar-laced cereal, usually consumed on a deliciously thick shag carpet in front of a TV set—television being another thing my mother didn't believe in or let us have.

Of course, now that Wal-Mart sells organic vegetables and sodas have been banned from schools, my yoga-practicing, bread-baking mother seems like something of a trendsetter. But this only confuses me more. Having lived such an aggressively clean life, why has she picked a mind-blowing narcotic as her "means of deliverance"? Not to mention the very narcotic that robbed her of a father and led to his premature death.

Had all those years of taking her Parkinson's medications muted her distaste for drugs? I doubted it. She'd always complained about taking her pills and used to deliberately *under*medicate herself. Back in her mid-sixties, maybe ten years into the disease, she spent months violently trembling and barely speaking above a whisper because she wasn't taking her full dose of dopamine. As soon as she increased the dose, she was, for a time, markedly more functional.

So why, I wonder, climbing back into bed, is she choosing to go out on a big, airy wave of drug-induced euphoria? Morphine is a drug I associate with madness and stupor and tragedy, not with my well-controlled and controlling mother. For her to voluntarily relinquish her mental faculties at the final moments of her life seems entirely out of character. Where is the woman who once insisted on having the full experience of childbirth, pain and all, and couldn't understand why I would ever choose to escape my "right mind"?

# Too Small

I sat at my usual spot at the foot of the long butcher-block kitchen table; Hannah on my right, then my mother. Next to her, at the head of the table, sat my father. Katherine used to sit next to him, across from my mother, but she was away at college.

I liked this seating arrangement because it meant I was as far away as possible from my parents, and only Hannah could see how little I ate.

But tonight I'd made the mistake of putting almost no food on my plate. This made pushing it around to obscure the fact that none of it was being eaten more difficult.

"What's going on, Zoe?" my father asked, frowning. "You hardly served yourself anything. Don't you like it?" My father was an excellent cook, a passionate devotee of Julia Child and Marcella Hazan. He made dinner almost every night. But he liked to be appreciated, and the first few minutes of every meal were invariably spent praising the food.

"I like it," I said, looking down at the steaming coils of pasta, the buttery clam sauce and crisp, leafy salad. "It's good. I'm just not hungry."

"Why not? You always say that and I never see you eat." He stopped chewing and regarded me intently. Comically, his own plate of pasta and salad was reflected in the lenses of his glasses, giving him two little plates for eyes, and I thought how appropriate that was. Sometimes I thought his whole life was about food: chopping, slicing, boiling and eating. He didn't seem to notice how disgusting it was, all those bloody juices and oozing particles of fat he so carelessly shoveled into himself.

"I do eat!" I said, disdainfully. "I *am* eating. Just not a huge amount. Anyway, I ate earlier."

Actually, I hadn't eaten normally since starting high school the year before. I'd lost all my adolescent chubbiness and then quite a bit more. My mother no longer weighed me or monitored my food; my body was finally beyond reproach.

Hannah snorted without looking up from her plate. "Like what?" she asked. "An orange slice?"

"Fuck off," I snapped at her. "What do you care?"

"Zoe, don't say 'fuck off.'" My mother held her fork midair, giving me a look. I ignored her. I'd say what I wanted and she couldn't stop me. I was stronger than she was. I was stronger than all of them. While they were at the mercy of their appetites, I didn't even *need* food anymore. I had no interest in it whatsoever.

"Well, it would be nice if you showed a little enthusiasm for your dinner," my father said, digging into his food. "A growing girl needs to eat, right?"

"Jonathan—" My mother put her hand on his arm and shook her head.

"I told you, I *do* eat."

Hannah shifted in her chair next to me, about to speak, but I shot her a warning look, and she just sighed loudly and went back to her food. Hannah was voluptuous but slim, and my mother had never worried about her weight. She criticized Hannah only when she looked too grown-up and sexy.

"Well, you're looking very svelte these days," my father persisted through a mouthful of pasta and clams, peering across the table at me.

"*Jesus,* Poppa! I'm fine. Just leave me alone."

"I think Zoe looks good," my mother said, smiling at me. "I think she looks just right."

I put the fork back down on my plate. I'd actually been thinking of eating something, but "just right" wasn't good enough. "Just right" was much too close to "too fat," which meant a return to being analyzed, dissected and scrutinized as though my body was a flawed science experiment: open for public commentary, on display.

Not eating kept me safe from all that. It also seemed to obstruct my mother's view of me, because no matter how thin I got, she never appeared to notice. Hannah and my friends noticed—even my father had finally noticed—but the only thing my mother ever said was how good I looked in clothes, how "healthy" I'd become.


Out in the backyard by the pool, I lit a cigarette and blew the smoke up into the humid summer air. No one was home, so I could smoke without anyone yelling at me. I took a long sip of iced tea and squinted down at my stomach. My hip bones rose sharply from the sides of my belly like the edges of a bowl. Pleased, I lay back down.

Soon, I'd gather my strength and walk the four or five feet to the edge of the pool and plunge into the cool, weightless water. I was already anticipating the rush of black particles into my vision, the loud knocking of my heart. But first I'd let the sun sear into my skin, watch the smoke rise from my cigarette, and admire the bones in my perfect, slender wrist.

———

Hannah passed me the "Style" section of *The Washington Post*.

"What's this?"

"Just read it. I think you have it."

"Have what? What are you talking about?"

I looked at the headline: "When Too Thin Isn't Thin Enough."

I looked up at her. She was staring at me, not in a critical way but in a kindly, concerned way. This scared me. I took a closer look at the page.

At the top, there was a photo of a girl in a bathing suit. Right away I could see there was something wrong with her. Her waist dipped severely inward, as if she had no internal organs, and all the bones in her body—especially her ribs and collarbones—were visible under her skin. Her elbows and knees looked weirdly large and square because the muscles that ran between her joints had disappeared.

I started to read. Hannah flipped noisily to another section of the paper, bending away to give me room. Feeling nervous and a little sick, I read that the girl in the picture had a disease called anorexia. It had started when she went on a diet. She'd lost weight but then, inexplicably, kept on dieting. She ate less and less, sometimes only an apple a day. Her weight dropped to eighty-four pounds. Then eighty. Then seventy-seven. She was hospitalized twice and had feeding tubes forced down her throat. She still thought she was fat.

My heart clanged as I skimmed through the article. "Anorexia largely afflicts white, middle-class girls in their teens or early twenties. . . . Doctors and health officials are concerned. . . . Anorexia is on the rise. . . . Some anorexic patients have died."

"Look in the box," Hannah said gently, leaning over to point at a grayed-out square of print on the side of the page. "It lists the symptoms."

My eyes skipped down the list:

Amenorrhea
Irregular heartbeat

Bone loss

Hair loss on the scalp

Light, downy hair elsewhere on the body

I looked down at my arms. They were covered in hair, hair that I'd never had before this year. It was also on my chest and face, a light fur that caught in the beam of the overhead bathroom light.

"You have that," Hannah said, again in that quiet, worried voice that was so unlike our usual joking tone.

I put the paper down, took a drink of coffee. "Yeah."

"You've got to start eating more." She sounded like she might cry.

"Yeah, I think maybe I do." I took another sip of coffee and felt it burn through my empty insides.

Later, after she went upstairs, I took the article into my room and read it again and again. I stared at the skeletal girl in the bikini. She looked like a corpse.

That night, for the first time in months, I put my father's food on my plate and, instead of rearranging it for twenty minutes, put a small amount in my mouth. I chewed and chewed and then I swallowed. I felt disgust as the particles of food slid down my throat and entered my pure and perfect body, but I was also relieved. Like the good witch in a fairy tale, my sister had broken the spell. It would take time to fully shake free of it, and in some ways I never would, remaining forever vigilant about both food and exercise, but my dance with death was at an end.

Having engaged in that duet, in plain sight of those I trusted most to protect and look after me, I never again counted on anyone to see me. I mean the truth of me, not just the external construct. Except perhaps Hannah who, at the age of seventeen, barely a year older than me, saw me—starving and covered with hair—and held up a mirror so I could see myself. In that terrifying moment of truth and love, she filled the place where my parents, but especially my mother, should have been.

# Death Diet

The day after we arrive in D.C., my mother and I avoid talking about the morphine or her latest change of date but spend the morning peaceably reading the paper together while my children wander in and out of the room.

Even confined to her bed, she finds little ways to connect to my girls. When Lane walks in wearing her favorite nylon ski pants, my mother tells her she likes the swishing sound they make, and Lane marches noisily around the room, beaming happily down at her chubby legs. And when Clara flings herself into my lap and complains she's bored, my mother suggests she take Bruno, her neurotic sheepdog, out for a walk in the yard. Clara runs to find a leash and spends the next hour dragging Bruno from one end of the yard to the other.

After lunch, Kendra herds them off to the park, and I immediately go over to my mother's bookshelf and gather up her handouts on "cessation of food and hydration" from a shelf neatly labeled "Hemlock Society." The moment I woke this morning, I knew I had to find them.

Morphine had seemed like a viable solution last night, but in the sober light of day, I know it's impossible. The only thing that made morphine more attractive than Seconal was the fact that it is a common palliative drug for dying patients, while Seconal is a sleeping pill. But an overdose is an overdose, and this is exactly the scenario that Hannah, Katherine and I wanted to avoid. Not only did the idea of watching my mother take pills or morphine repulse me, my sisters and I stood to gain financially from her death. What was to stop some overzealous prosecutor from deciding that we had grown tired of waiting for our inheritance?

Returning to my usual spot on the couch, I begin to prepare my case while my mother takes her after-lunch nap. The pamphlets are from Dr. Harmon, the psychiatrist who gave us the Seconal. It was on our way out the door that I'd asked him about the legal risks of being there when my mother took an overdose.

"I don't know of any cases where family members were investigated, especially when the death happened in the home, but it's theoretically possible," he told me. Then, turning to my mother, he added, "One thing you might want to consider, Mrs. Draper, is ending your life by stopping eating and drinking. I'd be happy to give you some literature on that."

My mother smiled politely. "Well, I guess we could take a look."

"As you'll see, there's surprisingly little discomfort after the first couple of days, especially if no liquids are ingested. It's actually a relatively quick and painless way to die."

"Although not as quick and painless as Seconal," my mother said. She spoke in a light tone, but I could hear the note of resistance underneath.

"That's true," he continued. "But the suddenness of a suicide with drugs can be hard for family members to digest. And while there haven't been any really good studies, research indicates that the families have an easier time accepting the person's decision to die when the death occurs over a period of days and in this manner. They feel that the person's commitment to dying is demonstrated by their continuing refusal to eat or drink."

"That makes a lot of sense to me," I said, thinking of the final days with my father. "It sounds closer to a natural death, if you know what I mean."

"I do know what you mean," he said, smiling at me.

"And no legal risks."

"True."

"Well, it's something to consider," my mother said, clearly done with the subject.

On our way home, we'd stopped off at a pharmacy on Connecticut Avenue—not her usual pharmacist. I was about to run in and get her prescription filled when my mother turned to me and said, rather stiffly, "I thought the point of ending your life was to avoid suffering. Not to find brand-new ways to suffer."

Flipping through the pages in my lap, I can see this isn't going to be easy. Frankly, even I found it difficult to believe Dr. Harmon. How could dying without food or water be quick and painless? But given the alternative—worrying about going to jail or letting my mother die alone—it was worth a try.


"But what if I can't do it?" she asks querulously after I show her the pamphlets. "I *like* to eat."

My mother looks exhausted and disheveled after her nap, her unwashed hair sitting in clumps on the top of her head. After watching her sleep for close to an hour, Bruno curled at her side, I'd woken her up. Kendra and the kids would be back soon and my friend Suzanne was due at three. This might be our last chance to talk privately this weekend.

"That's true," I say, lying on my side at the end of her bed, pamphlets spread in front of me. "And if you can't, you can't. There's nothing stopping you from deciding to start eating again."

"Well then, it doesn't seem like much of a solution, does it?"

"I don't know, Momma. It really depends on you. If you're as committed as you say you are, you should be able to do it." I hear how challenging this sounds and mentally kick myself. I don't want this to end in an argument.

"I'm damn well committed. I just don't relish suffering."

"It says you won't." I flip to a section I've underlined and read: " 'Once liquids are stopped, the body shuts down quickly and there is little sensation of thirst or hunger. If the mouth becomes uncomfortably dry, mouth lubricants or Vaseline can be applied and—although it slows the process—hard candy or ice chips can be offered as well.'"

"Oh, that sounds lovely."

My mother looks cross and I have a sudden urge to laugh. With her hair sticking up wildly around her face, and her quilt pulled tightly to her chin despite the warm sun filling the room, she looks like an angry porcupine emerging from its hole. But instead I say, more gently, "You're right. It doesn't sound like that much fun. But you're already weak. It's not as if it was someone in perfect health doing it. It probably won't take that long, especially if you don't drink."

"But why do it this way at all, Zoe? Why do I have to stop eating when I could just take the morphine or Seconal?"

I sigh. No matter how often I explain it, my objections remain abstract and shadowy to her. She never seems to remember them. But taking a deep breath, I go over it again. Stopping eating and drinking will allow us to be with her at the end, I say, without legal risk. It's that simple.

But as I speak, I realize that the legal issues are only part of it. Scanning through the handouts, I find the words that have been quietly resonating in me since our meeting with Dr. Harmon last year. Without preamble, I read them out loud, not wanting to reveal how much they mean to me:

> The friends and relatives of the dying person often find comfort in the person's ongoing choice to move forward with their

decision. Unlike other methods of self-deliverance, cessation of food and water allows the family members to be with the dying person, while they are dying, and to experience their commitment to death *over time*. Follow-up interviews and discussions reveal that this method of self-deliverance may be less traumatizing for family members than more rapid-acting methods, such as the ingestion of drugs.

I nervously wait for her response, not looking at her. Under me, I can feel the bed vibrate, as if her body is also working out its response. It suddenly seems imperative to me that she choose this method of death. Not just because it's the safest for the three of us but because it will make it easier for us—for *me*—to bear. By choosing this death, she will acknowledge the enormity of what she's asking.

"Well, it might not be so bad," she says slowly, after a moment. I glance up. Her face is thoughtful, no longer grumpy. "I could at least try it. If it meant you all could be here with me."

I quietly let out my breath. "It would! I mean, we could be here. We *will* be here, I promise. But are you sure?"

"No, but, well . . ." She stops, flushing uncomfortably. "It's funny, I was talking about this issue with Michael—my hospice nurse—last week, and he said I needed to listen to what you and Hannah and Katherine were telling me. And I realized that I can't do this by myself. I don't *want* to do it by myself. I want you here with me. That is the most important thing."

I nod, not trusting myself to speak. Not only because I might cry but because I don't want to talk her out of it. I want to let her words hang in the air, taking on weight and permanence, like a signature etched in the space between us.

I lay my head back on the bed, exhausted. It feels like I've been working toward this moment for months without realizing it and with no real confidence it would arrive. It's only a plan, but for the first time, there is a way forward. Yes, it's an unknown outcome, and yes, watching her starve might be worse than watching her swallow pills, but for the moment the clouds have lifted, the way ahead is visible. I close my eyes and my body uncoils on the soft quilt beneath me.

I'm startled awake by the doorbell. Bruno leaps off the bed and tears out of the room in a barking, skittering frenzy.

"It's Suzanne," I say, hurrying after him. Yipping hysterically, he gallops through the dining room and down the front hall, where he flings himself against the front door, snarling and snapping. Any attempt to control Bruno is useless—even his trainer has given up on him—but instead of yelling at him, grabbing him by the collar and forcing him into the living room as I usually do, I gently push him aside and open the door.

There on the doorstep is Suzanne, my sweet, funny friend who has left her own young children in New York to come see me because that's the way it is with us. For years, we've been as intimate as sisters, passing into and out of each other's families—both the original ones and the ones we've created with husbands and kids—except this sister is one I chose and who, luckily, chose me back.

"Oh my God, you're here," I exclaim and hold her tightly, soaking up the familiar feel of her slender frame beneath her tweed jacket, the brush of her long blond hair. We stand back and look at one another. Or rather, she looks at me, eyes squinting through her glasses as if preparing to put me on canvas, something she has done more than once over the years.

"Wow," she says, finally. "You look terrible."

# Drop Me a Feather

*"Hope" is the thing with feathers—*
*That perches in the soul—*

—EMILY DICKINSON

Suzanne and I spend the afternoon walking around Cleveland Park, stopping off at the local Starbucks for pastries and coffee, then heading down Wisconsin Avenue to the National Cathedral, several blocks away. Although the day is warm and clear, a strong wind sends trash and leaves skittering across the sidewalk and whips our breath away. Inside the Bishop's Herb Garden, a walled enclosure filled with flower beds and stone pathways, the air is mercifully subdued and we find shelter on a bench next to a small, manicured lawn.

We used to come here back in high school, usually to share a joint and buy rock candy—clumps of sugar crystals on a slender wooden stick—from the Herb Cottage, the gift shop just outside the garden. I can perfectly recall the warm, spicy-sweet air that surrounded me when I pushed open the door and the kind, blue-haired ladies who worked there. Somehow they never seemed to notice our glassy eyes and pungent breath.

"So," Suzanne says. "Do you think she's really going to do it?"

I look over at her, face flushed and windblown, and think how little she's changed since we met over twenty years ago. Her blond hair has a touch of gray, but her skin is the same warm brown and, behind her glasses, her blue eyes are lively and bright. Yet, I can tell from her posture and the pinched sound in her voice that she's upset. Her ability to read and share in my distress is the very thing that drew me to her all those years ago; it was from her I learned that empathy is not a weakness.

Yet I feel strangely resistant to answering. She knows nothing of this twilight world of parental death, I think, and how can I explain it to her? I can't even explain it to my husband, who lost his own father a few years ago but finds my mother's desire to end her life unfathomable.

I watch her scoop up a handful of pine needles and throw them to the ground, one at a time, and realize she's uncomfortable too. I grab some pine needles and throw them gently into her lap.

"I don't know, Suze, I really don't. She's certainly obsessed with doing it. It's all she talks about. But she's changed her dates three times now and sometimes I think she's going to die before she gets around to killing herself."

She looks surprised and I regret sounding so bitter. She's come to D.C. to say good-bye to my mother, and it'll be easier for her if she believes my mother is moving smoothly and purposefully toward death, not weaving and bobbing. But the hopefulness I felt this morning after our conversation about not eating and drinking has faded, replaced by niggling doubts: What's to stop my mother from jettisoning this plan like all the rest?

"How sick is she anyway?" Suzanne asks, brushing the needles off her lap. "She seemed so, I don't know . . . normal, when I went in to say hello to her."

I think of my mother's list of diseases and disabilities but cannot bear to speak of them. Those are her lines to recite, not mine. Besides, I no longer believe the answer lies in symptoms and prognoses; it comes from some murkier place where fear and will and identity meet and mingle. A place I can intuit but can't possibly explain.

I realize how deeply exhausted I am by this macabre drama, the way it looms over me like the enormous stone walls of the cathedral behind us. I'm stuck in its shadow, and it lives within me, coloring everything I do. Even the people I love—my husband, my children, Suzanne—seem far away and unreal, the effort to connect with them exhausting.

I jump up off the bench, suggesting we take a walk. Suzanne gives me a questioning look but gets up to follow. As we wend our way single file through the garden, fragrant with the smell of tulips and damp earth, I attempt to answer.

"I'm not sure it has anything to do with how badly off she is. Her desire to end her life is more about who she is than about how sick she is, if that makes any sense."

"Not really."

I laugh. "Well, if you think about it, not everyone with her particular physical problems chooses to die, right? People worse off than she is stick it out to the bitter end every day, no matter how long it takes them. So there's obviously something else, something in *her,* that's driving this decision."

"What do you think it is?"

"Fear of the unknown. Fear of losing control."

We reach the gates at the end of the garden and slip through them, then start up the wide steps facing the southern entrance to the cathedral.

When I was young, the kids from my school used to walk here on Friday afternoons for services in Bethlehem Chapel. My family weren't big believers in God, but the cathedral always gave me the shivers. It might not have been God in there, but it was definitely *something*.

"But not of death?" Suzanne asks.

"No," I say, looking up at the saints and angels etched into the enormous stained-glass window over the doors. "Not of death."

Inexplicably, my mood lightens. Nonbeliever that I am, there's something comforting about looking up at the familiar arches and turrets, the vast stone walls and medieval-looking doors. The place is such a testament to people's belief—in God, yes, but also in beauty, in orderliness, in work itself. Somehow, as I stand before it, my own drama feels small, and I find this comforting.

Throwing an arm around Suzanne's shoulder, I say, "Let's go home. Maybe you can talk some sense into her before she drives me completely nuts."


Lane and Clara are excited that Suzanne is here. Squatting on the floor of my mother's room with their bowls of macaroni and cheese, they shriek loudly when Bruno comes to sniff at their food, then race off to find him dog treats. After they go to bed, my mother, Suzanne and I order Thai food, and I bring in a fresh bottle of Chardonnay.

Settled in my usual spot on the couch, I watch with pleasure as my friend and my mother chat. Suzanne sits on a chair several feet from my mother's bed, conversing animatedly, waving her wineglass as she talks. My mother's face is remarkably mobile and expressive in response. She sits upright in her bed, listening and asking questions with great interest.

Suzanne tells my mother about her sons, both of whom are doing well in school: the older one gifted musically, the younger a social butterfly. As for herself, she's been painting regularly and has had two recent shows in the small town on the Hudson River where she and her husband moved from New York City several years before.

She tells my mother about Dia, the new art museum that's opening in the nearby town of Beacon, and they discuss the works of Richard Serra. My mother looks extraordinarily pleased. She's always enjoyed these kinds of conversations, about art and culture, especially with people willing to share their expertise. And she's fond of Suzanne, whom she's known for years.

With no pressure to join the conversation, I'm about to go check on my kids when I realize they've stopped talking about art and are talking about death.

"Zoe told me you were planning to do that," Suzanne is saying, her voice quieter and more serious. She gives me a questioning look and I shrug.

"Ah, I see the perennial topic has been introduced," I say, filling my glass and getting up to fill Suzanne's as well. "And I was just about to make my escape."

"There is no escape," my mother says playfully.

"That's so true," I respond, matching her tone. "Except, of course, the big one at the end."

"Exactly." She laughs.

"So, Margaret," Suzanne asks, hesitantly, "what exactly are you planning to do?"

"Well, as of this morning, the plan is to stop eating and drinking."

"Wow." Suzanne sits back in her chair. "That's intense. How long will it take to . . ." She looks toward me questioningly.

"Actually, it's surprisingly quick and easy," I say, giving her a pointed look. I need her to back me up on this. "People who fast say it's quite pleasant after a day or two. You stop feeling hungry and become calm and clearheaded."

Of course, I know this firsthand but don't mention it. I gave up talking to my mother about my teenage eating disorder years ago. She could never get beyond the basic supposition that, while mistakes may have been made, and I had perhaps been a bit thin, she'd saved me from a lifetime of obesity. "I mean, look at you, Zoe," she'd say. "In all these years, you've never had a weight problem." At this point, overcome by rage, I'd have to physically retreat or risk slugging her. Eventually, I vowed never to speak of it again.

"God, I don't think I could do that," Suzanne says. "I'm way too much of a pig."

"You don't look like a pig," my mother says, eyeing Suzanne's petite frame approvingly. "Actually, I'm not sure I can do it either. But I'm going to try."

"Well, I wish you the best. Although it sounds funny to be saying that."

"No, no. I appreciate it. I really don't know what to expect, so I'm glad for your support."

They seem so chummy, I wonder if either of them ever thinks about that Easter weekend when my parents came to visit Jack and me in Brooklyn and Suzanne and her husband, Max, invited the four of us to go hear Max's band play at a club in Red Hook. My mother begged off, saying she was tired, and retreated to her hotel, and I stayed home with five-month-old Clara, uncomfortable about leaving her with a babysitter. So there was no one there to stop my father when he drank too much and put the moves on Suzanne, asking her for a "little smooch."

Poor Suzanne had to come over to my apartment Easter morning and pretend nothing had happened. But she filled me in as soon as my parents left, and that night I called my father to confront him. He claimed to have no recollection of the incident; in fact, he expressed genuine confusion about it. It was, I realized later, a blackout. My mother said it actually scared him off drinking for several months.

I'd always wondered if, in some way, my mother held it against Suzanne, detecting—or imagining—a subtle coolness toward my friend, but my mother seems delighted to have her here tonight and is unusually warm and chatty. Perhaps Suzanne's lively, outgoing presence is as much of a respite for her as it is for me.

Having momentarily lost track of the conversation, I tune back in to hear my mother say, "The Tibetans believe the soul takes several hours to vacate the body. They chant and pray around the dead person until they feel that they have really gone, and this is followed by forty days of prayer. They don't want the soul to be left alone as it departs."

"So you believe we have souls?" Suzanne asks.

"I don't know." My mother looks thoughtful. "But I remember when Jonathan died, we stayed with him for quite a while before we called the funeral parlor to come get his body. Do you remember that, Zoe?"

I do. After his caretaker, Dalia, and I finished dressing him, Clara came in carrying a pinecone she'd been playing with, went over to his bed, and laid it in my father's hand. I then went and fetched a story I'd written and slipped it into the front pocket of his shirt. My mother put a computer disc with her novel on it and a tape of his jazz band in the pocket of his jeans. I placed an origami bird for Hannah, who'd left a few days earlier, on his chest and tied a string of ribbons and bells from Katherine's Morris dancing days onto his belt loops. Jack found a fishing lure in the hall closet and pinned it to his shirt. Someone, Dalia maybe, added blooms from the bouquet of flowers on his nightstand.

By the time we called the funeral parlor just after midnight, my father looked as though someone had emptied a drawer on top of him, and yet, thanks to the flowers and ribbons, unexpectedly jaunty and festive. I half expected the two pasty-faced men in dark suits who came to remove him to object to taking all that bric-a-brac along with the body, but they appeared not to notice his eccentric appearance and simply wrapped everything up in a sheet and carried him out the door.

"I don't know if his soul hung around after he died or not," I say. "But I know he—or it—would have appreciated the send-off."

"That was nice," my mother says, looking happy, and I too feel cheered by the memory. I remember how exultant we felt—my mother, Jack and I—to have chanced on this final, fitting ritual.

"It *was* nice," I say. "Maybe we'll do the same for you."

She laughs. "Oh, I think you should."

"And then, if you're still hanging around, you can give us a sign. You know, knock a book off a shelf or something."

They both give me a quizzical look and I realize I'm a bit buzzed from the wine. But the conversation has reminded me of a story I'd heard the author Rachel Naomi Remen tell at Gaia Books in Berkeley a couple years before, during her book tour for *Kitchen Table Wisdom*.

Like many of her stories, it involved her work with dying patients. One of her patients, an Asian man, had particularly moved her. When she asked him what he thought would happen after he died, he said he thought he'd return as a bird. A white heron. Several months after his death, she was waiting for an elevator and thinking about him when the doors opened and there, on the floor of the empty elevator, was a perfect white feather.

I tell Suzanne and my mother the story, half-expecting them to laugh or dismiss it, and jokingly add, "So when you die, Momma, you should drop me a feather."

To my surprise, she looks extraordinarily pleased with the idea and says, "I will. I absolutely *will* drop you a feather."

When Suzanne leaves a while later, instead of the heavy emotional parting I'd anticipated, she gives my mother a kiss and says, quite cheerfully, "Drop me a feather too, Margaret, okay?"

Once again I'm astonished at the expression of delight on my mother's face. "Oh, don't you worry, I'll drop you one," she says, giving Suzanne a jaunty wave. "Keep your eyes peeled."

I walk my friend to the front door and step outside with her into the cool night air, wishing she didn't have to leave. "I'm so glad you came," I tell her. "You have no idea. That was the liveliest I've seen her for ages."

She hugs me, then steps away, her face quivery and tearful in the front door light.

"I love your mother," she says, her voice breaking. "I can't believe she's really going to kill herself."

I think of my mother's face, beaming as she promised to drop me a feather.

"Yeah," I say softly. "I think she might actually do it."

I wave to Suzanne as she gets into her car. The roar of its engine fades away, but I'm reluctant to go inside. Pausing on the front steps, I look up at the sky and have a sudden image of my mother lying motionless in her bed with me beside her, as a pale, translucent bird rises slowly from her body and takes flight, its great wings unfurling, then beating powerfully up into the dark night air. It circles, then flies in the direction of the cathedral, its white wings disappearing over the trees.

# Jack

While we're waiting for our flight home the following Monday, I call Jack on my cell phone, knowing he'll be up and getting ready for work.

Standing where I can keep my eye on Clara and Lane, who are happily eating enormous muffins from Starbucks and watching the planes come in, I listen to the burr of the phone, soft and oddly comforting in my ear. I imagine my husband eating his breakfast in our sunny, rust-colored dining room, and I long to reach across the table and smooth the wild shock of hair over his forehead, reassure him that soon I'll be home for good and—*patience, patience*—love him and be his wife.

The receiver is lifted noisily just as the answering machine clicks on, and Jack's irritated voice barks, "Hello?" and then, "Shit. Hang on."

We both wait for the message machine to click off.

"Did I wake you?"

"Yeah . . . you did. What time is it?"

"It's after eleven, East Coast time. I figured you'd be up by now."

"Mmmm." He yawns noisily. "Must have forgotten to set the alarm."

This is unlike Jack, who maintains a highly regular morning routine: shower, breakfast, work by eight-thirty. But he's a night owl by nature and likes to stay up working or reading until three or four in the morning, especially when I'm not there to remind him to come to bed. Other more disturbing possibilities of what he might have been doing flit across my mind, but I dismiss them. Our marriage has been at a low ebb for months, but I still trust him. I have to. I don't have the energy or will to win him back. Not now, not yet.

They announce our flight just as he starts to say something.

"Sorry. What did you say?"

"Forget it. Just tell the girls I love them and miss them."

"Okay." Ordinarily I would have said, Hey, what about me? Don't you love me? But I've lost the right to joke about such things. I can't demand what I can't give.

I must have met other nice men in my life, but Jack was the only one I ever really noticed or fell in love with. Before him, it was all losers and bad boys.

The most compelling of them was Liam, a tall, sexy keyboard player with whom I fell horribly, obsessively in love at the age of twenty-one. We met in a bar in the seedy Boston neighborhood where I'd moved to finish up college. He lived down the street from me in a crowded third-floor walk-up that he shared with the other members of his rock band. When he wasn't working, he would hang around on the street corner waiting for me to get back from class, which seemed incredibly romantic at the time. In fact, being with Liam felt like being in some cool movie, edgy and intense, and not quite real.

But the good times faded fast and within a year we'd established the following pattern: he would cheat on me, I would break up with him, and then he'd pull out all the stops and desperately, passionately win me back. Rinse and repeat. This went on for almost four years, until some much needed therapy and a move to a new city finally freed me.

But despite my emancipation from Liam, the excitement of attending Columbia Journalism School, and my work at various magazines in New York, I kept choosing the same men: men with big personalities and loads of charm who were also unemployed or immature or substance-abusing or all three. Determined to avoid a repeat of Liam, I kept my expectations low and my emotions in check. As a result, my life was a blur of clubs, parties and casual hookups.

The arrangement suited me. I liked being outside the world of conventional relationships, and even felt sorry for couples I passed on the street or in cafés. How predictable they were, how trite and self-satisfied. I, on the other hand, was a sexual warrior, fierce and independent. When I heard women talking about getting "commitments" from the men they dated, I was baffled. Why would they want *that*?

But soon this no-strings approach to sex began to lose its appeal, kind of like drugs had back in high school. Holed up in my tiny sublet in the West Village, after a one-night stand with an alcoholic film director I'd met at a party, I began to suspect that what looked like power was actually fear. In my determination to avoid a repeat of Liam, I chose men like him—and yes, like my father—then rejected them before they could reject me. Which kept me "safe" but increasingly lonely and out of sorts.

It was at this point that Jack turned up. He rented a room in the same SoHo loft where my friend Suzanne lived. Tall, blond and boyish in his tight-fitting jeans, he was hard to miss. I agreed to meet him at a local café but explained that I'd just given up on relationships. Oh, and sex too. He laughed and said that was fine, he could wait, and because his response was so sweet and unexpected,

I made an immediate exception. Within days we'd embarked on a full-fledged affair. Ten months later we were living together and four years after that we got married.

For once I'd picked the right guy. The one who—miracle of miracles—showed up when he said he would, had a real job, and didn't hesitate to let me know he was crazy about me. He was honest, kind and startlingly intelligent. Amazingly, I didn't blow it, although I skated close more than once and was occasionally tempted to push him away.

Fortunately, he had a knack for making big, romantic gestures without being obvious or sentimental. Soon after we met, I had told him one of those random pieces of personal history that only a new lover could possibly find interesting. It was about how I used to sob hysterically when my mother dropped me off at nursery school every morning until the day she promised to bring me a lollipop if I let her go. When that worked, she brought me a lollipop every day, and one of my happiest childhood memories was watching my mother walk up the steps of the nursery school with a lollipop in her hand.

Weeks passed and it was Valentine's Day. Jack showed up at my apartment carrying flowers and a huge covered bowl. Inside were dozens, maybe hundreds, of lollipops, in a multitude of colors and shapes and flavors. He'd left work early to walk the forty or so blocks from his office in Midtown, stopping off at every Korean market, candy store, and five-and-dime along the way to collect them. I was seriously smitten.

I can't say it's all been easy. Like all opposites, we can make each other crazy. I'm impatient and opinionated, while Jack is slower, more deliberate, someone who thinks through ideas rather than blurting them out. One of the running jokes in our marriage is that he married a woman like his father—a fierce and dominating former fighter pilot, a man who never consulted anyone when he made a decision or formulated a plan—and I married a man like my mother.

I like to think I'm a more accommodating person than Jack's father, and Jack is certainly warmer and more physically affectionate
than my mother, but the comparison feels emotionally accurate.
My mother made me feel safe as a child, just as Jack does now, and
both of them are utterly loyal.

I'm counting on that loyalty and I'm worried about it. I've been
missing in action in my marriage for so long, I can't help but wonder
how far I can push this thing before it starts to collapse.

On the airplane, knees wedged uncomfortably into the back of the
seat in front of me while my kids watch some awful movie about a
dog, I feel simultaneously revved up and exhausted. The muscles at
the back of my left shoulder, which have been painfully clenched for
weeks, have turned into a red-hot spiral of pain, and I take a second
dose of Advil and try to relax against the harsh synthetic seat.

I can't shake the feeling that my mission has failed. Having
avoided telling anyone—even Jack—that my mother has dropped
the May first date, I'm dreading the announcement.

I can hear my sisters' indignation coming at me through the
phone and imagine Jack's slow burn of disapproval. The funny
thing is, I don't feel angry myself. Now that I'm starting to believe
she really is going to kill herself, in some perverse way, the date is
less important.

This lack of outrage figures to make me a target. I'll be accused
of letting her get away with something, of being "taken in." Just as
my sisters and I were forced to hold my father's secrets, to overlook
his difficult behavior, I'm now in that position with my mother. I've
become her apologist, her defender. And as the borders between
my mother and I diminish and blur, I worry that I will lose the support of my sisters and, more painfully, my husband.

I look out the plane window at the orange and pink cloud bank
that stretches like some fantastic mountain range just below us.

I remember how desperate I was to explore that expanse of soft weightlessness as a child, and how frustrating it was to be stuck on the wrong side of the glass, separated from all that beauty and adventure.

I let my hand rest on Lane's small knee, and she looks up at me and smiles. For a moment, the soft glow from the window illuminates her face and I'm reminded of all that is good and uncomplicated in my life. But when I turn to look back outside, the clouds have abruptly been leached of their light and there is nothing left but dingy colorless waves. I reach over and take my daughter's hand as we begin the long, bumpy descent to the ground.

# Editing

The summer my father died, I became my mother's editor. It started innocently enough. The family was gathered in Vermont for the month of August as usual when my mother came into the kitchen carrying an enormous manuscript to "show me." At that point, she'd been working on her book, an autobiographical novel, for over twenty years and I'd never read a word of it.

Grabbing a dictionary-size chunk—the manuscript was over fifteen hundred pages—I dug in, and was instantly hooked. Not by the writing per se, although it was generally clear and strong, but by the opportunity to see into my mother's mind, discover her secrets. It was intoxicating and frustrating at the same time. Intoxicating because there was so much juicy and revealing information in it. Frustrating because it was filled with pages of extraneous material and, given the number of years she'd been working on it, a shocking lack of form and structure.

What had all those editors she'd hired over the years been doing? Or rather, not doing. She'd spent so much time with some of them they'd practically become adjunct family members. There was Mr. Longstreth, a Henry Miller type who lived in Adams Morgan with his young Asian wife and typed without his shirt on. And a sweet, obese woman named Sheila, who lived on a remote hillside in Maryland. For over a year, my father dropped my mother off at Sheila's house for several nights every week. The two of them would work all day and watch movies together at night. I think my mother was one of the only people Sheila ever saw.

There were others as well, some friends, some professionals, but all of them apparently too lazy, kind, or deferential to tell my mother she needed to lose three-quarters of her book.

Not so with me, her blunt and uncompromising daughter. Within minutes, I was drawing lines through paragraphs and even whole pages and making suggestions as to where she should begin and end chapters. Although I had no formal training as an editor, I'd been writing professionally for ten years at that point, and my mother seemed happy and grateful to have my input. Flattered, I began working on the manuscript more systematically, driven by the possibility of shaping it into publishable form.

Looking back, I realize that becoming my mother's editor that summer was no accident. My father had died a month earlier, and we were both still shell-shocked and disoriented. Coming to Vermont had been unexpectedly difficult because the house was full of his things: fishing poles and waders, books and instruments, even a pair of his black-framed glasses left casually on his nightstand. Sad and a little eerie, these objects made his absence seem arbitrary and unreal, as if he might still swing through the door with a freshly caught fish or appear at the kitchen table with a drink and a book.

Having twenty-month-old Clara under my care kept me too busy to brood, and soon I was engaged in my usual Vermont activities, swimming and sailing and driving to Burlington to meet Jack, who flew up from New York on weekends. But my mother was clearly suffering. Stick-thin and pale, she floated around the house like a wraith, too tired and weak to swim or take a walk or even go to town. "I just don't want to see anyone," she finally admitted. "They'll say something nice to me about Jonathan and I'll cry."

In light of her grief, her decision to continue working on the book seemed a hopeful sign and when she offered to hire me as her editor at the end of the summer, I agreed. We soon established a routine. She sent me pieces of the manuscript and I read and edited them. Then, every four or five weeks, she flew up from Washington and we would spend several days together in my Brooklyn apartment going over my comments and suggestions.

These trips served to bring us together regularly, something we both needed, and I got to continue the strange and fascinating process of excavating my mother's childhood. I was familiar with much of it—in particular her father's alcohol and drug addiction, his troubled second marriage and brief incarceration on drug charges—but I hadn't known how much my mother had loved, even worshiped, him.

While not exactly a model citizen, Thomas Flynn DeLacey was a thrilling parent. Tall and slim with curly brown hair and piercing blue eyes, he was movie-star handsome, with a careless, grandiose manner to match. Rebellious with his stuffy, old world family, he was also a snob about their ancestry, telling my mother that the DeLaceys were descended from French aristocrats when they were in fact Irish potato farmers. She believed every word. He also convinced her she'd seen Santa Claus fly overhead on Christmas Eve, and that one day the two of them would get a monkey and live together on a houseboat.

Promises were invariably broken and, after divorcing my grandmother, Thomas left my very shy, five-year-old mother with his elderly parents in Boston and moved to Hollywood to work on screenplays. He was at the height of his career by then, having published two novels and various short stories in *Esquire*. But with the notable exception of allegedly bedding Lillian Gish, little came of his Western adventures, no doubt because of his escalating addictions.

In the meantime, my mother was left to fend for herself in a household of unfamiliar adults and she quickly receded into near catatonia. Her prickly Irish grandmother, Mary DeLacey, particularly terrorized her. A proud, insecure woman, Mary was convinced she was going to end up in the poorhouse despite the fact that she was married to a successful industrialist, one of the so-called Robber Barons of Boston, and they were a wealthy, socially prominent family.

Mary's main concern in loco parentis was that my mother turn out to be a proper lady. Affection was left to the nannies or "nurses." My mother's favorite was Maddie, an older French woman with dyed red hair and a gold tooth. The closest my mother came to rebellion was when she returned from school to find Maddie and all her belongings gone—sacked for some unknown, never-discussed transgression—and refused to come down for dinner.

Although her father was largely absent, he didn't totally abdicate his role as parent and would occasionally stand up to his mercurial mother. During one visit, he was outraged to find my mother wearing a back brace, apparently to correct scoliosis. Stopping his car on a bridge, he demanded she take it off and sent it sailing into the river below.

These visits were clearly the high points of an otherwise dreary childhood.

In the prologue of her book, my mother wrote:

My father lived in Hollywood and wrote for the movies. He drove a green Duesenberg roadster with T.F.D. on the door. His name was Thomas Flynn DeLacey. We didn't see him very often. It was a great day whenever he came to visit my grandparents and me. He always stopped at the top of our street and blew his Klaxon. *Ahooga, ahooga, ahooga.* Everyone ran to the windows. No one had a horn like his. Those were the cushy days when he was riding high and so was I. I remember sitting beside him, I must have been eight or nine years old. He took my hand and said, "The sky's the limit for you, old girl. You're really something." And I was.

The book was tentatively entitled *The Sky's the Limit*.

My mother's highly idealized relationship with her father stood in direct contrast to that with her mother. A tall, doe-eyed woman known as the "pretty one" in her family, Emily Custis Butler was a card-carrying Daughter of the American Revolution, a Southern aristocrat and a direct descendant of both George Washington's wife and sister, as well as of Lord Baltimore, who established the city of Baltimore in the 1600s under the auspices of King Charles I.

Enjoying a life of enormous privilege—private schools, trips to Europe—Emily flouted convention to elope with my handsome, ne'er-do-well grandfather at the age of twenty-one. A year later, she had my mother. Taking to neither marriage nor motherhood, she divorced him and moved to New York to pursue her dream of becoming a playwright.

When her writing career failed to take off, Emily launched herself on a world tour, in search of a titled husband, which she found just before the start of World War II. Friedrich von Kessler, a German baron, was more than happy to have the rich and lovely Emily arrange for him to come to America after the war, and they married soon after.

One fly in the ointment was that, despite his dashing looks, Friedrich was more interested in boys than in women. In the only photograph we have of him, he is posed with his arm around a skinny, brown-skinned teenager in Indonesia. According to my mother's cousin Maeve, despite Emily's travels and seeming worldliness, she apparently didn't have a clue.

Much to my amazement, none of this was in the book. I discovered these facts about Emily quite incidentally during our monthly get-togethers in Brooklyn. As my mother and I lay stretched out on my living room couch together, a plate of crackers or fruit between us, she answered my questions about Emily, but in the book she simply killed her off. In a car crash, no less. At the very beginning of the story.

When I asked her why she'd disposed of her mother so precipitously, she said, "Well, it *is* fiction," although, for all intents and purposes, it wasn't. Other than a few changed names, all the facts about my mother's life were fundamentally accurate.

But the more I learned about my glamorous grandmother, the more I began to understand how death in a car crash might be a fitting revenge. Not only had she neglected my mother for months and even years at a time, she'd exhibited a marked lack of warmth and interest when they did meet. After spending a few days with my twelve-year-old mother in an Atlantic City hotel, Emily had written in her diary, "Poor Margaret is just like her father, but with none of his charm." (My mother came across this lovely item after Emily's death.) And a few years later, when Emily rented a house on Nantucket for the summer, she invited my mother to come stay but then put her in a house on the far side of the island.

The story of Emily's wedding to Friedrich was, perhaps, the final straw. Although Emily hadn't bothered to invite her only child, my mother happened to be visiting friends in Jackson Hole, Wyoming, at the time and ran into her future stepfather at the post office.

"So you'd met him before?" I asked.

"No." She laughed. "I only knew it was him because I heard him give the postmistress his name. When I introduced myself, he insisted I come up to the lodge where they were staying. Turned out their marriage ceremony was scheduled for a few days later. Since I was there, my mother asked me to be in it. I remember I had nothing but jeans and cowboy shirts, and she had to loan me a dress."

My mother spoke as if her lack of a dress was as significant as the fact that she had to crash her own mother's wedding. I was immediately suspicious. Wasn't she hurt or furious at this casual, after-the-fact invitation?

"Not really," she said, sounding vague. "I'd barely seen my mother since I started college, although she wrote me letters once in a while. The wedding didn't seem like such a big deal."

Except that it was the last time she saw her mother. Apparently the altitude in Wyoming put a strain on Emily's already compromised heart—she'd picked the location despite her doctor's warnings—and she soon found herself in a medical crisis. Although she quickly traveled to lower ground, it was too late. She died in a hospital in San Francisco on September 11, 1949, at the age of forty-seven.

After her mother's death, von Kessler showed his true colors by suing my mother for her share of Emily's inheritance. My mother, an idealistic, Marx-reading college student at the time, informed her lawyers that as far as she was concerned he could have it. Fortunately, cooler heads prevailed. After patting her on the head and sending her back to Sarah Lawrence, my mother's lawyers fought her stepfather in court and won.

My mother's money was safe. As for my mother, I wasn't so sure.

I'd begun to seriously question all the years my mother had spent in therapy and to wonder if maybe her therapists had been as ineffectual as her editors. It was dawning on me as we worked on the book that she didn't have much understanding of her past, in particular how all this parental abandonment and family dysfunction had affected her. She seemed shocked when I suggested she'd married a man like her father and denied that her critical assessments of me and my sisters—especially when we were younger—

might have something to do with her own mother's coldness and neglect.

But mainly I worried about the book. The excessive length and lack of structure were fixable, but a deeper issue lurked: a pervasive emotional opaqueness that prevented the story from coming fully alive. Although capable of writing eloquently and powerfully about "what happened," my mother never wrote about what events meant to her. Emotions were rarely described and reactions to events, even shocking ones, were only barely alluded to or left out altogether. This left the reader to fill in extensive blanks, forced to imagine what my mother had experienced.

I knew then why daughters shouldn't edit their mother's books. As her editor, I could have demanded that she reveal more; as her daughter, I hesitated. Did I really want to be her editor *and* her therapist?

It was actually Katherine who encouraged me to confront my mother. She'd read my edited version of the book and, in her laser-like way, immediately identified its essential flaw. Fortified by her opinion, I broached the subject with my mother. Why had she never described her character's inner life? To my surprise, she seemed to welcome the question. It was an artistic choice, she explained. The character of the child—my mother—was meant to function like a blank screen, a canvas, on which the words and behavior of the adults could be projected. The reader was *meant* to understand more than the child.

I see, I said, although I didn't. Surely children have feelings even if they don't understand everything going on around them. Besides, she was a child for only the first half of the book. By the end she was a college graduate starting her life in New York; a thoughtful, intellectual young woman interested in psychology and literature. She must have had opinions and emotions.

But if she did, they—like Emily—were not in the book.

Looking back, I see that I should have made the argument that the manuscript would benefit from more personal revelation, but I didn't. Instead, I told my mother it was done. The story was coherent; it had a structure; she should try to get it published. I'd done as much as I could, and I needed to get back to my own writing.

And so, like so many others before me, I guess I failed her too.

I just didn't know how to tell her that she didn't have to be a blank screen.

Several months later, she called me. She'd found a new editor. The woman had some really good ideas, and she was back at work, revising the book yet again.

I don't know if this woman's ideas were good or not. I never read *The Sky's the Limit* again, even when my mother had bound copies made of the book, each with a picture of her father on the front, and gave them out to Hannah, Katherine and me before she died.

On the cover my grandfather wears a tweed coat. He strikes a lord of the manor pose, his Irish wolfhound at his side. The family's imposing summer house is visible behind him. My mother stands, pale and fragile beside him, squinting into the sun. She looks like a small monkey.


Several years later, when coming to Vermont for our annual August vacation had become a Herculean task for my mother, involving rented hospital beds, oxygen tanks and her caretaker, Rosa, I drove her over to see her old friend Sally, who lived on a small farm at one corner of the lake.

Sally ran a riding stable and used to board my mother's horse, Patrick, an overweight Percheron-Belgian mix, too ancient and fat for any of us to ride. She also had a degree in applied kinesiology and used to have sessions with my mother during the summer, working on her knotted muscles but also talking through any emotional issues that the physical work brought up for her.

When I went to pick my mother up that afternoon, she looked completely spent. Her face was red and puffy-eyed, and she could barely get herself to the car. Once in, she asked me to drive her someplace instead of going home. I turned down the road toward Craftsbury Common, a small, scenic town that we both loved for its large central green and view of the surrounding mountains.

"What's going on?" I asked.

She flapped her hands and looked away, unable to speak.

I continued to drive, following the familiar bends in the road past woods and open fields, wondering if I should say something more. I knew how much she hated falling apart in front of me and was afraid that the usual words of comfort would only make it worse.

"I had a dream," she finally said. "I was driving. Like this." Her hand jerked spastically toward the passing scenery. "Except I couldn't see. There was a shroud . . . over my head."

She started to cry. "It was *me*, Zoe. Me under the shroud. But I was also sitting next to it, driving. And the me that was driving was afraid to look under the shroud because I knew that underneath there was nothing there. I didn't exist."

She was sobbing now, gasping for breath. I glanced over at her. Her face looked squashed and broken, her eyes barely open. "I told Sally . . . it was . . . a metaphor," she said. "For the book—for me in the book. All you see is the outside. Because what's under . . . is dead."

Her body jumped and trembled, the heat from all that wildly misfiring electricity burning against my arm. I hoped she was done.

"It's me, Zoe. I'm dead too."

"You're not dead—" I broke in, horrified. "What are you talking about?"

"No, I am." She brushed her hand frantically in front of her face again. "That part of me. The child."

"It's okay, Momma," I murmured, staring straight ahead, my

hands numb on the wheel. I wondered if her dream was a response to my questioning of her book. I felt sick. "You *are* there," I told her, reaching over to touch her.

"Thank you . . . ," she said, her voice strangled. "You know, I've never told you . . . I wanted to tell you . . . I think of you as my friend."

I took her hand. The grass shimmered outside the window. The blood flowed back into my brain. My heart swelled.

# Home Again

"She's toying with you, honey," Jack says in a terse, aggrieved voice the morning after my return. "I doubt she has any intention of killing herself at all. It's just a weird bid for attention. And the worst part is, you keep falling for it."

He stalks around the room, pulling out drawers, slamming his closet door after retrieving a shirt and tie and refusing to look at me. I lie in bed, at the mercy of this rant, fighting the urge to pull the blankets over my head and cover my ears. My upper back pulls painfully every time I turn or move and the acrid smell of stale airplane air emanates from my skin and hair. The thought of taking a shower exhausts me and I seriously wonder how I'm going to make it through the day.

"Jack, please," I say, hating the worn-out sound of my voice. "I know it seems irrational—*she* seems irrational—but maybe killing yourself isn't an entirely rational process. I think we just need to give her some room to get there in her own way."

In the middle of putting on his shoes, he stops to glare at me. "She's never going to get there! Why do you keep believing all that crap? I understand you feel sorry for her—I do too. But you have to protect yourself. I mean, what about *your* life? *Your* needs? Does she care that she's completely taken over your life?"

I stop listening as he describes all the ways I've dropped the ball. "Unengaged . . . barely present." The words barely register. Ordinarily these accusations would have had me bristling with defensive anger, but my rage—once so easily accessed—has completely deserted me. I couldn't summon it if I tried. I know he's feeling more abandoned than angry and who can blame him? I'm basically a zombie.

I consider telling him about the conversation with Suzanne, my nighttime vision of the bird flying overhead, but this will get me exactly nowhere. My husband is skeptical of anything not tangibly evident. Despite having grown up in hippie-dippie Northern California, he's far more of a typical, hard-nosed East Coaster than I am. If he doesn't view my story as New Age drivel, he'll see it as a feeble attempt to defend my mother.

Standing at the foot of the bed, clean, brushed and suited up for work, he looks down at me. I feel laid out and exposed under this scrutiny, conscious of my unwashed face and messy hair. I attempt to assemble my features into something approaching normal and look steadily back at him; it's essential that I appear at least marginally functional.

"Look, I know this is hard," he says, a flicker of sympathy softening his expression. "But while your mother keeps us all in turmoil, time's going by. It's up to us—to you—to make her stop this endless planning for death. This has been going on for close to a year. How much longer are you going to put up with it?"

"I can't make her stop, Jack," I say, sitting up and shivering as the blankets slip off my shoulders. "The only way she's going to stop is by dying. I'm sorry, but that's what I believe."

He gives me a look, but then comes over to my side of the bed and puts his arms around me. I lean against him, breathing in his fresh, soapy smell. We stay like this for a moment, my cheek pressed against the soft wool of his suit. I'm grateful for the still, gingerly way he holds me. Anything more would crush me.

"It's all right, sweetie," he whispers finally. "We'll get through this. I'm on your side, okay?"

I nod, lean harder as the tears stream down my face, the warmth and pressure of his body absorbing my grief.

He kisses my hair, gives my shoulders a squeeze, kisses me again on the lips, and then gets up and leaves the room, closing the door quietly behind him.

I listen to him wake the children as I curl under the covers, wishing he would come back and lie down with me, breathe his warmth into my hair. Has he been there for me all this time? And if so, why haven't I sought his comfort more often?

I stare glumly at the bumpy expanse of red cotton quilt, dreading the onslaught of dressing, driving, shopping, cooking and cleaning that lies ahead. I long to hopscotch past it all, roll over and go back to sleep. I think of my mother lying in her bed and wonder, is this what she longs for? To be done with her day? Return to the oblivion of sleep, and ultimately the oblivion of death?

I throw off the quilt, jump up and hurry into the bathroom, rip off my T-shirt, and step into a scalding blast of water.

I am not dying, I tell myself severely as the water pounds against my back and neck. I am young and strong. I have years ahead of me. A husband who loves me and two children to raise. This is no time to lounge around longing for oblivion.

Jack looks surprised when I come into the kitchen in fresh clothes—a skirt, no less—my wet hair twisted into a bun. Lane waves happily from her booster seat, and sings out, "Mommy, Mommy. Daddy said not to wake you up! He said *he* was gon' take me to school."

Clara sidles over and stands silently at my elbow, still buttering her toast, and I reach out and pull her into a hug.

"I thought Daddy and I could both take you to school today. How does that sound?"

"Yes, Mommy! Yes! Yes!" Lane crows, struggling to climb out of her chair and come over to me. "That sounds good!"

Out on the sidewalk, Jack opens the car door for me and gives my butt a pat as I turn to climb in. "Good Mommy," he says, teasingly. "I'm proud of you."

"Thanks," I say, looking back at him. "And thanks for being nice this morning."

"You mean after I got mad at you?"

"Well, yeah . . ."

"Zoe, you know I want to support you, I just—"

"I know, Jack," I say, cutting him off. "And I know I don't make it easy for you."

"You do?"

"Uh-huh."

We stand looking at each other until Clara calls to us to hurry up, get in the car, *let's goooo!* He smiles and I feel lighter than I have for months. The car moves down the sunny street past small, flower-filled front yards, each one a perfect miniature. My children chatter excitedly in the back, and next to me my husband hums. I'm not sure what he's humming—he's tone-deaf—but it sounds to me like that song from *The Sound of Music,* when all the children line up to say good night.

> *So long, farewell, auf Wiedersehen, adieu,*
> *Adieu, adieu, to yieu and yieu and yieu . . .*

# Still Running

After Jack drops me back at home, I leave a message for Hannah telling her *not* to cancel her plans to visit me and to call me as soon as she can. Then I settle on our living room couch with my laptop and some Peet's, pleased that I've managed to go with Jack to drop the children at school and buoyed at how happy it made everyone.

The first e-mail is from Katherine. My back twinges painfully when I see it and I go wash down several Advil before opening it. Apparently, she has heard the news. Calling what my mother is doing sick and manipulative, she suggests we refuse to discuss any future dates with her. If my mother is serious about killing herself, she writes, then she will do it. But if she's just talking about it to get our attention, we shouldn't encourage her. She ends by saying that, given my mother's perverse behavior, she's decided not to be part of the "deathbed watch."

I'm frankly surprised she's so adamant about not being there, as I don't think anyone, except possibly my mother, was expecting her. But her e-mail is the perfect preemptive strike: she can opt out of participating in my mother's death and command credit for taking a firm stand.

I begin to craft a reply, making subtly critical references to her decision while praising her "clear boundaries." But in the midst of this effort, an image of my mother's gaunt, exultant face comes to me, the way she looked the night Suzanne asked her to drop a feather, and I find I no longer have the will to continue. Pausing midsentence, I delete my reply. There is something poisonous about these e-mails—their hostile jockeying for position, their utter lack of love or comfort—and I no longer want to engage. Katherine can do what she wants.

Looking into the lush branches of the liquid amber tree that grows in front of our house, I realize I've stopped fighting my mother as well. Almost without my being aware of it, my repulsion toward the idea of her killing herself has diminished if not yet dissolved. I no longer feel as driven to make her change her mind, convince her to live, to stick around and be my mother— as much as I'd like her to. I don't know if I'm ready to help her complete the act, but then, how can anyone know this about oneself?

Closing my laptop, I go change into my running clothes. My body feels sluggish after yesterday's flight, but the Advil has softened the knot in my back and I have a strong compulsion to move. The race in Sonoma is only a few weeks away and I still haven't run more than five miles at a stretch. My plan is to add a half mile this week and another half mile the next, making the last few runs a full ten kilometers.

Pulling on my shorts, I think about how this tedious accruing of minutes and miles sustains me, as if running provided a meaningful counterpoint—an inverse progression—to my mother's journey toward death. She gets weaker; I get stronger. But who am I kidding? At forty, I'm clearly starting on the downhill slide toward infirmity, sickness and death. Surely running won't stave off the inevitable.

I catch sight of my muscled calves and tanned shoulders in the mirror and decide I don't care. There may be no prevention for aging, no cure for death, but there is a stubborn joy in not conceding easily. And as long as my body does what I ask, I'm going to run.

# Hit the Road

Hannah has been in California for three days and this is the first chance we've had to be alone. Waking at dawn, we'd carried our toast and coffee to the car, leaving Jack and the four children asleep in the house. Eating and talking as we drive, we pass through the deserted urban landscape of I-80 and out across the rolling hillsides northeast of the city toward the town of Sonoma, where my race is scheduled to start in less than an hour.

We begin, as we often do, by discussing our children: how each of them has grown since Christmas, how my daughter, Clara, and Hannah's older daughter, Fiona—both eight—are up to their usual sibling-like tricks, passionately devoted one minute, squabbling the next. And how Evie and Lane, our two younger ones, three and four, are so much less intense and demanding.

We've finally gotten to my mother when we're interrupted by Hannah's cell phone. It's her husband, Dan. Impatiently, I listen in as they chat, waiting for the inevitable I love yous that will signal the end of their conversation.

Hannah and Dan always say "I love you" when they say good-bye, even if it's only to run to the store. This seems strange to me, because my family rarely said these words when I was growing up. In fact, Hannah and I used to laugh at families who were forever shouting "Love ya!" and I never heard my parents say "I love you" to each other. I imagine they would have considered it rote and sentimental if they considered it at all.

My father did tell me he loved me a few times during his final illness, but I always figured it was the right-brain injury talking. My mother rarely says it, although when we were children, she used to wrap up our arguments with a mechanical "Now, sweetie, you know we love you." All of which could explain why I find the words so hard to say.

I do occasionally tell Jack I love him, usually when he's traveling or I'm leaving on a trip, which is more a hedging of bets than anything else; a preemption of posthumous regrets. But with my children the words come easily and recently Clara has begun saying "I love you," unprompted, when I tuck her in at night, which delights me. To have a daughter capable of uttering these words without embarrassment seems a triumph.

"Okay, bye. I love you." My sister snaps the phone shut and drops it into her purse.

I glance over, admiring the way Hannah's fine, pale skin glows in the early morning sun. I note how dramatically her profile resembles my mother's—and my grandmother's, which I know only from photographs. All of them with the same high, rounded cheekbones and long chins, the thick, dark curls and fair skin.

I love you too, I think, but cannot bring myself to say it, even now, when the presence of death sits over us like a low pressure weather system, sucking up all the fresh air. I have a sudden image of the two of us walking hand in hand into a dark wood, sisters in a gothic fairy tale, orphans in the storm.

———

"So tell me about Momma. What's she saying now?" We're getting closer to Sonoma, and I'm worried we won't have time to finish talking before the race. Ever since her arrival, Hannah has been dropping hints, usually over the top of some child's head, that she and my mother have worked out "a mutually tolerable plan," and I'm anxious to find out what it is.

"Let me start with what *I* said," Hannah says. "I told her that I supported her decision to stop eating and drinking, but I needed to know if she was serious this time. I'll come down but only if she actually starts her fast. And as long as she doesn't take an overdose, I'll stay with her until the end. No matter how long it takes."

I'm impressed—and pleased. I've been feeling defensive about my mother's recent change of date, but I feel like my sister and I are back on the same side. Hannah's promise to my mother feels like a promise to me.

"So she's not planning to take the Seconal or morphine?" I ask, trying not to betray my excitement.

"Nooo," Hannah replies, a little less certain. "But she did mention that Michael the hospice nurse gave her an entire bottle of morphine."

"Right—Mr. Singing Bowls. But what do you mean? Did it sound like she was going to take it or not?"

It feels strange for *me* to be asking *her* these questions. I've been the point person between my mother and sisters for months. But I haven't talked to Momma since my last trip to D.C., and I'm feeling strangely out of the loop. I can't decide if I'm offended or relieved.

"Well, I have to admit she dithered a bit, but I told her those were my terms."

I remember the Gollum-like way my mother had held up the small amber bottle of morphine. "And you're okay with that?"

"Not entirely. I just hope she'll decide not to do it. I think the morphine is probably just a security blanket. A last resort if the fast gets too difficult."

"God, I hate that we have to worry about it! The whole point of getting her to stop eating and drinking was so she wouldn't take the drugs."

I can feel Hannah watching me but keep my eyes on the road ahead. "We can only influence her so much, Zoe," she says, after a pause. "We just need to be clear about what we're willing—and not willing—to do."

I like the sound of that *we*. Despite all the ways my mother has misjudged and underestimated Hannah, my sister is going to be there "until the end." With me.

I want to hug her. Tell her that I love her. But Sonoma's large village green looms just ahead, runners and walkers are streaming around the car, and I turn my attention to finding a parking place instead.


I give Hannah a wave as the starting gun goes off and the band on the village green belts out, *"Hit the road, Jack. Don't you look back . . ."* Bodies move around and past me in a rapidly accelerating wave. Swept up in the crowd of runners, I quickly reach the end of the green, turn the corner, and head up a long residential street lined with live oaks and small houses.

Struggling to get my breathing under control—the adrenaline rush of the music and the sound of the gun has put my system into overdrive—I settle into my usual measured pace, resisting the urge to compete with the faster runners ahead. My main goal is to complete the full ten kilometers without walking.

I start up a long, gently ascending drive through a small vineyard, still fighting for air. To relax, I force my mind to disengage from the running, go inward, a technique I use on long runs to distract myself from fatigue. But my brain feels strangely unfocused and all I can think about is how much I want to get back to Hannah.

Turning down a shaded, tree-lined street, I realize my bad shoulder has loosened and my breathing is deeper and steadier. I fall in behind a dark-haired teenage girl and her forty-something mother. Running just behind them, I imagine they are silently communicating, making small adjustments in pace as one of them tires, exchanging little nods of encouragement. I think of my own mother, trapped in her bed, in her malfunctioning body, and have the urge to tap them on the shoulder and tell them to enjoy those bodies. They won't last forever.

As I sprint past them, I realize that I'm running a race with my mother too. A race to the end—*her* end—but also a race to stay healthy and sane in the face of this crazy, unspooling situation. A race that makes this six-mile run feel like a skip in the park.

As I puff down the final stretch, my heart gives a little leap when I see the green of my sister's sweater. She's standing just past the digital clock that hangs between two posts at the finish line. Forcing my leaden legs to move faster, I stagger across the line and come to an awkward, arm-flapping halt next to her. I glance back. One hour and five minutes.

"Congratulations," she says, handing me a bottle of water.

"Thanks," I say, catching my breath. "Did I win?"

She laughs. "Yeah, if you don't count those total cheaters who came in half an hour ago."

"Assholes! I bet they ate up all the post-race goodies too." Together we walk over to the conspicuously empty tables, where only a few donuts and orange slices remain. "That's okay," I say happily. "I'm taking you out to lunch."

"You are? Why?"

"Because I'm hungry," I say, adding, "And I'm glad you're here."

"I'm glad too."

We walk across the parking lot, my thighs and calves tender and rubbery beneath me. The sky is a blazing Technicolor blue, and the sunlight gleams against the chrome door handles and windshields of the parked cars. A light wind cools my skin and dries the sweat in my hair.

At the car, Hannah climbs in, but I pause for a moment to let the day burn into me, vivid and timeless and static, as if it was something I could return to again and again. Like a photograph or a memory, but with all the beautiful sounds and smells of life.

# The Art of Happiness

Barely registering the undignified process of removing my jacket as I pass through airport security, I head toward the large, wood-paneled bookstore that's located at the end of the long corridor that leads to my gate. I have in mind something trashy, a celebrity gossip magazine or one of those shiny women's magazines that will tell me how to spice up my sex life or get my body bikini-ready for summer.

Not that any of these things are in my immediate future. Once again, I'm heading to D.C. Although this trip was supposed to be the "big one," it's not. My mother has asked me to come "tie up any loose ends," like how much money to leave her caretakers and what to do about the mulberry tree that's about to topple into her yard. I'd initially refused to go, citing the disruption to me and my family, but gave in when Rosa called sounding even more depressed than my mother.

Although she hasn't settled on an exact date, my mother still maintains she's going to stop eating and drinking in a couple of weeks. "You keep getting mad at me when I mention specific dates," she complained in our last phone conversation. "So I guess I just won't mention any."

Which is fine with me, but I'm not kidding myself. She hasn't let up one little bit on the idea of killing herself and has, in fact, started talking openly about it with her friends and caregivers. One reason I agreed to go this weekend is that my mother's caregivers—Kendra and the housekeeper, Sonia—are upset and worried about losing their jobs, according to Rosa. I can tell Rosa is also worried but is too polite to mention it. I tell her we'll talk when I get there.

Inside the bookstore, my eye is immediately caught by a large display of books by the Dalai Lama called *The Art of Happiness: A Handbook for Living.* There's a picture of him on the cover looking happy in a quizzical, playful sort of way, his forehead wrinkling upward over his dark glasses, his mouth pursed as if he's secretly amused by something. Living, I guess.

I buy one for my mother.

And so, with *The Art of Happiness,* a stack of bad magazines and *The New York Times,* I make my usual stop at the See's candy cart just outside the bookstore. I buy a large box with extra nuts. Fortunately, we both like nuts. My mother gets first dibs, but I invariably eat a third of the box.

I walk to my gate and sit, waiting to board the airplane. The muscles in my upper back are already aching and I'm dreading how I'm going to feel after five hours in a plane. Maybe I've been in California too long, but I've come to view this constant, inexplicable tenderness in my back as the physical manifestation of my mother. Or, rather, the *pain* I feel about my mother. And I've been hauling it around for so long, it feels like a part of me, an extra limb, so familiar I barely notice it.

The door opens and Rosa reaches for my bag. She neither smiles nor gives me her usual cheery greeting and I notice there's a disorganized, almost shabby look to the front hall, as if people have stopped cleaning or straightening up. The large DO NOT CALL 911 sign over the hall phone has come undone and hangs down, brown and curled at the edges.

Most of the lights in the house are off—it's after ten—and heading down the long, gloomy hall and through the darkened dining room past Rosa's bed, I have the sensation of walking into a cave. The high ceiling looms darkly over me while the corners vanish into fuzzy blackness.

I continue into my mother's room and find her propped up in bed, her head floating, disembodied and starkly illuminated under her bright gooseneck lamp. Her face looks craggy in the harsh light and she doesn't smile when she sees me.

I lean over and give her a kiss.

"Are you all right?" I ask. "Is something going on?"

"I'm fine," she says, peevishly.

"Rosa didn't look too happy," I say mildly, sitting on the edge of her bed.

"She wants to go to Florida," my mother bursts out, her head and torso beginning to tremble. "To see her son."

"She does?" My jet-lagged brain can't compute this information. "So, why can't she?"

"I need her here!" my mother snaps. "She can go after I'm dead."

"Did you tell her that?" I ask, only half-serious.

"I did. I told her what I was planning to do and asked her to wait."

"What did she say?"

"She doesn't understand why I want to kill myself." Again, the sulky tone.

"Well, it's not surprising. She cares about you."

"But she said she wouldn't stop me if it was what I wanted."

There's a quiet knock on the door and Rosa's muffled voice. "Can I get you something to eat, Zoe?"

I jump up and open the door. "No, no, Rosa. I'm fine. You should go to bed." I smile at her. She looks worn out and smaller somehow, stripped of her usual effervescence.

I sit back down on my mother's bed. "I brought you some presents," I say. "Chocolates. And a book by the Dalai Lama. It's called *The Art of Happiness.*"

She gives a rueful laugh, acknowledging the joke. "I'm all for happiness," she says.

"Good," I say. "I'm glad to hear it."

"It's just . . ." She glances at the Dalai Lama's picture on the cover and puts the book down.

"Just what?"

"Well, I guess I'd have to say there's a time and place for everything. Happiness really isn't my goal right now."

"Fair enough." I hadn't really believed this last-ditch attempt would work and I feel a little foolish. It was a reflex, I suppose.

She smiles, grimly. "Thanks for trying, though."

"No problem. Want a chocolate?"

She eats one and closes the box. After a few moments, her face takes on the familiar rigidity of sleep and the box of chocolates slips down off her chest.


Walking into the kitchen the following morning, I'm greeted by a fraught and sudden silence. Rosa and Kendra stand side by side by the table, while Sonia, a heavyset Hispanic woman who comes in to cook and clean three or four times a week, hovers fretfully at the sink, glaring at them. Everyone looks ready for combat and for a moment I feel confused, wondering which side, if any, I should join.

Although hostilities have erupted since my last visit, the battle lines were drawn months ago. Sonia, who's been here the longest, resents Rosa and Kendra, not just because they get paid more but because, as home-care workers, they have more intimate access to my mother. She's especially jealous of Rosa, my mother's clear favorite, but also dislikes Kendra, perhaps sensing my mother's ambivalence toward her or, who knows, finding her youth or race objectionable.

Rosa used to try to win Sonia over, chatting to her in Spanish and even helping her do housework. But when Sonia asked my mother to help her buy a car a couple of months ago, claiming it was too hard for her to take the bus, Rosa was furious. Not only was the request overreaching given Sonia's marginal usefulness around the house, Rosa felt Sonia was pressuring my mother and encouraged her to refuse. My mother, who I believe would ordinarily have forgiven Sonia, has turned against her, even requesting that she stop bringing in her meals. Needless to say, this has further marginalized Sonia's position in the household.

Glancing over at Sonia, who stands with her hands on her hips, her plain face a study in misery and defiance, I feel sorry for her. She's the oldest of the three, well over sixty, and clearly no match for Rosa and Kendra.

On the other hand, maybe she deserves their ire. Now that the gloves are off and everyone has started to complain, Kendra has told me how little Sonia does and how bossy and mean she can be, careful to add, "Of course I put up with it, because what can you do?" to demonstrate her own reasonableness.

Turning back toward Rosa and Kendra, I see they've assumed more neutral expressions and Kendra even manages a smile. Her large eyes and small features give her an almost doll-like prettiness, and her hair is arranged in its usual fuchsia weave, but caught in the bright band of sunlight from the back door, she looks strangely unkempt. Her skin is blotchy and she's wearing an enormous, stretched-out sweatshirt over her jeans.

Rosa looks worse. Her red hair has a wide swath of gray at the roots and her face is lined and droopy. I remember what my mother said about her wanting to see her son and wonder if I can find some way to help.

"Good morning!" I say, trying to keep the irony out of my voice. It's so clearly *not* a good morning, but I don't want to open the door to their grievances yet. Not before I've had my coffee, and not while they're en masse.

"Good morning," they reply in unison, and the standoff dissolves. Rosa busies herself straightening the table, while Sonia turns back to the sink and Kendra says, "I'd best be going. I've got to get that prescription filled for Mrs. Draper. Is there anything else you need, Rosa?"

"I need Windex," Sonia says in a harsh voice without turning around. "A big bottle. Buy it at Long's when you pick up the prescription."

Kendra turns and shoots Sonia a narrow-eyed look, her body tense, and I freeze, waiting for her to lash out at the older woman. But Rosa rushes between them, saying, "That's fine, Kendra. Take some extra money from the jar and buy some Windex."

Kendra shakes her head, makes a disgusted face in Sonia's direction and then glances at me as if to say, *See how bad it is?* I give her a sympathetic smile.

"Unbelievable," she mutters.

Sonia whips around and glares at Kendra but then, eyes flickering in my direction, turns away.

Shit. This is not good. I can feel how close the situation is to blowing up and am afraid someone is going to quit. We could replace Sonia easily enough, but losing Rosa, or even Kendra, would be a disaster.

"Listen," I say, addressing the room generally, "I know how hard you've all been working and I just want to say how much I appreciate it. It makes a huge difference to my sisters and me knowing my mother's in such good hands."

Kendra is the only one who replies. "We're happy to help, Zoe," she says, scooping up her purse and my mother's car keys. "See you later, Rosa," she says, ignoring Sonia but giving me a grin on her way out.

I go to the refrigerator and rummage for food, ignoring the silence behind me. Sonia mutters something about needing to clean upstairs and is gone by the time I've assembled toast and jam and poured myself a cup of coffee.

Rosa leans against the counter, watching me. "Your mom's glad you're here," she says.

"I know."

"She loves it when you come. Even now. It's all she can talk about."

I chew my toast and wonder what she's getting at. Does Rosa want me to move here and help her take care of my mother?

She pulls out a chair and sits across from me. "Did your mom tell you I want to see my son?"

"She did. She wasn't too happy about it."

Rosa grimaced. "I know. But I told her this morning I won't go until, you know . . . after." She gives me a pained look. "She told me what she plans to do. I can't say I support it, but I promised I'd stay with her. I wasn't there when my own mother died and . . . I want to be here with your mom."

"Oh Rosa, that's great. Thank you!" I choke up and have to stop eating. "I'm really grateful. That'll mean so much to her—and to me. Just tell me if there's anything I can do to make it easier for you. Can I get you more help? Maybe have Kendra spend some nights?"

"Kendra's offered, but your mom doesn't want her. She wants me." She raises her eyebrows in mock despair. I can tell she's flattered but detect a note of desperation as well.

"Do you want me to talk to her about it?"

"No, no. But just so you know, your mom spoke to Kendra. About her plans." She gets up and closes the kitchen door. "Sonia doesn't know anything, although she's figured something's up. But

Kendra's been crying all week. She really loves your mom and she has her son to support. She's worried about being out of a job."

"Won't the home-care agency place her somewhere else?"

"They will, but it can take a couple of weeks. I don't think she can afford not to work, even for a few days."

"Well, I know my mother's planning to leave everyone some money. I'll make sure it gets to all of you right away so you don't have to wait for her estate to be settled. It's one of the reasons I came this weekend."

Rosa winces at my bluntness, but I want her and Kendra to know that they'll be covered financially when my mother dies. What I don't know how to address is their personal loss. I don't want to romanticize their attachment to my mother, but I know this isn't just about losing a job. They care about her, whether she realizes it or not.

I look at the clock. I know my mother's lying in there, wondering where I am. I've got to work fast.

"I'll call the home-care agency and give them a heads-up about Kendra. But what about you, Rosa? Should I ask them to line something up for you as well?"

"Oh, me. I'm going to take some time off. Go see my son in Miami for a while. Maybe go back to Chile and live with my husband again."

Rosa talks about her husband as if he were a particularly difficult child, but I can hear her affection for him. "That husband of yours," I say, smiling.

She laughs. "He drives me crazy, but I do miss him. It's just better if I go there. That way, if I need to get away from him, I can come back here, get another job. Maybe in Miami this time."

Miami? For some reason the idea saddens me. *But we'll never see you if you move to Miami,* I want to say. But then I realize we'll never see her if she stays in D.C. either. I can't imagine what would bring me here once my mother is gone.

I look across the table at Rosa and think how much I've come to like and admire her. I mentally add her to my list of approaching losses.

My mother is extremely agitated by the time I go in, much worse than the night before. Apparently, the pain in her shoulder has been bothering her and she was up much of the night, something Rosa hadn't mentioned. Feeling anxious about a repeat of the excruciating pain she experienced in February, I suggest she take some morphine. After calling Rosa in to discuss the dose, she takes a dropperful in a glass of juice.

Almost immediately, she grows sleepy and relaxed but continues to fuss and complain, mainly about the overgrown mulberry tree that hangs sloppily over one corner of the yard and the tall trees that line the back fence. She is sure that one of them is going to come down during one of the many fierce thunderstorms that pass through D.C. in the summertime.

I'm only half-listening and it takes me a minute to realize the absurdity of the situation.

"Wait a minute," I interrupt her. "Why are you so worried about the trees?"

"I told you, I'm afraid one of them could damage the roof or knock out a window or . . ."

"But chances are you won't be here when that happens, right?"

She looks confused for a moment. "Well, maybe not, but . . ."

"Then why not let *us* worry about it. Or even better, let whoever buys the house worry about it."

"Hmm," she says, doubtfully. "I suppose I could do that."

"You remind me of Jan," I say.

Jan is our elderly neighbor in Vermont, the widow of a famous writer. She's a lovely, intelligent woman who likes to lightheartedly complain about her bachelor son, Nathaniel. We were having lunch in Manhattan a couple of years ago when she leaned over and, in her plummy Upper East Side drawl, said, "I just wish Nathaniel would get married so I don't have to worry about him when I'm dead."

I tell my mother this story and she laughs, then screws up her face again. "I'm worried about Rosa."

"Why Rosa?" I ask. I'm lying at the bottom of her bed and can feel her body trembling. Her sheepdog, Bruno, nestles between us, groaning with pleasure when she pats him.

We've discussed how much money to give Rosa and Kendra, as well as my mother's accountant, Sherry, and the young woman who comes in to help her with her writing and correspondence, Tina. (Sonia won't get as much as the rest of them, but she's getting enough to tide her over until she finds another job.) I've agreed to call my mother's lawyer on Monday morning to arrange for all this money to be put aside.

"Well, I'm glad she's going to put off seeing her son, but I think you should also ask her to stay here for a while. I mean after I'm gone. She can help keep the household running and answer the door and things. You're going to have a lot to do."

I stare at her. There's actually something funny about this need to control things from beyond the grave—or, to be strictly accurate, *before* the grave. It's so typical of my mother.

"Momma, we'll figure it out. Really. I'm sure one of them will be able to stick around a bit and help out. You don't—"

"I know, I know. I don't have to worry."

Her head sinks back and her eyes close. Her skin is so colorless, it's almost gray. "It's just . . . strange."

"What's strange?" I say, softly.

"To imagine . . . not being here."

"So, um, you're not rethinking this thing, are you?" Reflex again, I think, glancing over at the Dalai Lama's book, which now has both chocolates and morphine sitting on top of it.

She shakes her head, slowly. "No, no. Not rethinking."

Her eyes close and she starts to snore.

Even asleep, she frowns and looks pained. She's impatient to be done, I think, to finish this thing. And for the first time I start to wonder if my objections, my resistance, has been prolonging her misery.

That afternoon, my mother has two visitors. The first is Michael, the hospice nurse, a middle-aged guy with a potbelly and a ponytail. He has a calm, quiet way of talking, although you can see the hard living in his face. He comes to check her vital signs but also to talk and meditate with her. I wait until they're done and stop him in the hall.

"So, how's she doing?" I ask as Bruno leaps around between us, barking.

"I should ask you that. How do *you* think she's doing?"

"Actually, she seems kind of pissed off," I say, irritated at having my own question thrown back at me.

He chuckles, unperturbed. "Well, I imagine she's a little different with you. She seems pretty much the same to me."

"Did she tell you we gave her some morphine today? For her shoulder?"

"No, but that's okay. You *should* give it to her when she's in pain. Just remember, and I've told your mom this, the morphine is for pain management. Nothing else."

"What do you mean?" I know what he means, but I want to hear him say it.

He gives me a bland look. "We don't give out morphine to facilitate people taking a lethal dose."

Again, I feel irritated.

"But you can't really stop her, can you?"

He smiles his round-faced, Buddha smile. "No. We can't."

We look at each other for a moment. Then he opens the door

and says good-bye. I'm not sure what just happened. Did he just give me tacit permission to give her an overdose of morphine, or was he warning me? I close the door, unsettled. Michael is one more person who could blow the whistle on us if my mother decides that fasting is too slow.

The second visitor that day is the writer and painter Anne Truitt, a neighbor and friend of my mother's. She's a tall, stylish, white-haired woman with a confident, unfussy manner. My mother admires her tremendously. It was after one of her chats with Anne that my mother informed me that, despite having never been published, she'd lived a writer's life. I wasn't sure what she meant, but it seemed to resolve something that had been bothering her.

I show Anne to my mother's room but don't go in with her. She emerges while I'm in the kitchen talking to Rosa and I jump up to see her out.

In the hall, she turns to me and says in her strong, clear voice, "Your mother is very brave, isn't she? I think what she's planning to do shows incredible strength."

Quite unexpectedly, I begin to cry. She wraps her arms around me and we stand holding each other.

"I guess it does," I say, my voice muffled on her shoulder.

"It's not easy for you, though, is it?"

I shake my head, embarrassed by my tears and this unexpected physical contact. Yet I can tell she's comfortable holding me, which is strange. Of all my mother's friends, Anne is probably the one I know least well.

"You need to be strong," she murmurs, finally. "Your mother needs you."

The words pierce me, but what makes me sob harder is the thought that I should be crying in my mother's arms instead.

# Final Call

Heading back to the airport, I'm once again in the back of Derrick's Lincoln Town Car, sitting in an exhausted heap behind his broad, suited shoulders and chiseled profile. Outside, the familiar stores and restaurants of Georgetown slide by as we head down Wisconsin Avenue toward Key Bridge.

Letting my head flop back against the headrest, I close my eyes. I cannot bear the sight of all those people out there with their packages and their coffee drinks and their busy, important lives. Rush rush. Buy buy. They make my stomach hurt.

My body slides down into the smooth leather seat. I want to wave my wand and disappear like a character in a Harry Potter novel, only to reappear in some other town, some other life. A life without traffic or Starbucks or suicidal mothers. Is that too much to ask?

Then, like one of those old movie projectors that have to be cranked up by hand, my mind lurches into action, tossing up images and facts and bits of conversation like some wild, colorful thought salad. I see my mother's white box of a bedroom, her face lit harshly by the gooseneck lamp, Sonia saying, "I need Windex," Michael saying, "We can't stop her."

Rosa: "I want to see my son."

Momma: "She can go after I'm dead."

Anne: "You need to be strong. Your mother needs you."

Sonia: "I need Windex."

Me: "Why are you so worried about the trees?"

The words come faster and louder. They blend together, making a loud buzz that bounces and echoes around my brain. I shake my head and take deep breaths, trying not to attract Derrick's attention. Rolling the window down as we start across the bridge, I inhale the ripe, sulfurous smell of the river below.

*Your mother needs you.*

I think about the Dalai Lama's book lying on her bedside table covered with chocolates and morphine, the portable commode, the oxygen tank, and my mother's frozen, unhappy face. I cover my own face. I've been trying so hard to keep her here, to convince her to accept her fate—to be *happy* about it, for God's sake—that I've missed the bigger truth: My mother has ended up exactly where she didn't want to be.

I lean my head out the window and let the rush of warm air press against my eyelids, filling my nose and mouth until I can barely breathe. The tears fly across my face.

I've just walked into the house and dropped my bags when my friend Cynthia rings the bell. Lane's preschool is on summer break, and Cynthia offered to take her today while Jack was at work and I was flying home. The two of us are planning to take Lane and Cynthia's daughter, Sarah, over to the Bay Area Discovery Museum in Sausalito for the afternoon.

Cynthia is a slim, lively woman, a musician whose husband's work dropped her into the Bay Area around the same time mine did. I give her a hug and spend a moment holding Lane in my lap listening to her stories about the weekend—an afternoon in a neighbor's hot tub, a trip to Ben & Jerry's with Jack and Clara.

As thrilled as I am to see her, I need to get to the phone. My brain has been burning since those devastating moments in the back of Derrick's Town Car, and even now, with my daughter on my lap, I feel distracted and impatient.

"I'm really sorry, honey, but there's something I need to do before we go," I say, jumping up and giving Cynthia an apologetic look while gently untangling Lane's arms from around my legs. "Why don't you guys grab a snack in the kitchen and I'll be right back."

I race upstairs and into my bedroom. Closing the door, I spend a moment composing myself, gazing out over the rooftops toward the bay, which looks like an Edward Hopper seascape, all sunny waves and dotted sails.

I pick up the phone and dial.

It rings four times and her message service comes on. Listening to my mother's recorded voice, I feel strangely serene, as if some deeper, more instinctive part of myself has taken over and is in control.

"Momma, this is Zoe calling. I just have a brief communiqué. I'm heading out for the afternoon with Lane but I wanted you to know that I think you should feel free to do what it is that you need to do and that I feel ready to, well . . . let go. And you should know that.

"I also think you should stop worrying so much about what actually happens at the very end, that it will work out whatever you end up doing, and we'll be there. It's going to be okay.

"We're going to have to play it by ear to some extent, but you shouldn't worry or feel that you have to work out every last detail ahead of time. And don't worry so much about all the stuff around your house. That will get taken care of too.

"So, that was my thought. I was feeling maybe you needed to hear that. That you should feel free to do what you are doing and not be held back by everybody questioning it. I'm going to be gone all day, but I'll talk to you soon."

I place the phone back in the receiver.

Two weeks later, on the twenty-ninth of June, my mother began her fast.

When I arrived three days after that, I found a transcript of this call typed up by her assistant, Tina, tucked into her calendar.

# Fast

SUNDAY

Hannah and I arrive with our children on July first. Unlike my bleak visit a little over two weeks earlier, the house feels bustling and alive. The children greet each other excitedly in the front hall, then race off through the large downstairs rooms with Bruno barking loudly behind them. When they get to my mother's bedroom, they run in, and I hear them laughing and talking over each other before rushing out again.

Dinner is a noisy, chaotic affair, but I'm pleased to see Rosa and Sonia exchange friendly looks as they serve up plates of pasta and vegetables and bring glasses of milk to the table. Even when Evie chokes on a string bean and begins to cry, the mood stays cheerful, and I'm relieved to see that, for the moment anyway, Rosa has regained her usual animated manner.

My mother had called Hannah and me on Thursday, three days earlier, to tell us she was beginning her fast. We immediately booked our flights, not letting on to the children that this was anything other than a routine visit. As soon as we arrived, Rosa confirmed that my mother hadn't eaten anything since Thursday night and was only drinking enough water to get her medications down.

When we first went in to see her, she looked pale and her lips were chapped, but she was propped up on her pillows and waved cheerfully. "I'm so glad you're all here!" she enthused, as if, instead of being summoned, we'd arrived spontaneously. "It's wonderful to see everyone."

I wasn't sure if her good mood was due to having us here, or relief at having her fast under way, or both, but with the kids moving in and out of the room, it was impossible to talk. Hannah finally asked how she was feeling, and she shrugged and said, "A little hungry. But not too bad."

I found it difficult to reconcile the family reunion feel of our arrival—complete with excited children and cheerful granny—with the fact that we were here to witness her starving to death. Going through the usual motions of greeting her, I felt awkward and off-balance, as if still subjected to the turbulence that had plagued our flight. When I leaned over to kiss her, a blast of cold air from the vent above her bed blew down my neck. And the bedroom itself, lit by the murky evening light that filtered in from the windows and French doors, had a dank, claustrophobic feel that made me long to throw open the doors and let in the steamy summer air.

Hannah hovered at the end of the bed, looking similarly discomfited. My mother, on the other hand, seemed relaxed and chatted about how much fun it was to see "the girls" and how sweet they were to come in to see her. I wonder if she's called Katherine to tell her she's fasting, but I don't ask. Mumbling something about needing to get dinner on the table—we weren't bringing our plates into her room as we usually did—we made our escape.

"That was weird," Hannah muttered as we passed through the dining room and into the kitchen.

"She seems awfully happy for someone who hasn't eaten in three days," I said.

"Yeah, and she looks remarkably good. I have a feeling she's going to last awhile."

"Who's going to last awhile, Mommy?" Lane was standing in the doorway to the kitchen and grabbed me around the waist.

"You're going to last, sweetie," I told her, reaching down to pick her up, bringing her round face up to mine and making a funny face at her. "You're going to eat so much pasta tonight, you're going to last forever."

She giggled. "That's silly. I can't eat *that* much. Can I?" She looked a little worried.

"What are you *talking* about?" Clara asked disdainfully as she helped Rosa pour everyone's drinks.

"I have no idea," I said, tickling Lane until she laughed and then gently setting her back on her feet. "All I know is I'm starving. Hey, Rosa, any chance I could get a glass of wine?"


After dinner, I go in to say good night and am once again struck by my mother's lighthearted manner. There are no complaints about missing dinner or feeling hungry and apparently no need to share her thoughts about starting her fast. Not tonight anyway. Tonight she seems happy to talk about how her neighbor Petra is coming over tomorrow with copies of the children's story she wrote so she can hand them out to the kids.

I can see how pleased she is at having gotten this done, and we chat about the book and the illustrations by Petra's friend. I'm interested in seeing it, of course. I'd asked my mother to write something for each of her grandkids before she died, nothing too heavy, just a short letter to remember her by, and she'd tried but quickly given up. "I'm just not good at that kind of thing," she'd complained. "I always feel so stiff and pretentious."

Then she came up with the idea of writing a story. "It's about a family of geese," she'd explained. "At first I was thinking of cats, but that seemed too sentimental and clichéd. Geese are so much better. It's called *The Goslings Visit Grandpa Gander and Nana Goose.*"

Listening to her talk about it makes me think about her novel, a subject I'm reluctant to raise. But then, as if sensing my thoughts, she mentions that Tina is bringing over a box of copies the next day. Hannah and I have already received ours, as have many of her friends, but she wants us to give them to people after she dies, "if, of course, they're interested." It seems *The Sky's the Limit* is finding its audience after all.

I'm impressed that she's managed to organize these two projects. Perhaps this is what's put her in such a good mood. And why not? I'm familiar with the particular euphoria induced by completing a piece of writing. But, like a dog who keeps circling the same worn piece of carpet, I can't help but wonder: Why not stick around and enjoy the payoff?

Claiming that I need to get Clara and Lane into bed, I kiss her good night. What I really want at this point is to fetch the rest of the wine, grab Hannah, and find a private corner of the Big Room to talk.

Much to my disappointment, Hannah is too exhausted by her day of travel with the vomit-prone Evie. She and her girls are staying in Katherine's old room—as I suspected, Katherine has no plans to be here—and I hear them moving around in there as I help Lane brush her teeth and search under the bed for Clara's stuffed dog.

I feel bad about these sleeping arrangements. Katherine's large, shadowy room makes me uneasy and I know Hannah doesn't like it in there either. I consider offering to move my daughters in with me and letting her have her old room back, but my girls are so used to sleeping in there, they consider it "their room." Also, not knowing how long we're going to be in D.C., I'm reluctant to give up the one place I can be alone.

I think about going downstairs to call Jack but am not sure what to tell him. He's planning to fly here Friday and I see no reason to change his plans. He'll be disappointed if he doesn't get to see my mother before she dies, but I have no way of knowing if she'll be around by then or not.

Crawling into bed, I pick up my book, a murder mystery by P. D. James, but am unable to focus. I turn off the light and curl into a ball, listening to the familiar whoosh of cars driving by on the street, each one like a searching question sweeping through my head. Is she really going to follow through with this and, if so, how long will it take? Whoosh. Will she be dead by Thursday? Or Saturday? Whoosh. What if it takes longer and we're stuck here for weeks, like inmates under house arrest?

Another car passes, but the questions are coming faster than the cars and there's a massive freeway pileup in my brain. What's going to happen to her body as she fasts? Will she become gaunt and skeletal or shrunken and curled into herself, like my father? Will it be painful to look at her? Will *she* be in pain? How will the children deal with watching her die?

Eyes wide open, heart pounding, I stare at the dim rectangles of light where the streetlight filters in through the curtains, anxiety ricocheting through my body like an exploding fuse box. I can't do this. I can't watch my mother deliberately waste away! The idea is repugnant, obscene. Why had I thought this was a good idea?

I sit up higher, pull the sheets under my chin, and stare fiercely around me, letting the very ordinariness of the room—the white painted bookshelves, the footlocker of old sweaters under the window—calm me.

Whatever lies ahead, at least the drama is coming to an end.

Or . . . is it? What's to stop her from changing her mind again, coming up with a different plan? As she's so amply illustrated, planning your departure also means being able to postpone it.

> Don't sing love songs, you'll wake my mother.
> She's sleeping here right by my side.

Exhausted and utterly spent, I begin the slow downshift toward sleep. My body, recently on high alert, grows lax and soft, expanding across the cool mattress. The sound of the passing cars comes faintly now, the soft echoes of a whoosh. More questions without answers and then . . . finally . . . no questions at all.

# The Grateful Dead

## MONDAY

The day after we arrive is clear and sunny, and Rosa opens the French doors that lead from my mother's room out to the pool. My mother looks noticeably gaunt in the bright light and keeps dozing off, but when she is awake, she seems relaxed and glad to see us.

At eleven, I go help Kendra get the four girls ready for an outing to the playground on Macomb Street, several blocks away. Closing the front door behind them, I stop by the kitchen and grab an apple before returning to my mother's room.

In a white tank top and print skirt, her legs outstretched on the bed next to my mother, Hannah looks fresh and summery but also clearly irritated. She and my mother are arguing about Bruno.

My mother wants her dog trainer, Binky, to take him after she dies, but Binky already has three dogs and a cat and is concerned about how Bruno is going to fit in. Hannah wants my mother to contact Bruno's breeder and make her take Bruno back. I decide not to get involved; Hannah has stronger opinions about animals than I do, and I'm happy to let her deal with it.

Settling on the corner sofa, I pick up *The Washington Post,* which Rosa still brings in every morning, although my mother rarely glances at it. I don't immediately notice when they stop talking.

"Zoe!" Hannah says, sharply.

"What?" I say, looking up to see them both staring at me.

"You're eating."

I look down at the half-eaten apple in my hand. "Oh, sorry. I forgot."

Feeling stupid, I take my apple and leave, intensely aware that my mother hasn't said anything. She must have wanted me to stop eating too, but I'm grateful she didn't. Being told not to eat brings up bad memories for me.

In fact, watching my mother fast is making me think a lot about my old eating disorder. For both of us, not eating was an attempt to control our bodies but—more important—to control how people *saw* our bodies. I didn't want to be seen as fat, my mother doesn't want to be seen as helpless and incapacitated, and neither of us want to be pitied or ridiculed. Of course, while I'd been willing to risk death to achieve my goal, for my mother, death *is* the goal.

I toss what's left of the apple into the kitchen sink and switch on the disposal. As the blades roar, I feel sad for both of us.


When I return, Hannah is accusing my mother of being totally irresponsible.

"His barking is going to drive Binky and her boyfriend insane!" she says, her face flushed. "She'll be desperate to get rid of him but feel like she owes it to you to keep him. That's a terrible position to put her in. Let me get in touch with Bruno's breeder and see if she'll take him."

But my mother is worried about what the breeder is going to think of Bruno—and of her as well. Convinced that getting animals fixed is cruel and unnatural, a belief that led to a series of out-of-control, badly trained dogs when we were growing up, my mother has insisted Bruno remain "intact," which has added to his territorial aggression and general excitability. Inconsistent discipline over the years has compounded the problem, giving rise to a number of unfortunate habits, including peeing and defecating in the house.

"Why do you care what she thinks, Momma?" Hannah asks, her voice shrill. "You're going to be dead!"

"Well, that's true, but I still don't want her to think badly of me."

"Wait a minute," I jump in. "Shouldn't she take responsibility for the fact that she bred the little freak of nature?"

"He's a good dog," my mother replies, patting the hairy heap next to her on the bed.

"A good dog? You told me he snarled at Rosa and lunged at her when she came over to the bed last week," Hannah says. "You're just lucky he's never bitten anyone!"

"He has bitten someone," I say. "He bit that nice woman in Vermont when she came to clean our house last summer. Doris."

"That's true," my mother says. "But she let herself in without knocking and she came into the house in a very aggressive way."

Hannah and I laugh.

"Well, if that isn't codependency in action," Hannah says softly so my mother can't hear just as the doorbell rings. Bruno stands up on the bed and begins barking and growling, legs stiffly extended on either side of my mother's body.

We hear Rosa greeting someone at the front door. "It's Ray, Binky's boyfriend," my mother shouts over the noise, trying in vain to get hold of Bruno's muzzle to make him stop barking. "Stop it, Bruno! He's been walking Bruno recently. Bruno, no! Helping Binky out. *Bad dog!*"

A very tall, middle-aged man with a ponytail and beard opens the door and strides into the room calling Bruno. Bruno leaps off the bed still barking, but Ray calmly reaches down and snaps a leash on his collar. "That's a good boy," he says, cheerfully. "Time for your walk."

"Ray, these are my two daughters Hannah and Zoe."

"Happy to meet you." He gives us a casual wave and then, as if he's used to hanging out in his clients' bedrooms, just stands there looking around. Hannah and I exchange a glance.

"Hey, Margaret, I forgot to give you something the other day," he says, finally. "I have a present for you."

Swinging a small backpack off his shoulder, he opens it and pulls something out. Taking several steps to the bed, he lays a large tie-dyed T-shirt over my mother's lap. She lifts it up and reads: "The . . . Grateful . . . Dead. Gosh, Ray. Thanks."

He laughs. "You've heard of them, right?"

"I have," my mother says gamely. I used to play Dead records back in high school, but I'm amazed that she remembers their name.

"I've always known this is what I want to be buried in. So in case you want to do the same, it's yours."

"Thanks." She gives him an impish look. "I hadn't really thought about what I was going to wear, but this is just the thing."

"No problem." He gives her a slight bow. "Anyway, I guess I'd better get this little guy outside. Let us know when you want us to come get him. Binky can pick him up tomorrow if you like."

"Okay, Ray. Thanks again."

"See you, Margaret. Come on, boy."

As soon as we hear the front door close, we both started talking at once.

"You *told* him you're fasting?" Hannah asks.

"They're taking Bruno away *before* you die?" I ask, shocked and dismayed. One of the most heartbreaking moments of my father's illness was when he was stuck in the hospital and we had to put Paddy—Bruno's predecessor—to sleep because of a sudden, debilitating illness. I was devastated that my father never got to say good-bye to the dog he'd owned and loved for over ten years. And now my mother was planning to hand Bruno off before she had to?

"Certainly I've discussed my plans with Binky," she says, turning to Hannah. "I wanted her to take Bruno, so I had to. And obviously she's told Ray. In fact, he's told me several times how much he admires what I'm doing."

"Apparently," Hannah says, drily. "He's just made you an honorary Deadhead."

"Well, it may seem funny to you, but I think it's sweet."

"Whatever," Hannah says, getting off the bed. "Just don't let your aunt Marianne know you're planning to be buried in a Grateful Dead T-shirt. I think it would kill her."

My great-aunt has developed a rather charming childishness in recent years, but we all remember those uncomfortable lunches—the "good" clothes, the polite conversation—at her enormous house in Baltimore when we were young.

"Don't mention my fasting if Marianne calls," my mother says, quickly. "It would only upset her. Besides, I was thinking of having the T-shirt in the coffin, not wearing it."

"Who cares about the stupid T-shirt?" I burst out, impatient with this exchange. "I want to know why you're sending Bruno away. Don't you want him here with you?"

I realize that I've been nurturing an image of him curled up next to her as she died, and the idea that she would banish him, disposing of him like all those lousy dog owners who get rid of their dogs when they grow too large or "inconvenient," infuriates me.

"No, not really," she says, mildly. "It just makes everything more complicated. I don't want to have to worry about him with everything else going on."

I look around the room. "What exactly is going on here that would affect him?"

"The children, for one thing. He gets terribly excited around them and I'm just worried he's going to get more anxious as the week goes on. . . . I just think it's easier this way."

"Easier for him or for you?" I ask, thinking how unhappy my kids will be if Bruno leaves. Despite his failings, he's surprisingly good with them.

"Both."

I sink back on the couch, cross my arms, and stare up at the ceiling, too upset to speak. My mother's lack of feeling for her dog embodies everything I find painful and distressing about her. I'm surprised she hasn't decided having her grandchildren here was inconvenient!

I'm about to light into her when I see she's dropped off to sleep again. She looks tiny under the rumpled white sheets. Even her head seems smaller.

"Oh, fuck it," I say, under my breath.

Hannah, who's been pacing around the room, looks over at me. "It's a little late to want to change her now, don't you think? What did you expect anyway? She's always been like that about her animals."

"I just feel bad for the dog," I reply, surprised that Hannah isn't more understanding.

"You feel bad for us."

I dig my nails into my crossed arms to stop my eyes from stinging. "Yeah, well that too."

She gives me a sympathetic look. "You know, it might actually be easier on Bruno not to be here. Let's just focus on his long-term prospects."

She stops in front of my mother's bedside table and picks up the bottle of morphine.

My mother's eyes fly open, startling both of us. She shifts onto her side in order to look at Hannah. "That's another thing I need to talk to you girls about," she says, hoarsely, pausing to clear her throat several times. "I think it's time for me to take that." She gives a nod toward the bottle in Hannah's hand.

"Momma, I don't think—"

"Let me finish. It's been four days and as you can see I don't seem to be dying very quickly here. Maybe because I'm still drinking enough to take my pills. But I don't think I can go on much longer. I'm not hungry, but my mouth feels terrible and my stomach hurts. I'd like to pick a day this week . . ." She gives the bottle a nod.

The couch feels suddenly itchy against my back and the air drifting in through the open door, which has felt fresh and clear all morning, seems humid and unpleasantly hot.

"Momma, why don't you just wait and see where you are in a few days?" Hannah asks. She holds the bottle gingerly between her outstretched thumb and index finger, as if poised to drop it.

My mother's expression hardens. "I don't want to suffer."

The words drop into the warm air like small chunks of ice.

"*Are* you suffering?" Hannah asks.

"Yes," my mother says. "I am."

# The Deep End

"Do you think she's in pain?" I ask, leaning my head back against the tiles at the edge of the pool, watching the light flicker across the side of the Reynoldses' enormous white clapboard house, a mesmerizing effect produced by the reflection of our underwater floodlights. Next to my head, the water slaps noisily against the tiles, still churning from Hannah's and my vigorous swim up and down the length of the pool.

Hannah drapes her body against the large circular steps leading to the shallow end, her head tipped skyward. Several times she turns to peer up at the house and I know she's worried about hearing Evie if she wakes up. We've opened the window on the stair landing overlooking the pool, but the darkened house stands behind us like a thick and forbidding wall. Tucked into their beds, our girls seem far away and unreachable, like fairy-tale children in an enchanted castle.

"I don't know, Zoe," Hannah says, her voice loud and echoey in my ear. "She seems comfortable enough. She's actually pretty damn strong and healthy. The idea that a few days of starvation was going to kill her was a fantasy. But of course now she feels justified in taking the morphine."

My mother had agreed, after a tense discussion, to wait until Friday—four more days—to take an overdose. Neither of us is happy with this plan, but we're relieved she hadn't insisted on taking it sooner. I know she talked to Katherine on the phone today, but I have no idea how my sister feels about this new plan. Katherine hasn't been in touch with either Hannah or me.

There's a loud sucking noise as Hannah sits up abruptly and water rushes in to fill the space around her. "I *knew* this was going to happen," she says. "This is exactly what I was determined to avoid."

I don't answer, afraid for a moment that if I agree too quickly she'll do something rash like insist on going back to Canada with Fiona and Evie. The idea of being left alone with my mother terrifies me. Hannah had promised to be there "until the end," but that was contingent on Momma having a drug-free death. A defection would be entirely justified.

"This is what she wanted all along, to die like this," Hannah continues, sweeping her hands violently through the water, as if trying to push it away. "Any idea of surrendering herself to her body, to the natural process of death, is completely beyond her."

For some reason, Hannah's words remind me of a black-and-white photo of my mother that sits on her desk upstairs. In it, she's maybe twenty-five, perched on a chair, legs crossed, knees bare, wearing a dark fur coat and cloche hat. With her head tilted to one side, her mouth pursed in a sexy pout, her expression is challenging and coy. Only a vague hint of secretiveness, a shy holding back, reveals that she's putting it on, playing at being a femme fatale.

What struck me when this photo appeared several years ago was how much she liked it. I'd never seen my mother look like that in my entire life, yet this was the image among hundreds that she'd chosen to represent herself.

"It's funny," I say, "how she managed to project this stylish, sophisticated image to the outside world when she was actually so insecure about her looks. I doubt if even her friends know how much of a strain it's been maintaining that façade, and how much she's hated her physical deterioration over the last few years."

"That's it!" Hannah replies, settling back against the side of the pool. "It's the fear of deterioration that's driving this whole thing. She can't bear the idea that people might see her as weak or ugly or—"

"A drooling half-wit?"

"Exactly. Which, if you ask me, is still better than a dead half-wit."

Relieved at this unexpected note of humor, I quietly exhale, letting my body sink down into the water. It had been silly to think Hannah would leave. My sister is nothing if not loyal. Still, I understand her frustration. My mother has a way of quietly plowing over our objections, mainly by acting as if they don't exist. I don't even think she's aware of doing it. Our objections *don't* exist for her.

"You know, Han, for the first time today I really felt like it was all about her," I say, turning to look at her. Her face is a ghostly green in the reflected pool light. "I mean, just casually signing off on her dog after all these years? It made me wonder if we aren't all sort of incidental."

Hannah laughs. "I don't think *you're* incidental exactly, Zoe, but I'd say our concerns, especially about the morphine, are incidental. And listen, it's not like I don't feel sorry for the little fucker, but keeping him here for a few more days isn't going to make any difference to him. We just need to find him a home where someone actually likes him and doesn't end up abandoning him somewhere."

"Yeah. I guess maybe I'm identifying with him a little too much."

Hannah laughs again and pushes herself off the stairs toward the center of the pool. "Should we swim some more?"

Her anger has subsided, but I'm not ready to let go of my own. I still want to bitch and moan about the ways my mother has run roughshod over us during this last year and is continuing to do so now. It bothers me that I always have to suppress my rage and distress in order to placate Hannah or make my mother feel better. Like Bruno, I'm a ball of frustration, ready to leap up and bite someone.

Pushing off the wall, I swim toward Hannah, who is already in the deep end. One thing my sister and I have barely discussed is the phone call I made to my mother two weeks ago. I'd been startled to discover it typed up in her calendar but even more shocked to come across it today saved on her answering machine. It was eerie to hear myself saying, *I think you should feel free to do what it is that you need to do.*

Hannah seemed to think I'd done the right thing; she even said it was a relief having my mother start her fast instead of just talk about it. But given the enormity of the consequences, I remain uneasy. How was I going to feel someday knowing I was a catalyst for her suicide? Proud for helping her make this final leap, or guilty for helping her over the edge? Either way, one thing was clear—my giving her "permission" had meant something to her. Perhaps my part in her drama was not so incidental after all.

# Letter from a Friend

The next afternoon, my mother's friend Marilyn Fletcher comes to read to her. She's a tall, lovely woman whose gray bun manages to look youthful rather than fussy or old-fashioned. Unlike many of my parents' friends, who dropped away after my father's death, Marilyn and her husband have stayed in close touch with my mother. It didn't surprise me when I saw Marilyn's signature on the bottom of my mother's "statement of intent," a shaky handwritten paragraph that I'd found lying on a stack of books in her room yesterday.

> *I, Margaret F. Draper, of sound mind, have decided to stop eating*
> *and drinking. I have had Parkinson's Disease for 24 years and*
> *congestive heart failure and chronic pulmonary disease. In recent*
> *months I have had periods of paralysis and dyskinesia. I have lost*
> *consciousness for 5 or 6 minutes at a time. I may need help from*
> *my care workers to take morphine prescribed by Hospice to ease my*
> *chronic pain and make me more comfortable.*

It was signed by my mother and witnessed by Marilyn. I was surprised and pleased that my mother had thought to make such a document, thinking it might afford us some protection if, God forbid, we were accused of helping her kill herself, but I wonder if maybe she's forgotten about it. She hasn't mentioned anything to us.

After showing Marilyn into my mother's room, I take all four girls out to the pool, where the air feels sticky and hot after the air-conditioned house. Evie and Lane splash around the pool stairs looking like comic book superheroes with their bright yellow water wings while the two older girls, Fiona and Clara, set up a series of highly competitive swimming events: racing the width of the shallow end, holding their breath underwater, and staying up in a handstand.

They watch each other's performances with great sighs of irritation, and soon Fiona accuses Clara of not counting fairly when she does a handstand and stomps angrily out of the pool. Immediately, Clara swims over and throws her arms around me, saying, "Let's go to the deep end, Mommy!" as if her fight had just been a ploy to spend time with me.

I kick off from the side and do a slow breaststroke with her hanging lightly around my neck, remembering how I used to swim like this with my own mother, the thick synthetic material of her black one-piece bathing suit rubbing against my legs. Somehow the memory makes me feel heavy and middle-aged, a slow-moving tug pulling my sprite of a daughter through the water.

At the end of the pool, I help her reach up and grab the diving board, and we both hang there, facing each other, her long blond hair plastered against her neck and shoulders. Looking past her, I can see Marilyn through the French doors. She's sitting on a chair holding a book. Using her legs to twist her body so she can look too, Clara says, "Who's in there with Nana, Mommy?"

"It's Nana's friend, sweetheart."

"Oh." She sounds a bit miffed. My mother was asleep when Clara and Lane went in to see her both yesterday and today. "Does Nana have *lots* of friends?"

"Yes, she does."

"Doesn't she mind them seeing her in bed?"

I laugh. "No, I don't think so. She can't really get up anymore, but she still wants to see people."

I notice Clara struggling to hold on to the board and suggest we let go. Immediately, she drops into the water, then grabs my hand so I can pull her over to the side. We both hold on to the edge, looking toward my mother's room, kicking our legs out behind us.

"How can they talk to her if she's so tired all the time?" she asks, slicking her hair back off her face with one hand.

"Well, it's hard, sweetie, but her friends know that she's really sick. That's why they want to make a special effort to see her. They don't know how much longer she's going to live."

I've been slipping in these kinds of statements since we arrived, careful to keep it casual, but I see Clara's face tighten with worry.

"She wasn't that sick at Christmas." She twists her face toward me and gives me a skeptical look.

"No, but Nana's actually been sick for a long time. And sometimes when people are very old, and they've been sick for a long time, they can get a lot sicker and weaker pretty quickly."

"But do they always have to die?"

"Eventually they do."

"I don't think Nana's going to die, Mommy. I think she just needs more sleep. So she can get better."

"Maybe, sweetie. But she might die. And if she does, we'll all be really sad. But Nana won't want us to be *too* sad because she's had a long life and done lots of wonderful, interesting things and that's a good thing. Does that make sense?"

"No," Clara says, giggling at her own audacity.

*"No?"* I ask, with mock outrage.

"No. No. No." She scuttles down the wall away from me. "Can Kendra get me a Popsicle?"

I send a little wave after her. "No. You can get it yourself. Ask Lane and Evie if they want one too, okay? And Fiona if you can find her."

*"Lane! Evie!"* Clara's long, skinny arms fly wildly along the side of the pool until, taking a big breath, she pushes out into the water and begins her flailing, churning swim toward the shallow end. Arriving at the stairs, she grabs Lane in a tight hug and whirls her around and around in the water. "We get Popsicles, baby! One for each of us!"

Lane squeals and kisses her while Evie does a funny little knee-bending dance on the stairs.

I push off from the wall and let myself float out into the center of the pool on my back, smiling up at the hazy summer sky. For the first time since I arrived in D.C. I think it's going to be okay. We're going to get through this.

"You know it's the anniversary of his death, right?" Hannah asks me as I head out for a run later that afternoon.

"I do." My father died on July third, exactly seven years ago, although by the time the men from the mortuary showed up it was after midnight and his death certificate says the fourth. "Did you mention it to Momma?"

"Yeah. She didn't have much to say about it."

"Well, she was never big on anniversaries."

Hannah looks pained for a moment. "Well, I feel sad. Especially now that the kids won't have either grandparent."

"And we'll be orphans," I say, trying to get her to smile. But inside I'm thinking that as long as we have our children, losing our parents isn't so bad.

————

Two more of my mother's friends show up before dinnertime, a couple that she and my father knew from his late-in-life discovery of art. Paul Horowitz was a teacher at the Studio School in Georgetown, where my father took painting classes during the three or four years between retiring and getting sick. Paul and his wife used to visit my parents in Vermont, and several of Paul's paintings hang in our house.

After they leave, I go in to see my mother. She looks exhausted, and I notice that the undyed roots of her hair have grown in considerably, making a white halo effect around her face. There's something odd about this last-minute show of vitality from her body, but then I remember reading somewhere that hair and nails continue to grow even after you die. The visuals on this have always bothered me.

"So, you're having quite the social day," I say, brightly. "Does everyone know you're planning to die this week?"

"Well, not everyone, but I admit I have called quite a few people." She gives me a funny look. "I called Mitzy up on the Cape. She told me she did not approve of what I was doing. She said I was being selfish."

"Really?" I have to admit part of me agrees with her, but I also feel protective of my mother. "And is Mitzy drinking these days?"

Mitzy, who had brought my parents together in her small New York kitchen fifty years ago, had moved to Washington soon after they did and—sadly—become a severe alcoholic, perennially on and off the wagon. I'd been friends with two of her sons growing up and I knew how unpleasant she could be when she was drinking.

"Oh, it's hard to say," my mother says. "She did sound a little fuzzy. But it's okay. I don't expect everyone to understand. Marilyn and the Horowitzes were certainly supportive." She looks teary all of a sudden. "Paul said Jonathan would have been proud of me."

"Mmm. That's nice—and true. I think he would have."

Funny, I've never wondered how my father would feel about her decision, but it suddenly strikes me that he's the one person who would have wholeheartedly supported her. He hated the idea of dependency even more than she does and neither of them was sentimental in the least. Is this perhaps the source of her tears, her wishing he could be here to cheer her on?

"He talked about what great competitors Jonathan and Joan Reynolds were in his art class," my mother says, using a humorous tone to cover her tears. "Joan was a better painter—she'd been doing it for years after all—but Jonathan was determined to best her. And he wasn't bad."

Our neighbor, Joan Reynolds, was one of the few women whose personalities had been a match for my father's. She'd never stopped ribbing him for confiding in her one day at lunch that all the women in the art class were in love with him. She and her husband, Ben, had remained close friends with my parents even after they'd moved down to Georgetown several years ago. I wondered aloud why they hadn't been by.

"Oh, they're in Europe for the summer," my mother explains. "They came to see me before they left. They were going to spend a few days up in their house on Cranberry Island and then leave from there."

She turns and with considerable difficulty pulls open one of the drawers of her nightstand. "I have a letter from Joan in here somewhere," she says. "She sent it to me after she left."

I get up to go help her. It's stuck between some Hemlock Society pamphlets and one of her "Don't Call 911" notices.

"You can read it."

Sitting back on the couch, I pull the letter out of its envelope. I'd always liked Mrs. Reynolds, although her deep voice and big personality scared me a bit when I was young. I can still remember every room in their house in vivid detail—the sweeping grand stairway, the pink bathroom that Sharon and her sister shared, the pantry where their dog had puppies—almost as if it were a second childhood home. When the new neighbors offered to show me around after remodeling it a few years ago, I turned them down, wanting to hang on to the house I'd known.

Written on June 7:

*Dear Margaret,*

*It is early morning on Cranberry and I want to talk to you before we go away this Sunday. We have had such a long life together that I cannot leave you without telling you some thoughts.*

I look up, not wanting to be watched as I read, but my mother's eyes are closed and she is breathing heavily.

*What you are about to do or are maybe doing by the time you read this is an extraordinary thing, but I respect your decision and I admire your perseverance and your ability to make such a decision. Not to be able to see you again is a very very difficult thing to accept. But that is my problem. You have made your mind up to do what you want and Ben and I have tried to adjust our love for you to accept that. And we have. So now I want to tell you about some of my thoughts these past days.*

*Do you remember the time we had Joseph Campbell in our back yard? You had told me about your interest in myth and about having studied with Joseph Campbell at Sarah Lawrence. And there he was sitting in our garden having been brought by unannounced by our friend on the way to the airport. We had not been in Cleveland Park for very long and I was just discovering what a delving scholar you really are. I was so excited to be able to present you with this "white rabbit." I do not remember what we talked about . . . just how much I wanted to find a wedge into your "other life." I have always been so in awe and envy of your ability to pursue an area of interest or an "intellectual" question. One of the great joys about living next door were the afternoons you and Judy and I spent with Henry James, Conrad, Joyce, etc. Thank you for those times.*

*Then I remember going with you and Jonathan and a friend of yours to an inaugural ball. You had on a long fur coat and you walked or glided through the crowds with the most glorious ease I had ever seen. I thought you were utterly beautiful. So when we went camping and you and I went down to take a swim and I discovered we both had on the same kind of black underwear I thought maybe I had learned something. It was a joy to me to bring you back a bunch of black tights from London. Do you remember that? The store thought I was a spy for some other outfit. Well, you really introduced me to black tights. And goodness we have certainly kept up that tradition. So I thank you for a corner of your glamour.*

*All our dinners. How did we do that? Children, guests, food, liquor, music, tensions, competitions. And throughout it all you seemed to keep a calm that was beyond belief. You may have been a jumble inside but it never surfaced. Just a steady gracious acceptance of whatever came on the scene. I would lose control but there you were. I sometimes wanted to strangle you because you were so willing to let Jonathan "show off." But after becoming such a friend of his at the Studio School I can understand it all a bit better now. He needed you and you were there. I can see you holding his hand as he was dying. Thank you for your example of patience and wisdom.*

*Well, we did have fun . . . on our trips to Oxford, Jackson Hole. Our "over the fence" life. It is wonderful that some of our children are in touch with each other as well as with Ben and myself. And they have memories so different I imagine than ours of living side by side. It was a long time we were all there. I am thankful we had those times. Not many people have.*

*We love you,*
*Joan and Ben*

The light is nearly gone when I am done and my mother's bed is swathed in blue shadows. Wiping my eyes, I replace the letter in the envelope and go over and place it on her table. I lie down next to her on the bed, looking around the room and out through the windows as if to see and memorize what she sees lying here day after day, because I'm afraid she's going to leave before I know who she is, and I will be left with only words and images, the mere outlines of my mother's life.

# Fireworks

WEDNESDAY

The sky is a shimmering blackish gray by midafternoon. The line of tall, skinny trees at the back fence shakes and sways like possessed spirits in the hot, gusty wind. The first heavy drops of rain hit the large picture window facing the backyard just as a sharp crack of thunder wakes my mother, who's been sleeping next to me on the bed.

"Oh, boy," she says, looking around the darkened room. "It got so late."

"No, it's a storm," I say.

A flash of lightning flickers.

"Oh, goody," she says, sleepy and childish, trying to sit up higher.

"It's going to be a good one. And you've pretty much got a front-row seat."

She turns and looks out the window at the swaying trees.

"Gosh, I hope none of them fall down."

"I wouldn't worry about it. They've survived storms worse than this one. I just hope this is over in time to set off the firecrackers tonight. I got a bunch of good ones up at that stand by the hardware store. The kids are pretty excited."

"Oh, Zoe, do you think that's a good idea? It's so dangerous."

"Yes, I do," I say happily. "I can't believe they're actually legal here. It's going to be a blast."

She gives me a look. "Ha. Ha. But are you sure . . . ?"

"Don't worry, Momma! I'll be really careful, okay? No one's going to get hurt. Plus, I only got a couple of really dangerous ones. You know, the ones that blow your hands off. . . ."

"Very funny." Her head sinks back down and she closes her eyes, but I see that she's smiling.

For several minutes we stay silent together, enjoying the storm. Rain pelts the French doors, turning the room into a noisy, sea-swept darkness. The thunder alternates between long, angry bellows and short cracks followed by blinding flashes of incandescent light. I remember racing out to the porch swing during storms like this with my sisters when we were little, the three of us huddled together under a blanket, sometimes with my mother there as well, shrieking with excitement when the thunder broke overhead or a sudden gust blew a cold slap of rain in our faces.

The next rumble of thunder starts slow, more of a deep vibration than a noise, then seems to invade the room itself, filling the air with its rolling presence. Like some giant bellowing beast, it moves across the house, claiming it until, fully ensconced, it throws back its head and roars a shattering, bone-tingling roar.

I can hear the girls yell upstairs.

"Holy shit! That was a big one." I jump up to look out at the backyard, which is now flickering wildly like some crazy disco ball. Even the black trunks of the trees look silver as they dance back and forth in the light. I wonder if perhaps one of them *will* crack and fall. Maybe even crash through my mother's skylight or slam into the main roof of the house. They must be at least eighty feet tall.

My mother jerks upright behind me on the bed. "Is everything all right?" she asks. I realize she's drifted off.

"Everything's fine," I say. "Do you want me to go check?"

"No, no. Stay here."

The door bursts open and Lane and Evie come flying through, shrieking in two long, wailing notes like sister sirens.

"Did you hear that, Mommy?" Lane yells, heading toward me. "Did you hear that? The house is falling down! The house is falling *down*!"

"Hey, you two. I thought I heard some screaming going on up there." I squat down and they run into my arms. "What makes you think the house is falling down? This house is as strong as a fortress. A little thunder can't hurt it."

"We heard something *breaking*," Lane yells right into my ear, as they both jiggle up and down in my arms, nearly knocking me over. I can tell Lane's already over her fright, but Evie is still trembling in my arms.

"That's what thunder sounds like," I say, giving her a squeeze. "Like something breaking. But it's really just two clouds running into each other. Isn't that right, Nana?"

The three of us turn to look at her from our position on the floor. She lies with her arms crossed over her chest, eyes closed, her mouth hanging open.

"Did you say something?" she asks softly, eyes still closed.

I smile at the girls. "I think Nana's trying to sleep," I whisper as another deep rumble shakes the house. "How about we tiptoe out really quietly and go see where Clara and Fiona are?"

"They're under the bed in our room," Lane says in a piercing whisper, glancing over at my mother.

"We were hiding with them," Evie says, still jittery and wild-eyed, "but we got too scared. We couldn't find my mom so we had to find you." Her arms tighten around my neck like a vise, as if she's afraid I might also disappear.

"Hey," I say, giving them both a little shake. "Do you think I could carry both of you at the same time? Or are you too big?"

"Carry us! Carry us!"

I help them up onto the couch and place one onto each hip.

"Nana," I say, softly. "I'm going to take these girls out. I'll send Rosa in, okay?"

"Okay," she whispers. "Don't worry. They won't fall down."

I pause, confused, then turn to go. She opens her eyes and gives me a sharp look.

"The trees," she explains. "They won't fall down."

At eight o'clock, with our dinner eaten and the dishes cleared away, Hannah and I take the girls outside, past the pool, to the small lawn at the end of the garden, where my mother can see us through the picture window. The sky is overcast and unsettled and there are still regular flashes of lightning on the horizon. A light mist floats across the yard, and the leaves and branches drip noisily. The grass feels squishy and matted under my bare feet.

I lay out the boxes of fireworks along the top of the stone retaining wall, ten or twelve feet from the back of my mother's room, as the girls race happily around on the grass above it. The deep bluish gray light is perfect, dark enough to show off the fireworks but light enough to see what I'm doing.

"Do you know what you're doing?" Hannah asks, skeptically eyeing my pile.

"You mean do I know how to set off fireworks?" I ask cheerfully. "It's not exactly rocket science." I look down at the box of Roman candles I've just opened and laugh. "Well, actually it *is* rocket science, but you know what I mean."

She laughs too. "Okay. Just don't blind yourself or blow up one of the kids."

"I'll try not to," I say. "Here. Why don't you get started with the sparklers?"

Soon the yard is swirling with small points of exploding lights as the girls dance and wave their arms.

"Go show Nana," I tell them, and they line up on the small pebbles outside her window, whirling their sticks in the air. Looking over my shoulder, I see Rosa standing by my mother's bed. My mother is propped up on her pillow. They are both waving.

"Careful, girls!" Hannah warns, staying right behind Evie, who looks about ready to whirl off into space with joy. "Be careful with those things. Stay away from each other."

"Okay, my dears," I announce dramatically as I light the first match. "Stand back. The show is about to begin!"

I quickly move down the line of rockets, lighting them and, after a moment's sizzling hesitation, they go speeding straight up into the air and explode with a loud, satisfying bang, filling the sky with a descending arc of green and blue and yellow stars, each an ephemeral umbrella of lights.

There is a brief silence as everyone stands looking upward.

"*Cool,* Mom!" Clara says, as the last sparks fall into the grass. "Do it again!"

"Do it again! Do it again!" Lane and Evie chant, jumping up and down.

"Hey, look at Nana, you guys." Hannah points toward the window, where Rosa and my mother hold up their hands to show that they're clapping.

I'm already busy setting up the next line of fireworks. After lighting them quickly, like some wild-eyed pyromaniac, I stand back as they zip up past the dark outlines of the trees. We all gasp when one of them climbs ten or fifteen feet higher than the rest and offers a double explosion of lights. In a concentrated frenzy now, I set up the next round, light them quickly and set off more, barely aware of the children's cries, I'm so intent on keeping the air filled with color and light and sound and glory.

My nose stings from the smell of sulfur and a thick cloud of smoke envelops the yard as I come to my last firework. Glancing over my shoulder at my mother, I shout: "This one's for you, Nana! It's the last one!"

She waves and I wave back at her, turn, and strike a match.

Leaning back, I watch the last small ray of light go whistling up into the dark, and as it explodes into a patriotic red, white and blue, I raise my arms in the air and give a shout of triumph.


Wet and dirty, we all troop back into my mother's room, chatting noisily about the fireworks. Still buzzing with the exaltation I'd felt out in the yard, I need a minute to appreciate that my mother is also pleased, even elated. She has both Fiona and Clara by the hand, and the three of them are talking and laughing animatedly, heads bobbing up and down in the small circle of light from her bedside table.

"Did you see the sparklers, Nana?"

"Oh my God, Nana, I thought my hand was going to burn off!"

"I did too! I did too!"

"I had to drop the whole thing onto the grass!"

"Me too!"

"I loved the rockets, especially when they all went off in a row."

"Could you see them from here, Nana?"

"I could. They were *tremendous*."

Hannah steps forward, with Evie on her hip. "Listen everyone, I have to get Evie to bed. It's way past her bedtime. But I have an idea. Let's all hold hands in a circle before we say good night, okay?"

"Okay, okay."

Fiona and Clara line up beside the bed while Evie and Lane climb up next to my mother. The rest of us move closer around the bed. Once we all find a hand—I have Clara on one side and Hannah on the other—the room grows suddenly quiet.

"Now," Hannah whispers. "I'm going to send a pulse of energy around the circle. When you feel it come to you, send it around to the next person."

Everyone stays silent, and in a few seconds Clara squeezes my hand and I squeeze Hannah's hand and then, a few seconds later, the same thing happens.

"Did everyone feel it?" Hannah asks in a hushed voice.

"Yes! Yes!"

"So, do you know what this means?"

"No! What?"

Her voice drops even lower. "It means," she says, looking at each person around the circle, "that it's time to . . . say good night to Nana and *go to bed!*"

The kids pull apart laughing, and then race to give my mother a hug and kiss her good night. She looks radiant even as some of their hugs leave her wincing.

"Mom," Fiona says, grabbing Hannah's hand on the way out. "We should do this every night."

"We should," my mother calls after them. "We absolutely should."

# The Morning After

For hours after the fireworks, I'm unable to sleep. Finally dozing off at three or four in the morning, I dream of bombs detonating over Washington and all of us—Hannah, Rosa, the children and my mother, who has magically regained her mobility—rush up to the third floor to huddle together at the windows staring out at the fires that burn toward us across the city.

I awake in a foul mood, an apparent hangover from blowing things up the night before, and force myself out of bed. Swept up in the razzmatazz of thunder and lightning, sparklers and exploding rockets, I'd managed to escape everything else: the tedious hours at my mother's bedside, her steadily shrinking body, the specter of a morphine overdose on Friday. Returning to it feels unbearable.

Putting on my running clothes—a punishing run seems the best antidote—I head downstairs. I follow the sound of the television and find all four children sprawled on the living room couch watching *Annie*, a video they've seen numerous times over the last few days. Aware that they must also be suffering the effects of an overstimulating evening, I'm nevertheless irritated at the sight of their blank, vacant faces, the clutter of half-eaten dishes of cereal and fruit lying across the glass coffee table and floor. A glob of pink yoghurt drips off Lane's chin and there's a smear down the front of her pajamas. None of them are dressed although it's almost noon.

Rather meanly, I insist that they turn off the television and take their dishes into the kitchen. Marching along behind me, right on my heels, Clara complains bitterly that they were *just* in the middle of the movie, it was *so* unfair to turn it off, and there's *nothing to do*. I promise I'll go swimming with them later if they'll just please go play a game or read a book or do something—anything—for a while. They can't sit in front of the TV all day.

Kendra, who's been straightening the kitchen and listening to this exchange, says softly, "I'd be happy to take them to a movie, Zoe. *Shrek* is playing down on Connecticut Avenue this afternoon."

"Yes! Yes! Please! Please!" Their glum faces are instantly transformed, and Lane and Evie jump up and down, clutching each other.

Annoyed at having my attempt at discipline totally undermined, I'm tempted to say no, but my desire to have the children out of the house is stronger.

"Okay, fine, but don't think someone's going to take you to the movies every time you can't figure out what to do."

"We won't, Mommy." Clara grabs me around the waist in a fierce hug, then looks up at me with her best Poor Little Match Girl face. "We can get popcorn, right Mommy? One for each of us?"

Once they're out the door, with the entire contents of my wallet, I eat some toast and head toward my mother's room. Rosa is just coming out, and she stops when she sees me. With no meals to bring in, she seems a bit lost, although she's as attentive as ever, regularly swabbing my mother's mouth with glycerin, helping her take her medications, and changing her.

"I was just going out," she says, "to do a few errands." She pauses, standing between me and the door. I can see that she wants to talk, but in my current state, it's not a good idea. I don't want to hear about my mother's deteriorating condition, conflicts between Kendra and Sonia, calls we should make, or medications we should change. I know it's unfair, because Rosa has no idea how close we are to the end, but at this point my main goal is to stave off a total meltdown.

"That's fine, Rosa," I say, giving her a harried smile and moving to squeeze past her. "Take your time."

The room is warm and bright, the sky through the windows a deep poststorm blue. My mother is asleep, the blue quilt tucked up under her chin, the oxygen tube running out of her nose. Hannah is lying in my usual spot on the couch, reading the new mystery by Elizabeth George, an author we both like.

"How is she today?" I ask grumpily, not sure I want to know.

"Pretty out of it," Hannah says, looking up from her book. "I've been here since nine and she's been asleep most of that time. Michael, the hospice nurse, came by and checked on her about ten. They did some meditating and playing the Tibetan bowls or whatever it is they do. When I came back in, I saw him checking to see how much morphine she has left."

"Great. So when she takes the whole bottle tomorrow night, he'll know exactly how much she took."

"Yep. But I haven't told you yet. Katherine called this morning and suggested Momma *not* take the whole bottle. Apparently the first time her friend's aunt tried to overdose on morphine it made her sick—I mean, literally sick. She threw it up and then didn't die. So now Momma's planning to take only three-quarters of the bottle."

Interesting that Katherine is weighing in at this stage of the game and that she still has so much sway with my mother. I'm also surprised she didn't check with Hannah or me before giving my mother this advice. But maybe taking Katherine's suggestion about the morphine is a way for my mother to keep my older sister involved. And maybe for Katherine it's a way to stay connected with my mother, despite not being here.

"Great," I say, dropping heavily into one of the chairs next to my mother's bed. "Now I'm really looking forward to tomorrow."

"Yeah, you and me both." Hannah gives me a look. "You don't look so good. What's going on?"

"I don't know." I look over at my mother, who is sleeping heavily. She looks visibly smaller today, as if her body had started to dissolve into the bed. "Burned out, I guess. All that excitement last night was too much for me. Actually, last night was incredible. It was so much fun. Facing another day of this feels relentless."

Hannah puts her book down. "It's going to be over soon, Zoe," she says quietly, looking at the bed. "Whether she takes it tomorrow night or not. She's getting weaker. She asked me this morning where Dan was. She seemed to think he was here. Then she asked if he'd just left. She's definitely getting confused."

My upper back gives a painful twinge, and I stand up and shove the chair aside. "Listen, Hannah. I know you've been in here all morning but I need to go out for a run. I'll be back soon, and I'll stay in the rest of the day. I promise."

"Yeah, it's fine." She opens her book and starts to read. "I'm at a really good part anyhow. But don't be too long, okay?"

"You're the best."

"Uh-huh. Just do me a favor and be careful out there. This would not be a good day for you to get hit by a bus."

Once outside, I feel immediately better. The air is unusually clear—more like a summer day in California than in D.C.—and jogging down Ordway Street toward Wisconsin Avenue, I take deep, steady breaths. Inhale two steps, exhale four. Inhale two, exhale four.

I pass the two boxy, modern houses at the end of the block that were built by a famous architect, and the pretty stone house on the corner that's owned by a blond public television star. Turning down Thirty-fifth Street toward the National Cathedral, I pass houses that belonged to childhood friends, houses where I trick-or-treated, houses where boys I had crushes on lived, and a huge oak tree where the little neighborhood boy I used to walk home from school once peed.

Like one of those old-fashioned movie montages where the pages fly off the calendar, the houses of my childhood fly past me as I run, and I have the sensation that I am traveling back in time, growing younger on every block, until I'm no longer a forty-year-old mother but an awkward girl with big feelings, big fears, convinced she has to keep them hidden in order to stay safe.

So uncanny is this sensation that I actually look down at my body, at my toned runner's knees, to remind myself who—and where—I am. But the eerie feeling persists as I start up the long curved drive that leads to the northern entrance of the cathedral. I pass the familiar shaded courtyard with the modern fountain splashing noisily in the middle, the stone corridor that leads to the lower floor of the cathedral and, if one enters and turns left, Bethlehem Chapel, where I used to pray and sing hymns every Friday afternoon. My body feels oddly remote and mechanical, as if the person I was back then is more real than the person I am now, as if I am the memory and that other self—the one I'm remembering—is the real me.

Rounding the corner to the front of the cathedral, I wonder if this strange sensation of existing in both my past and my present is my body's way of preparing for the end. Not just the end of my mother and her house and these streets and sidewalks but the end of the girl who existed here. As if I've run back for a final look at her before the door between us closes for good.

I see Ray and Binky in their dusty red Saab while I'm jogging slowly up Thirty-fourth Street to Ordway. As they pass, I realize Bruno is with them. It's another good-bye, but this one is my mother's alone. I've asked Binky to bring Bruno back after she dies. We're going to keep him for a week and then put him on a plane to Ohio. Hannah spoke to the breeder yesterday. She said she had the perfect home for him: an older woman who lives alone and just lost her dog, also a Hungarian sheepdog. She can't wait to get him.

That night, once again, we stand around my mother's bed and send a pulse of energy around the circle. My mother looks noticeably thinner, her shoulders more hunched, but she's wearing a pretty navy blue shirt with little white anchors on it that I gave her a few years ago and she beams sleepily around the circle. Each child gives her a hug and a kiss and it's only when they're gone and she sinks back into her pillow that I see how depleted she is.

Lingering for a moment before we head up to put the children to bed, Hannah and I ask her how she's feeling. "Not too bad . . . that was nice." Suddenly Clara and Fiona burst back into the room, rush over to my mother's bed and, standing hand in hand, begin to sing a loud, theatrical version of "Tomorrow" from *Annie*: *"Tomorrow! Tomorrow! I love ya tomorrow!"*

Incredulous—do they *know* what's going on?—I turn to look at Hannah and see that her eyes are red.

The girls continue to sing.

*"You're always a day away . . ."*

# Night of Morphine

FRIDAY

The day is hot, well into the upper nineties. Dense, thick haze hangs over the back garden like a California fog but without the welcome cooling effects. In contrast to the weather, my mother is more clear and alert than she's been for days. She's also tense and irritable. After listening to her complain about not being able to brush her teeth or find the remote control to lower the shades on her windows, I have to bite my tongue not to ask: "Is this really how you want to spend the last day of your life?"

When she snaps at Rosa for forgetting to put chlorine in the pool, I ask her if she's feeling nervous about tonight.

"No," she says sharply. "I'm looking forward to it."

I raise my eyebrows, tempted to challenge her, but think of something Stephen Levine wrote in one of his books about how people die the way they live. My mother's inability to acknowledge any fears or concerns, even at this point in the game, is nothing if not characteristic. "I'm *not* mad," she used to say in a furious voice as she stamped around the house. *"There's nothing wrong."*

And just as I once scampered after her begging her to tell me why she was angry, I can't stop myself from trying to get at what she might be feeling now.

"So, you're completely ready to die?" I ask, trying not to sound doubtful. "No last-minute requests? No final words of wisdom?"

She's silent for a few moments, looking down at her shaking hands, which are cupped against her chest like two quivering animals.

"I think you're going to do very well without me," she says finally, looking up at me, her voice neutral and controlled. "And . . . I want to say how much I appreciate everything you've done for me all these months. I know it's been a lot to take on."

*You have no idea,* I think, although it was never the cross-country flights, the doctors' visits or even the phone calls that did me in: it was the continuous anticipation of losing her. But perhaps she knows this.

"No problem," I say, giving her a smile.

She chuckles, acknowledging the joke. "You and Hannah have been bricks. I'm lucky to have you."

Pleased and embarrassed, I look away.

This is my moment to tell her that I've been "lucky" to have her too, that I love her and will miss her, but somehow I can't. The words seem too small, too constrained. Like something wild stuffed into a box.

There's still time, I think. She's not going to take the morphine until after the kids go to bed tonight. That's hours away. I'll have time to tell her later.

After a long, quiet day, Jack arrives just after the nightly circle with the children. After grabbing a quick snack and helping put them to bed, he comes directly into my mother's room.

Rosa's just finished getting her ready for bed. Despite being dressed in her white and pink nightgown with the ruffle at the neck, my mother is delighted to see him. Warm and chatty, she asks about his flight, his work, and whether he found something to eat.

In his usual easygoing way, Jack answers her questions, even going into detail about the breast cancer drug his company is currently trying to patent. I've told him that my mother is planning to take an overdose of morphine tonight but am beginning to wonder if he's forgotten or is just thrown off by her gracious hostess manner.

But then, without breaking stride, my mother opens her bedside drawer and pulls out the morphine. "I was wondering if you could help me figure out how much three-quarters of the bottle is."

Hannah, who's sitting next my mother's bed, reaches over and takes the bottle, looks at the label for a moment, and hands it to Jack. Mesmerized, I watch from the couch as my husband takes the bottle and turns it toward the light to examine it, as unfazed as if my mother had asked him to help her lift a heavy box or open a car door.

I start to shiver and pull my knees up against my chest. The light from my mother's bedside lamp encircles the three of them but doesn't extend to the darkened corner where I sit, watching them. It's like viewing a performance onstage, distant and unreal.

They are talking about milliliters and ounces and droppers. It's a conversation I can't follow. I'm riveted by my husband's long fingers on the bottle, my sister leaning forward and taking it from him. I can see their mouths moving but can barely hear them over the roaring voice inside my head: DON'T TOUCH THAT BOTTLE.

Except it's too late, they've touched it. Both of them. And all I can think about is that their fingerprints are on it and that, when we're arrested for murder, I'll be the only one able to say I had nothing to do with it; the bottle was never in my hands.

Which feels wrong—unfair—like I'm planning to rat them out and save myself. Peering over my knees, wishing I could disappear behind them, I watch them talk and gesture and pass the bottle back and forth as casually as if it were a child's toy. Feeling like I'm spiraling down into some dark, alternate reality, I cower in the corner, filled with paranoia and dread while everyone else seems perfectly calm.

*Why am I the only one freaking out here?*

I want to say something, make them stop, put the bottle down. I start to speak, to interrupt the endless flow of words between them, but the numbers and calculations keep popping out of their mouths like cartoon bubbles and I cannot figure out how to interrupt them, or even what to say if I could. I scoot farther back on the couch, close my eyes, and wait for it to be over. For the next terrifying act to unfold.


It's settled, the amount of morphine. My mind can't make sense of it—the number is meaningless—but to my relief the discussion is over.

My mother thanks Hannah and Jack for their help and drops back onto her pillow. I feel I no longer exist. I've stayed entirely outside what may be the last important human exchange in my mother's life and now she's forgotten me.

"It's okay, Momma," Hannah says, placing the bottle back within reach on my mother's bedside table. "Just remember, we're not staying in here while you take it."

"That's fine," my mother says. "But don't go yet. Let's talk for a bit."

*Talk for a bit?* I look across the room at Jack for some confirmation of the awfulness, the strangeness, of this request, but he's gazing at my mother with polite friendliness: the good and helpful son-in-law. I realize with a stab of guilt that I shouldn't have let him walk unprepared into the middle of this. Half his brain is still in another time zone—another reality—and he's sitting too far away for me to communicate with him, even by the touch of a hand.

I feel totally alone, marooned in the darkness.

But then Hannah turns and locates me in my dim corner and I see I'm not alone. Deep lines run between her eyebrows, and her mouth is rigid and pale. We stare at each other for a moment, and the distress and apprehension that passes between us seems to take an almost palpable form, like an apparition hovering at the foot of my mother's bed.

She grimaces, looks away, her expression so pained and despairing that I'm released from my paralysis, becoming once again *of* the scene, not outside it.

Looking around the room, searching for something to say, I catch sight of the Grateful Dead T-shirt on my mother's bookshelf. Its garish yellow and fuchsia swirls glow in the dark over Jack's head.

"Hey, Momma, don't forget about Ray's present," I say, pointing toward it. "You're going to need it tonight, right?"

"What's Ray's present?" Jack asks, giving me a puzzled look.

"My mother's dog trainer's boyfriend, Ray, gave her a Grateful Dead T-shirt," I explain. "He thought she might want to be buried in it."

"I don't want to be buried in it," my mother says sharply, giving me an annoyed look.

"Oh. Well, forget it then," I reply, taken aback. Apparently her former amusement over the T-shirt has disappeared. "But you have to admit it's kind of perfect. I mean, the Grateful Dead, right?"

"Why is it perfect?" Again the combative tone. "It's *not* perfect."

"Momma, it's the *grateful dead*." My face feels hot and I pull my knees even closer to my chest. "Haven't you been saying you'd be grateful to be dead? Isn't that what this is about?"

"I'm not going to be grateful to be dead." She is positively angry now and I am deeply regretting having brought it up. "I feel that I have no choice about ending my life. But that doesn't mean I feel *grateful* about it."

I stare at her. *No choice?* Is she mad? Has she forgotten how she's single-mindedly been dragging us toward this moment for months if not years, despite all our efforts to dissuade her?

I want to argue, defend myself from this unfair and unexpected attack. I am furious, but also deeply distressed at finding myself in this argument—at having *any* argument with my mother right now. Why is she doing this? I look over at her, shocked at the sight of her stormy, resentful face, and think of the morning I was returning to California and she said: *I need a parent.* Is that what she wants me to be—her parent? To absorb her fear, reassure her, overlook this sudden display of temper? Why had I believed her this morning when she said she wasn't afraid? *Of course she's afraid.* But I'm also afraid and I also need a parent.

I feel the three of them waiting for me to speak and I know this moment will torture me forever unless I can somehow get it right.

"It's okay, Momma," I say, forcing myself to smile. "I guess I misunderstood you. Anyway, let's not have our last conversation be an argument about a Grateful Dead T-shirt, okay? I'm sorry I brought it up."

"That's all right. I just never said I was grateful about dying."

She still can't let it go. I throw Hannah a desperate look and notice Jack is no longer smiling.

"No one is saying you're grateful about being in the situation you're in, Momma," I try again, speaking more gently. "But given that you *are* in this situation, you have to admit you've . . . embraced death. That's all I meant."

"Yes, well, that may be true." She looks less fierce and, after a moment, gives me a look I choose to interpret as apologetic.

"Are you sure you want to do this, Margaret?" Jack asks in a soft voice. "I don't think I fully appreciated what was happening."

We all turn to look at her. As if on cue, her body gives an involuntary lurch and her lips flatten against her gums, revealing her teeth. For one brief moment, her emaciated face looks like a death mask. It's an expression she only started making this week, since she stopped eating.

"I'm sure," she says, almost brusquely, recovering herself. "And I think it's time. If I wait too much longer, I'm going to be too tired." She turns to look at Jack. "Thank you for helping me," she says. "You've been very nice."

He looks stricken. "Well, I haven't really done anything, Margaret."

"No, no. You have. And thank you, Hannah and Zoe. I love you both."

"We love you too," we both say in unison.

She sits up and slowly swings her legs out from under the covers. Hunched and small, she perches on the edge of the bed in her oversize nightgown. She's wheezing, and both Hannah and I look over at the oxygen tank. But she hasn't wanted to use it all day and neither of us suggests it now.

"Well . . . here we go," she says, taking a short, whistling breath. "Could one of you hand me that bottle before you leave?"


"This is bad," Jack says quietly, his warm hand on my back. Hannah stands on the far side of him. The three of us huddle together in the darkened Big Room, its extravagantly high ceiling looming over us. "I knew she was planning to take the morphine tonight, but she seemed so . . . casual when I got here. I mean, I can't get over how quickly we went from 'Hi, how was your flight?' to 'How much morphine should I take?'"

He shakes his head and I can see how upset he is. "I know," I say, leaning against him. "I'm sorry."

"It's a hell of a thing to walk into," Hannah says, also in a low voice. We're pretty sure Rosa is in her bed in the dining room but are concerned she might wander into the adjoining kitchen and overhear us. "You handled it really well."

I think about him "handling" the morphine bottle but don't say anything. What's done is done. And I suppose we could always wipe the prints off the bottle, although I've read enough murder mysteries to know this could also raise suspicions.

"Why was she so determined to take three-quarters of the bottle anyway?" he asks. "Why not the whole thing?"

We explain about Katherine's phone call, and he gives us a skeptical look. "That doesn't sound very helpful. So much would depend on the person's body mass."

"I guess." I rub my bare arms, which feel chilled. I want to move closer to Jack, have him wrap his arms around me, but I don't want to leave Hannah out. It's the three of us now. We need to stick together. "Well, never a dull moment," I say, using one of my mother's expressions.

Jack shakes his head. "Can we get a drink?"

He's just poured us each a glass of wine when Rosa appears in the doorway in her nightgown and robe. "Your mom's calling for you," she says, unsmiling. "She wanted me to come get one of you girls. She needs your help with something."


"She dropped it," Hannah says, coming slowly back into the room without looking at either of us. She sits at the kitchen table and stares straight ahead, as if transfixed by some internal picture too complicated or painful to communicate, just as my father did on the morning he took to his bed.

Jack looks at me, raises one eyebrow.

"So . . . what happened?" I ask, putting a glass of wine down next to her.

"I gave it to her."

"You mean it didn't spill?"

"A little did. But most of it was still in the bottle."

Her voice is flat and she doesn't look at us.

"Hannah?"

"I just didn't like handing it to her," she says angrily. "I just really didn't like that."


She's lying on top of her quilt, eyes closed, when we go in a few minutes later.

"I took it," she says. Her voice is raspy and I can see her chest moving slowly, exaggeratedly, up and down under her nightgown.

I walk to the far side of the bed, climb onto it and take her hand. Hannah sits on the closer side of the bed, takes her other hand. Jack goes over to the couch behind me.

"Are you okay?" I ask.

For a moment her eyelids flutter wildly, as if she's trying to open her eyes, but they stay closed.

"I feel . . . *wonderful*," she says. Her voice is childlike and happy, and she smiles a broad, loopy-looking smile that I've never seen before.

She's totally high, I think and feel laughter bubble up inside me, threatening to escape. I glance past Hannah at the Grateful Dead T-shirt sitting on the bookshelf. It would have been just the thing after all, I gently admonish her in my head. Going out on a wave of drugged-out bliss was something Jerry Garcia would have totally understood.

Hannah gets up, lights a couple of candles and turns off the harsh gooseneck lamp. Despite its high ceiling and blank white walls, the room feels warmer, more intimate.

"That's nice," my mother says sleepily, without opening her eyes.

Hannah looks at me. I can tell she's still upset about the dropped bottle. I want to tell her it's okay. That she did what she had to do. And I want to tell her how much I owe her for stepping into the breach tonight, taking on the heaviest burdens while I cowered fearfully in the corner. I want to let her know how much I've always loved her, but never so much as tonight.

I reach out and touch her arm.

*We can do this,* I say, silently. *The worst is over.*

We turn to gaze at my mother, each of us holding her hands, like figures in a Victorian deathbed scene. The candlelight flickers across her face. I imagine us as characters in a 19th Century painting. It would be inscribed: Dutiful Daughters Attend Mother's Deathbed.

"So nice," she says, smiling her funny, stoned smile. "So nice . . . to have you here like this."

"We're glad to be here too," I tell her, stroking her hand and then her arm, which lies relaxed and warm on top of the quilt. I block out the picture of her struggling to reach the fallen bottle, too weak and unsteady to get down on the floor. I stop thinking about the fact that my husband and sister's fingerprints are pressed against its slippery sides. In fact, I try to forget about the bottle all together. It's time to acknowledge the more pressing reality. My mother is finally dying.

"Momma?" I say.

"Mmmm?"

"I just wanted to tell you . . . you've been a good friend."

"Thank you," she says, still smiling. "You too."


An hour later—or is it several hours—my back aches from sitting unsupported on the bed, Jack has dozed off on the couch and is snoring, and Hannah has started absently unraveling a small piece of my mother's quilt. One of the candles has sputtered out, the other is burning low.

My mother is still alive.

Hannah sighs and looks at her watch.

"We should go to bed," she says. "It's after midnight. It'll be weird if Rosa comes in here for some reason and sees us like this."

"She seems to be breathing okay," I say, stretching out alongside her, bringing my face up close to hers. She actually looks pretty good. Despite the visible bones, the sharp cut of her brow and chin, her mouth is soft and relaxed, and whether it's the candlelight or my imagination, her cheeks have a flushed, healthy look to them.

"Momma?" I say, right into her ear. She doesn't move or respond in any way.

"I think she's unconscious," I say, crawling back to the end of the bed. My body has that deep, overtired bone ache, and I want nothing so much as to curl up in my own bed. But when I look back at her, lying there in the candlelight, it seems wrong to leave, to make her depart the world on her own.

"It feels strange to leave her," I say.

Hannah, who is standing at the edge of the bed, hunched and stricken, her hands knotted at her waist, nods. I think she's crying.

"What is it?" I ask, going over to put my arm around her.

"It's just so much worse than I thought it was going to be."

"You mean watching her die?"

"No. I mean helping her die."

"Hannah, it's what she wanted. You did the right thing. She would thank you if she could. Profusely. You know that, don't you?"

"Yeah. I guess so."

"C'mon. We need to go to bed. You go ahead, I'll get Jack. She won't even know we're gone. We've done what we could."

"No, we did what we had to," she says, going over to kiss my mother's face. "It's not the same thing."

"No," I say, putting my arms around her. "It's not the same thing."

# Traveling

All night I keep waking up, not sure if I'm in my bed or down in my mother's room, as if part of me cannot accept that I'm away from her. I wake, startled and disoriented in the dark, and look for her. I bump into Jack next to me in the bed and think it's her.

When I fall asleep I dream of her, except it's more like a journey than a dream. In it, my spirit body gets up, goes downstairs in search of her, while my physical body stays behind in the bed.

Whether dreaming or actually traveling in space, I repeat the same actions over and over again: sit up, put my feet on the floor, stand, open my bedroom door, walk down the stairs in the dark, go through the dining room past Rosa, open the door to my mother's bedroom, walk toward her bed.

Except I never get there. Either I wake up terrified and panting, sure that I'm about to reach out and touch my mother's dead body, or, just when I get to her room, the air starts to buzz and shimmy around me as if the molecules in the atmosphere have suddenly gone wild. Electromagnetic currents shoot through me like static radio waves. The air turns thick and black. I can't see.

I stagger forward, blind and disoriented, not sure where I am or where she is, but *I need to get to her.* My body starts to vibrate and dissolve, absorbed into the molecular soup that swirls around me, and I find myself back in my own bed.

"Zoe, Zoe, wake up." My mother is shaking me, her hand warm and heavy on my shoulder. "Wake up. I need to tell you something."

I'm so tired. I can't open my eyes. "No," I whisper. "Leave me alone. I have to sleep. I'm so tired."

"Zoe, are you awake? Can you hear me?"

I hear you, I think, pulling the sheet up over my face. But please go away. I'm too tired to wake up right now.

"I went down there. She's not dead."

"*What?*" I open my eyes. Hannah is crouching next to the bed. Dim light filters in from the windows. I cannot make sense of anything. What happened to my mother? Wasn't she just here? *Who's* not dead?

"Did you hear me?" Hannah shakes me more gently now. "Momma's not dead."

# The Passing Parade

## SATURDAY

Daylight is a revelation. A thing of joy.

I'm like Persephone emerging from the underworld, delivered from darkness. I stare happily at the sunlight on the rug, the bland expanse of my closet doors, and let the terror and confusion of the night recede. Did I really get up, go downstairs, or was that just a trick of my sleeping mind? And if I did go—because it truly feels like I did—why was I never able to reach my mother? Was I too frightened of what I would find? Or had some ghostly entity or entities prevented me from getting to her?

It was after Hannah's dawn visitation, her own torturous night having culminated in a frightening sojourn to my mother's room to check on her, that I finally relaxed and fell into a blank, exhausted sleep. When Clara and Lane came in several hours later to rout out Jack, I lay basking in the familiar sights and sounds of my brightly lit bedroom, the squirming presence of my children in the bed.

When I finally get up, I realize I'm in no particular rush to go downstairs and see my mother. I'm free of the nameless horror that pursued me all night: the fear that my mother was dying alone with no one to comfort her or witness her departure, and that Jack, Hannah and I were somehow responsible for her death.

Walking into the bathroom, I expect to be greeted by a wrung-out, haggard version of myself, a dry and witchy hag, and am surprised to see that I look . . . okay. Lips still plump, eyes clear. Not young exactly but vital. Intact. I run my hands down my cheeks and along the sides of my neck, press my flattened palms against the soft skin on my chest, feel the faint tap of my heart.

This sense of renewal stays with me as I make my way downstairs—oh, the blessed sunlight!—and into my mother's room. She's in there alone, eyes closed, her breathing deep and regular. She opens one eye as I approach the bed.

"So," I say, reaching down to take her hand. "You're still here."

The words are sweet on my tongue—jubilant even. The great morphine overdose was a bust! A dress rehearsal instead of the real thing. With all its secrecy and fear and late-night hauntings, last night was not the final ending after all.

"Yes." Her voice is slurred so the s comes out in a soft hiss. And then, "It was . . . *wonderful.*"

I laugh. The darkness recedes another notch. We've returned from the brink, been given a reprieve. Not from death—my mother is still going to die—but from *that* death. And now she gets to do it again. A different one. A better one.

For hours, "It was wonderful" looks like it's going to be the last thing my mother says. Both Hannah and I try to elicit more from her, leaning in close and asking her questions, but she doesn't respond. Either she's experiencing the lingering effects of the morphine, which could wear off, or the overdose along with the lack of food has put her beyond speech.

"She's changed," Rosa says sadly, laying her hand against my mother's forehead and peering down at her. "She never really woke up today. Even to take her medications."

Hannah and I give each other a worried look. Does Rosa suspect something? I fuss with a loose strap on my sandal, not wanting to meet her eye. But then she turns from the bed and, in her usual tone, asks what we'd like for dinner. We give her some suggestions and she goes to tell Sonia.

Hannah groans and lies back on the couch, while I stretch out on the bed next to my mother. "Do you think she's wondering about last night?" I ask.

"I don't," she says, staring up at the ceiling. "Although I'm surprised she isn't. We were in here so much later than usual." She turns to look at my mother, who has rolled onto one side. Her jaw is slack and she's breathing heavily, wheezing lightly every time she inhales. "I think Rosa just figures it's the lack of food catching up with her."

I reach over and push a piece of hair back from my mother's face. "Hey, Momma. Can you hear me?" I say, right into her ear. I can smell the citrusy smell of the glycerin mouth swabs we've been using on her lips and gums. She doesn't react in any way.

"She was talking at five-thirty this morning," Hannah says.

"Oh yeah? What did she say?"

"Well, I told her she was still alive, which, strange as it sounds, I thought she might not know. Then I asked her if she was all right with that—with being alive—and she kind of smiled and said, 'It's fine. I feel great.'"

"She told me last night was wonderful," I say. "I guess she got her big deathbed scene after all. And even got to review it the next day."

"Well, I'm glad *she* enjoyed it," Hannah says, shaking her head. "I'm just damn glad she didn't die."

I look out the window at the brilliant sky, the slender trunks of the trees along the back fence. Funny, how death and darkness are such natural allies, while sunshine brings an illusion of safety and well-being. I'm reluctant to look back into that darkness but find myself going over the scene at my mother's bedside.

The worst part was the sheer panic I'd felt watching my husband and sister handle the morphine. I was so convinced that they were in danger, and yet, in the light of day, my reaction seems irrational. Did I really think that hiding in the corner not doing anything to stop my mother from taking an overdose would make me any less culpable? I was, after all, the one who'd given her permission to go ahead and kill herself—and there was proof of that in writing and on her answering service.

But even if I hadn't been worried about fingerprints and murder investigations, I'm convinced the three of us would have felt guilty if she'd died last night. Even knowing we'd done *everything possible* over the last days and months to keep her from taking the damn stuff. I look over at the Library of Death and wonder if they covered *that* in their rosy-hued descriptions of "self-deliverance." If they did, she never mentioned it.

Not that I blamed the books. If assisted suicide was legal, and we hadn't been forced to spend so much time worrying about getting caught, we might have been able to better prepare ourselves. To figure out what it meant to be here at this profound moment of my mother's life. As for her . . . well, there's no doubt it would have been easier. She might have even chosen to stay alive longer if her doctors had been able to discuss her plans with her, and be there when she did it, instead of leaving her fumbling with a partially spilled morphine bottle, forcing my sister to step into the breach.

And maybe I wouldn't have resisted her so long, and been so afraid to help her.

It still would have been hard, but not so torturous and confusing.

"I've got to tell you, Hannah," I say, scooting down to the end of the bed and leaning forward so my mother can't hear. "That may have been the worst night of my life."

"Like staring into the abyss," Hannah says glumly, glancing over at my mother. "Until I went back in and picked the bottle off the floor, I was sort of okay with it. I was being helpful and doing what needed to be done. But at that moment, when I had the choice to hand it to her or not, I saw that the situation was much bigger—and much worse—than I'd realized. Suddenly, I was in the position of determining whether she lived or died, and that was way more power than I wanted."

"I'm sorry you had to do that," I say, looking into my sister's pale, exhausted face, feeling a little shiver of gratitude that it hadn't been me.

"The funny thing is, in some strange way, I also admire her for doing it."

Glancing over my shoulder at my mother's huddled body, I realize that I do too. Despite all her waffling and changing of dates and our reluctance to participate, she hadn't blinked an eye last night.

*And in her right hand, a silver dagger . . .*
*Leave you alone to pine and sigh.*

We're both still in my mother's room when Michael the hospice nurse arrives. He takes one look at my mother and goes directly to the bedside drawer with the morphine. He fishes out the near-empty bottle and looks at it, then over at us. But instead of saying anything, he simply puts it back and closes the drawer. Then he steps closer to my mother's bed and starts checking her vital signs.

A few minutes later, he says he has to go but to call him if we need anything. I realize I was wrong about Michael. He's been expecting this to happen for days. After all, the man had meditated with her, and talked with her about what she wanted, for weeks. And there was no point in his asking us what part we had or hadn't played. It was better for him not to know.

Katherine calls around eleven. I walk out to the yard to make sure no can hear us talking. Wandering around in the grass, I recount everything I can remember from last night, minus my sleep travel. She listens intently, interrupting only occasionally for clarifications, but in a subdued voice. When I mention that Momma took three-quarters of the morphine based on her advice, she's concerned that we'll be mad at her.

I flop down on the grass, cross-legged, and look out over the pool, which appears flat and colorless in the midday sun. "No, no," I say. "It was better this way, believe me."

"Oh," she says, sounding pleased if a little puzzled. "Well, that's good. But why? I would have thought you'd want the whole thing over with."

I consider how to respond. Part of me feels she's simply too removed from the situation to explain it, but her tentative tone softens me, and I try to convey how the three of us would have felt if Momma had died last night and why we were glad she hadn't.

"I see," she says, after a moment. "I have to say I'm shocked she went through with it. I really didn't think she was going to do it. I thought it was all talk and getting our attention."

"Actually, I think she was totally serious all along. She certainly was this week. Remember, even before the morphine, she hadn't eaten anything in eight days. And she'd had almost nothing to drink."

"Huh . . . I guess you're right."

Again, there's that pensive note in her voice and I wonder if Katherine regrets not being here. I consider asking her if she wants to come down, but I doubt she will. Deathbed scenes aren't easy for anyone, but especially when so much remains unresolved, and coming here would involve dealing with Hannah and me and, once again, being the odd person out.

I promise to call her and we say good-bye. I lie back on the grass and look up at the hazy, blank sky, the jutting green branches of the giant pine tree that towers over this corner of the yard. I remember being frightened as a child that the earth would drop away below me and I would fall up into that endless sky.

I recall, too, how afraid I once was of Katherine. Of her anger and bitterness, her bottomless yearning for things she couldn't have, and the way her rage and frustration would bubble over onto Hannah or me. Even now I wonder: Did my parents fail more with Katherine than with us, or was she just more vulnerable to their failures?

They certainly seemed to miss how left out she was, all alone in that room at the top of the stairs, parents on one side, sisters on the other. Despite Katherine's attempts to win me over when we were children—picking me as her "favorite," asking me to sleep in her room—Hannah and I had always been a sisterhood of two. I think of us last night, shoulder to shoulder on my mother's bed, and the many ways we've stood by each other over the years.

Thinking of Katherine as isolated and lonely instead of tough and scary is new and, for a few moments, I lie on the grass trying to absorb it. I wonder if now that my mother has proved she was truly intent on dying, Katherine will reevaluate, soften toward her. Forgive her some of her failings. I hope so, if only for Katherine's peace of mind. But if she doesn't, I hope that one day she and I'll be able to talk. Not only about this extraordinary choice my mother has made but about her choices as well. And I hope I'll be able to listen and understand.

That night, when the children come in to form a circle around my mother's bed, they are restless and silly and loud. Clara "calls" that she wants to start the pulse going, and she and Fiona argue about it until Hannah intervenes. None of the kids seem particularly aware that Nana isn't opening her eyes anymore or talking. They've all been in to see her today and seem to accept that this is her new state.

After the circle is over, Clara pushes me onto the couch and sits on my lap, at which point Lane climbs on me as well. Next to us, Fiona tells a noisy story about losing her hair clip in the pool and crashing into the side while coming up for air, and Evie, who's straddling Hannah on the bed next to my mother, keeps yelling, "Giddyup, Mommy! Giddyup!"

Even when we convince the children, after much persuasion, to go get ready for bed, promising that Jack will read to them if they do, they keep rushing in and out of the room.

And then, in the middle of all the chaos, my mother says, "Ah, the passing parade," in a clear, cheerful voice.

Hannah and I whip around and stare at her, then at each other to make sure we heard her right.

"Momma? Did you say something? Are you okay?"

We rush over and ask again, but she doesn't respond.

# Excavation

Hannah hands me a crinkly sheet of beige stationery covered with my mother's familiar scrawl. March 18, 1938.

> *Dear Grandfather, Thank you for sending me my allowance. Please tell Grandmother that all the other girls are jealous of the matching hat and cape she sent me. They will be perfect for Easter. I like them very much. I haven't heard from Mother or Poppy. Do you know if Poppy is coming to visit me over break? I am working hard and can't wait to see you this summer.*
>
> *Love, Margaret*

"Wow, that's sad," I say, letting the letter drop into my lap. "Both her parents were missing in action and her relationship with her grandparents was all about keeping them happy so they'd pay for everything. The only thing she had going for her was a new outfit."

"And the fact that her friends were jealous."

Hannah takes back the letter and pulls out another pile of envelopes and notebooks. We've been going through a huge trunk of letters and journals that Hannah found in the basement and brought up to my mother's room. We've spread them out on her bed next to her and across the blue couch.

It's Monday, July ninth, the third day since she took the morphine. Her body has shrunk, and she lies curled up on her right side, facing the window and the expanse of bed next to her. Even after Rosa comes in to change her, she returns to this position. Michael has suggested we put her on her back or left side to avoid bedsores, but it's no use. She always returns to the same spot.

Hannah and I have been in the room with her constantly since the morning after the overdose, leaving only when Rosa changes her. I know my mother wouldn't care if I stayed, but there are images of her I don't want to have. I've seen enough of her ravaged body, her pain, over these months and have even begun to forget who she was just a few days ago, before the morphine, before she stopped talking.

I turn to the letters and diaries as if maybe they will give her back to me, and in a way they do. I read the words she wrote as a child—mainly to her absent parents but especially to her father, begging him to come see her—and I have this vivid picture of her as a little girl with a pale face and dark red curls, serious and shy.

From her letters when she was a teenager, I discover that, despite her parents' ongoing neglect, there *were* adults in her life who cared about her. One of them was her father's brother, her uncle George, who wrote to her in both boarding school and college, giving her support and encouragement. The other was her paternal grandfather who, despite his formal, old-fashioned style, expressed a lovely, gentle warmth in his letters. (When relations between my mother and her grandmother grew distant, my grandfather begged my mother to contact her and be "the honest, sweet young woman I know you are.")

Reading through all this is like watching that old TV show *This*

*Is Your Life,* except it isn't my life, it's hers. I wonder if my mother is engaging in her own internal version, flipping back through the years to relive the highlights and traumas while lying there in a ball.

"Boy, she didn't suffer fools gladly," Hannah says, handing me a black leather journal. "Read this."

It's an entry from the summer my mother spent at a "dude" ranch in Colorado. A sophomore at Sarah Lawrence, she had developed a serious, if self-conscious, identity as a scholar. Between long, essay-like musings about Freud and Jung and Nietzsche, she complained about how the other girls at the ranch were not intellectual. "They care more about clothes and boys instead of pursuing real ideas."

"Ah, the life of the mind," I say, and Hannah laughs. But despite my gentle scorn, I know what a lifeline it was for my mother to join this larger world of ideas. Finally, she had some tools—philosophical, psychological—to make sense of her messy, out-of-control upbringing.

Later, she turned to therapy and dream analysis for guidance. We find a large box of tapes filled with her dreams, recordings she made in the bathroom every morning while my father slept. We play one, and her voice sounds scratchy and soft and eerie. "I'm walking up a big hill. . . . In the distance, I see an animal. . . . I think it's a dog . . ." Even the written versions, conscientiously typed up to take to her therapist each week—ever the good student—are too opaque and personal to read, and we put them aside.

Digging further into the trunk, we unearth draft after draft of her book, her great, unfinished work, and I think how appropriate it is that I'm helping her finish her story once again. And yet, as we excavate, I realize something: The part of my mother I knew, the part that sprang into being at my birth and existed only through my eyes, is but a narrow slice of the whole. The realization is both humbling and freeing. In gathering and holding these various pieces of her—child, teenager, young woman, wife, mother, writer—I can let go of my solipsistic belief that the "us" was essentially interchange-able with the "her."

I have the exhilarating sensation that I've finally found her. Not just the specifics but the entirety of who she was. And far from being sad that this is happening just as I'm losing her, I feel grateful to have found her at all.

We take turns eating lunch in the kitchen, and when I return, Hannah hands me a bundle of my parents' letters to each other with the terse directive "Read."

Looking through them, I discover how persistently, almost desperately, my father had pursued my mother. During their almost five years of courtship, which included several years of living together—a daring step at the time—my father had proposed repeatedly to my mother while she dodged and demurred. In one of these demurrals, she pulled my father up short in surprisingly straightforward terms.

"I wish you didn't always talk about yourself so much," she wrote. "You never ask me what I'm doing, or how I feel about anything, and when you tell me things about yourself, it is never how you feel or what you are thinking, it is always who you had lunch with or your plans for the weekend."

"Well, she had his number," I say.

"No kidding," Hannah replies. "Guess she just wasn't ready to listen to her own better instincts. Still, it seems like she loved him. Enough anyway."

I look down at a diary entry from the mid-seventies: "There are things I just don't want to know about Jonathan. Who he sees. What he does." And farther down, "I'm so glad I have the girls. They keep me from feeling lonely."

"Was it enough?" I ask. "It's hard to say."

"Well, no marriage is perfect, Zoe, and I'm not saying theirs was, but there were things they both loved and shared. Books, mainly, but also this house. How modern and hip it was. And they loved Vermont. I think they always had this image of themselves that made them feel good. You know, the bohemians in Paris, and then the bright young things bringing in a new day when they moved to D.C. after Kennedy was elected. Then there was their seeker phase in the seventies—est and meditating—although I'd have to say Poppa drove that train."

"The Great White Guru," I say, remembering how my father used to ask me what shape and color my headache was, believing he could cure me. "And you have to admit they were both creative. All that writing, playing music, painting and cooking. It's just hard to forget Poppa's betrayals. The affairs and his drinking. I think Momma just sort of checked out, pursuing her writing behind closed doors and shutting him out."

My mother shifts on the bed next to me and purses her mouth as if she wants to say something.

Hannah, who's been sitting on the floor, climbs onto the bed to look at her. "I bet it's killing her that she can't join in," she says, softly. "I mean, here we are, summing up her life and deconstructing her marriage."

"She's probably thinking, 'What do they know?'"

"And why do they always insist on focusing on the bad things?"

"Okay," I say, turning to address her next to me on the bed. "I'll give you one good thing. You and Poppa were really sweet with each other when he was dying."

Hannah laughs suddenly. "God, I was just thinking about all those crazy things Poppa said when his tumors came back. He wanted peanut butter on his toast one morning and he kept asking if someone could please land an airplane. Momma was so confused. '*Why* do you want an airplane, Jonathan?' Until finally she asked him where he wanted it and he pointed to his toast and she figured it out."

Next to me, my mother stirs again. This time, when I look down at her, she has a huge smile on her face.

"Oh my God, she can hear us? Can you hear us, Momma? Do you remember that?"

She raises her eyebrows, gives a faint nod.

"And do you remember when I was down here visiting and we went to Sutton Gourmet with Poppa?" Hannah sits next to me on the bed, talking right to her. "It was just a few months before he died and he'd lost so much weight. He was ordering something at the bakery counter and suddenly his jeans fell down. Right to his ankles. And he just thought it was so funny. I felt terrible for him, but both of you were laughing so hard and it *was* kind of funny although I'm not sure anyone else thought it was. The lady next to him looked kind of horrified."

Again, my mother smiles and her face, which has looked so vacant for days, is fully alive again.

"And don't forget his singing along with Willie Nelson when he was supposedly in a coma," I add. "Kind of made you feel like he was having a good time in there."

She gives a small nod.

Excited and amazed, I look at Hannah. "Keep talking," she mouths at me.

So for ten or fifteen minutes we share stories about my father, and my mother listens to us, smiling at the ends of anecdotes, or sometimes just nodding, but never saying anything or opening her eyes. Eventually she stops responding, and Hannah and I fall quiet. We lie there next to her on the bed, letting the joy of this unexpected offering settle inside us.

# Singing

I'm lying on the bed next to my mother, my arm around her waist. Her face is turned away, something I'm grateful for, as she would not want me looking into her stiff, closed-up features, her half-open mouth. I'm singing to her, quietly but continually, one song after the next, convinced that she recognizes and is comforted by the sound of my voice.

"Shenandoah." "Red River Valley." "Shady Grove." My voice is soft and clear, the songs are exquisite and sad: the ones she sang to me when I was a child and, I imagine, were sung to her. Not by her parents, who were too glamorous and distracted to put their only child to bed. Nor by her stern grandparents. But by one of her beloved childhood nurses who, from pity or loneliness, would sing my mother to sleep.

Most of the time I don't feel sad lying here, although sometimes the thought that I'm singing to my dying mother makes me tear up, as if I am watching myself in a movie. Mostly I'm in that surreal, out-of-body state I experienced as a new mother, when the edges of my being disappeared as I endlessly, exhaustedly rocked or nursed my tiny daughter, every cell in my body tuned to her tenuous progress toward sleep.

I start the final chorus of "Wild Mountain Thyme."

> *And we'll all go together*
> *To pick wild mountain thyme*
> *All around the blooming heather*

The sun sinks behind the bamboo trees at the back of the garden. My mother's breathing is easier now, lighter, less necessary. I can't see her face, but I know she has drifted further away, the music grown faint, a string of notes stretching in a loose trail behind her. I imagine her going forth, drowsy and weightless, cushioned by the sound of my voice.

# Flight

By Tuesday night, the twelfth day of her fast, my mother has become nearly invisible. As she lies curled in a ball facing the center of the bed, hands tucked as if in prayer under her chin, her face looks shuttered and small.

Hannah leaves to call her husband, and I begin to sing to my mother, as I do when we're alone. *"From this valley they say you are going..."*

And then I stop.

Something feels different, something subtle, like a shift in temperature or a sudden absence of sound—sound you've been only vaguely aware of. I look around the room, trying to identify what's changed, but it looks the same. Everything is tidy and in its place. Her papers are put away. The visitors' chairs are pushed back against the bookshelf. The oxygen tank is unhooked and sitting in the corner. Through the picture window by the bed, the sky is a hazy purple-gray with a few last streaks of orange, just as it was a minute ago.

I look down at my mother, her profile etched darkly against the pillow. Is it her? Is she dead? My eyes move down her body, find the gentle rise and fall of her ribs. Relieved, I lay my hand alongside her arm, feeling the hardness of bone, but sense no answering frequency, the "being there" that usually answers me when I touch or sing to her. That responding presence—her presence—is missing, like a background hum that's dropped away, or a breeze that's ceased to blow, leaving only still air behind.

The circle tonight is brief. The children seem eager to leave the room, and we let them go. Hannah and I have been sleeping in my mother's room since Jack returned to California Sunday night, taking turns between the bed and the couch, but tonight my limbs ache from fatigue and my mind feels flat and dull. I want to wrap myself in the comfort of my children, feel their breath on my face. They lie tucked in and waiting for me in my old childhood bed.

"Good night," I tell my mother, kissing her head. "I love you."

Again, I have to look carefully to see that she's breathing.

"Are you okay, Hannah?" I ask.

She gives me a look that I cannot interpret. I wonder if she also feels this unsettling absence, but am too exhausted to ask.

"I'm fine. I want to stay. You go on."

"Wake me if—"

"I will."

My legs are stiff and slow on the stairs, while the rest of me is just numb. No sadness. No loss. Just empty. Like all my feelings have disappeared.

I've been waiting for Hannah to arrive and I bolt up from the bed before she can speak or touch me. For a moment, we stare silently at each other in the dim light from the window and then, still without speaking, I grab my robe and follow her down the stairs. The bedside light is on and Rosa is there in her nightgown. Praying, I think, and crying a little. My mother lies on her back, her mouth and eyes both open.

"I'm not sure why I woke," Hannah says quietly, standing next to me, "but I noticed that her breathing had slowed. Her last few breaths were several minutes apart and then she . . . just stopped."

I nod, unable to speak. And then, remembering how Dalia and I had closed my father's eyes, I go over to her, reach down and gently lower her lids. They feel waxy and cool under my fingertips. I look down at her face. *Good-bye,* I call to her silently, except in my head, my voice is warm and strong. *Good-bye, good-bye, wherever you are.*

Rosa lights a candle and Hannah turns on the CD with the Tibetan monks playing their singing bowls. The three of us stand and look down at her. I feel peaceful and almost happy, as if we've completed some monumental task.

Then Rosa says we should dress my mother's body before she gets stiff, and I choose the dark blue blouse with white anchors that used to be mine and a pair of navy blue pants. Hannah goes to call the hospice while Rosa and I slip the nightgown over my mother's head and, with surprising ease, pull on the blouse and pants. Standing back to look at her, we realize she needs something on her feet and we add a pair of wool socks.

When she is dressed, Rosa wraps a soft black scarf under her chin and over the top of her head to keep her jaw from falling open. It's what they used to do in Chile, she says, when people were laid out at home rather than by undertakers, who wire the jaw closed. It makes my mother look bundled up, as if for the cold, but also gives her the austere, romantic look of an Italian saint. Her face is pale and smooth now, as if death had erased all the laughter and worry lines.

She looks beautiful.

It would have pleased her.

Hannah comes back and says the hospice told her to call the

medical examiner's office. Apparently no one at the hospice was available to come over and sign her death certificate. It's been over four days since she took the morphine, so I'm not worried about that, but I reflexively glance over at her bedside table. The morphine bottle is gone. In fact, all her medications are gone. I feel pierced by loneliness.

Hannah and I sit outside on the front steps waiting for the medical examiner. It's some time after four and the air is hot and heavy, the kind of night that makes your body feel liquid and uncontained, as if nothing separates your skin from the air around it.

Peering up at the smudgy orange-black sky, I think of the night Suzanne came to visit and my vision of a great bird rising from my mother's body. I think that perhaps the bird flew and we missed it. That sometime between when she "surfaced" while Hannah and I were talking to her and our circle last night, my mother left the premises without our noticing. Not with a great beating of wings but quietly, humbly, without fanfare. Leaving her still-breathing body behind as a decoy.

*People die the way they live.*

Big public gestures had never been my mother's style and now that I think about it, I see that the dramatic deathbed scene with the morphine wasn't her at all. Slipping away unnoticed in the midst of an ordinary afternoon was her all over. I kind of laugh, tip an imaginary hat toward the sky. After all those months of discussion, the false starts and failed attempts, my proud, determined mother had died on her terms, grace and dignity intact.

Hannah asks why I'm laughing and I try to explain.

"Yes! I totally felt that," she says. "Like her soul, or whatever you want to call it, was gone when I lay down with her last night."

"I think that's why I went to bed," I say, thinking back. "I was planning to stay with her to the end, but then . . . there was nothing holding me there. It was just . . . over."

Hannah, who's pulled her T-shirt down over her bare knees, rocks back and forth without speaking for a moment. "I told Momma that if she ever stopped eating and drinking, I would stay. Until the end." Her voice cracks as she tugs on her shirt. "I needed to keep that promise."

"You did, Hannah. Even with the morphine. And I'm sure she appreciated it."

I wonder suddenly if I'd let my mother down, not being there at the moment of her death.

"You were her biggest comfort, Zoe," Hannah says softly, as if I'd spoken. "The one she counted on the most. You know that, right?"

We sit there quietly, side by side, listening to the drone of the cicadas and the crickets and, eventually, the bright trill of birds. The sky turns from black to royal blue. Another day begins.

# Feather

*Well I told that undertaker*
*Undertaker, won't you please drive slow?*
*For that lady that you're haulin'*
*I hate to see her go.*

In the end, I'm just too damn tired to stay up for the medical examiner and head back to bed. According to Hannah, he was a tall, soft-spoken African American man, very gentle and sympathetic. He carried a large doctor's bag and finished his work quickly.

My children wake me at nine and immediately I tell them Nana is dead.

"Does that mean she's not in the house no longer?" Lane asks, squirming in close to me, her round face next to mine on the pillow.

"*Any* longer," Clara corrects, flopping across my shoulder.

"No, she's still here," I say. "She's down in her room. It's just that she isn't breathing anymore."

Both of them are quiet for a moment.

"Are we going to keep her?" Lane asks.

I laugh. "For a little while. Long enough for everyone to say good-bye to her, maybe give her something, the way we did when your grandfather died. Remember I told you about that? Each of us found something small to send along with him, like a flower or a note."

"But how do we give her things if she's dead?" Lane asks.

"We just put them next to her on the bed, sweetie."

"Then we bury her?" Clara asks, breathing heavily into my ear.

"Well, not exactly." I'm starting to sweat now. Both of them press heavily against me and the room feels hot and stuffy despite the air conditioner. "There are people called undertakers who are going to come and take Nana with them in a special car. They have a box for her body and all the nice things we give her, and then when we go to Vermont we'll bury it—bury the box—in the cemetery next to your grandfather."

"Wait, how do they get her into a box?" Clara asks.

"It's just something undertakers know how to do," I say, unwilling to go into urns and coffins, ashes and burning bodies. I give her a kiss on the forehead and sit up abruptly so they both tumble back on to the bed. "C'mon, sleepyheads. Let's go say good-bye to Nana."


I slip into my parents' bedroom while my children are getting dressed and call Jack.

"Oh boy," he says, inhaling sharply. "Are you all right?"

"I think so."

"And the kids?"

"Fine. A little confused about some of the details."

"The details were a little confusing."

"It was okay, though . . . in the end."

"That's good." He sighs. "She sure didn't make it easy, did she? On any of us."

"No."

I lie back against the pillows on my parents' bed, close my eyes. Would my mother's death have been any easier if she'd died "naturally"? Is death ever easy? I open my eyes, look around the empty expanse of bed where my parents' warm bodies once lay, now covered by a bluish white sheet.

"Jack?"

"I'm on my way."

At Hannah's suggestion, we form a final circle. My mother's hands lie at her sides, so I simply rest one of my hands on her shoulder while, on the other side of her—up on the bed—Evie leans comfortably against her hip.

There have been many questions about the scarf. Why is it wrapped around her head? Is she cold? Does she still have hair underneath?

"It's a custom," I explain. "Something Rosa taught us."

When the circle ends, they all seem remarkably cheerful and chatty, bickering good-naturedly over the inexpensive stone necklaces that hang on a stand on my mother's bookshelf, each wanting to pick one out to "give" her. Fiona and Clara both write her notes, which they fold into tiny squares and hide under her arm. Evie picks an orange from the ornamental orange bush in the dining room and drops it casually off at the end of the bed.

Pretty soon, the whole thing has taken on the madcap feel of a treasure hunt. None of the children seems the least bit uncomfortable or afraid of my mother's dead body as they rush around finding small items, including rocks and flowers from the garden, to bring in and deposit. Rosa puts a small rosary in my mother's hand and crosses herself, and Hannah tucks a favorite silk scarf into her pocket. I place a copy of her novel on her chest and a pair of my father's wooden drumsticks at her side.

I lay the Grateful Dead T-shirt on top of her feet and then lean over and gently tuck it in around them, liking the incongruous dash of color against all that blue.

Hannah says she'll call Katherine and, while she does, I run up to Katherine's old room. Filled with Fiona's and Evie's belongings, the bed a mess, the room looks small and innocuous, certainly not the shadowy dungeon I remember from the nights I spent on the floor next to Katherine's bed.

I spy a wooden penny whistle propped up on top of her bookshelf, its round holes filled with lint. Wiping it off on my shirt, I hurry back downstairs and lay it in the crook of my mother's arm.

It's almost ten and the undertakers are due any minute. I wander restlessly around the ground floor of the house, still searching for something to give her, something just from me. I go into the living room and stand looking at the paintings, books, instruments, records, masks and photographs that line the walls—the relics of our family history—but nothing feels right.

Crossing the front hall, I enter the Big Room. Again, I survey the room, letting my eyes travel up the huge floor-to-ceiling bookshelf that covers the wall in front of me, its shelves stuffed with old childhood art projects, crayons, paints and board games.

Then I see it, sticking up out of an old marmalade jar among an assortment of abandoned pens and paintbrushes. An enormous brown and white feather with a curling black tip. Reaching up, I grab the jar and pull the feather out, gently run my fingers down its soft sides, releasing a small whirlwind of dust particles into the clear, bright air.

I place the translucent white quill between my thumb and index finger, feel its dry, spiny strength, and then, holding it tightly, walk back to my mother's room and place the feather carefully under her hand.

# After

The day of my mother's memorial service, my friend Suzanne and I drive out to the C & O Canal. It's a perfect day, clear and not too hot, and the dirt towpath next to the canal is breezy and shaded. An occasional bicyclist or jogger passes us, but we mainly have the path to ourselves.

Both of us are still wearing our "funeral clothes," and pretty soon we take our flimsy sandals off and walk barefoot in the dirt. We talk about the memorial, which was held downtown at the Florida Avenue Meeting House, a large, sun-filled building ringed by gardens and a tall iron fence.

It was a Quaker service like my father's and, once again, we'd asked a few people to speak at the beginning. My cousin Anna Curtis read a poem, and Hannah talked about the peaceful way my mother died, losing her composure only once, when thanking my mother's caregivers for their love and hard work. They sat in a group across from us, Kendra with her young son on her lap, Rosa and Sonia in stiff black dresses, all of them dabbing at their eyes.

At one point, the bench I was sitting on lurched and, looking down, I saw Clara, Lane, Fiona, Evie, Katherine's son Peter and her daughter Shannon get to their feet.

"We love Nana and we'll miss her," they blurted in staggered unison before dropping back to the bench looking embarrassed.

I began to cry a little, and Jack squeezed my hand.

Neither Katherine nor I got up. I hate public speaking almost as much as my mother did, and what I had to say felt tucked too deeply inside of me. I hoped someone would bring up the fact that my mother had chosen her death, but mainly people talked about her glamorous style, her writing and scholarly interests. I began to despair that this critical truth was going to go unspoken when my mother's friend Marilyn rose to speak.

"Many of you have mentioned Margaret's physical beauty," she began. "And she *was* beautiful. But she was also strong. And on this occasion I want to salute that strength and in particular the brave choice she made at the end of her life. By her example, she has given us all a tremendous gift. As each of us faces our own death, we'll have the memory and knowledge of how Margaret faced hers. From her, we can draw strength and hope and possibility."

As Marilyn resumed her seat, Hannah and I exchanged glances and nodded. Then she turned to signal her husband, Dan, to start the music.

He played "Hand in Hand" on the banjo, his thick fingers flying across the strings.


Suzanne and I come to a bend in the canal and have to scramble over some large boulders covering the path. Distracted by my tender feet, I don't notice the bird right away. Even when my eye first lights on him, he's so still that I am not sure it is a bird. He looks more like some odd, vertical branch poking up from all the horizontal branches around him.

As we get closer, I see that he's an egret. Losing track of my conversation with Suzanne, I stare across the canal at him. The branch where he sits hangs out over the water, drooping slightly under his weight. Just as we draw even with him, he plunges down from his perch, almost as if he is coming straight at us, then banks to the left and swoops up the river, a powerful blur of white disappearing in the distance.

Suzanne grabs my arm.

"Zoe!"

"I know."

We laugh and hug each other.

"I can't believe it!" Suzanne says, her eyes shining. "She did it! Your mom did it."

Arm in arm, we walk down the middle of the towpath, our long, skinny shadows dancing along ahead of us.

# Acknowledgments

I want to express my enormous gratitude to the many people who shared their stories with me while I was writing this book. From you I learned that there is no "right" way to go through these experiences, only difficult decisions and occasional moments of grace. And to the doctors, nurses, hospice workers and home health aides who help people complete their final journey every day, you are my heroes.

I also want to thank Sarah Barron, Susan English, Hindy Bare, Ros Wyatt, Anne Connor, Diana Gittins, Jane Gunther, Peter Samis and Janice Shapiro (Thing One) for reading my early drafts and giving me their frank and helpful responses. Many more thanks go to my generous, talented Wednesday night writing group for their excellent feedback, and their willingness to hear the same passages read numerous times: Nelle Engoron, Gina DePaulo, Elizabeth Maynard Schaefer and Connie Hanstedt.

I'd also like to warmly acknowledge Betsy Rose and Elizabeth Whitney, and my "cottage sisters" on Manana Way in Point Reyes Station, where all my best writing happens. And to say how deeply grateful I am to Katherine Forrest for her wisdom and insight into the manuscript, and to Judith Barrington and Ruth Gundle for our lively, inspiring discussions at Almàssera Vella, and for the "wind studio" at Soapstone.

A very special thanks goes to Amanda Murray at Simon & Schuster for her kind and intelligent editing; to Sharon Skettini and Flip Brophy at Sterling Lord Literistic, for opening the file; and to David Rosenthal for opening the door.

Last but not least, I want to express my boundless love for my daughters, both of them storytellers in their own right, and for my husband, who talked me down from the ledge of writerly despair more than once, and who steadfastly supported me every long step of the way.

# Imperfect
# Endings

*Reading Group Guide*

# Introduction

Zoe FitzGerald Carter's mother, Margaret, is a beautiful, independent-minded woman who has suffered from Parkinson's and other ailments for over twenty years. Knowing that her future holds only further debilitation and the slow erosion of both her body and her pride, Margaret decides to "end things"—and asks her three daughters to be there with her when she does it.

For months, Margaret discusses possible means of suicide and repeatedly sets and changes her "death dates." Zoe and her sisters begin to wonder if she is serious and, if she is, who among them is willing to take on the emotional and legal risks of being with her at the end? As the "good daughter," Zoe wants to help her mother achieve a good death but is distraught at the prospect of losing her. Revisiting difficult scenes from her past—including memories of her larger-than-life father, her glamorous, stubborn mother, and her warring sisters—Zoe finds herself examining her own desire for approval and control. Eventually there is compromise, love and courage, and her mother ends her life surrounded by family and friends.

Wrenching, provocative and ultimately uplifting, *Imperfect Endings* is the story of a woman finding the courage to die; of a daughter finding the strength to parent her mother; of a family learning to love and to let go.

# Discussion Questions

1. This memoir transitions between the time leading up to Zoe's mother Margaret's death and vignettes of her childhood growing up. Did you like this narrative structure? How did it impact your understanding of the main characters?

2. This book is about life as well as death—the flashbacks give glimpses of the young family, and Margaret's grandchildren are full of energy and excitement. How did this contrast with Margaret's desire to die?

3. The sisters, and their mother, all have different reactions to Jonathan's alcoholism. Discuss their different ways of dealing with his problem. Are any effective?

4. Margaret does not seem to notice significant problems with those around her, such as her husband's affairs and Zoe's anorexia. Yet she is very picky about little things, such as appearances. Do you believe she was innocently naïve and unaware of those larger issues, or was she perhaps willfully blind?

5. Jack, Hannah, Katherine and Zoe express feeling that Margaret is being selfish in her wish to die and have them help her. Is that too much to expect from a loved one? Does she truly

have the right to end her own life, even though it has such an impact on those around her? Is there anything she could have done to make it easier on her family?

6. Throughout her life, Zoe constantly craves others' approval, especially her mother's. She even goes so far as to neglect her own family and marriage to go to her mother whenever she calls. Why does she do this? Why do you think it means so much to her when her mother calls her a friend?

7. Mother/daughter relationships are the backbone of this story. Skim pages 80–84. Talk about each daughter's relationship with her mother, and with the other daughters. Does Zoe really resent being pigeonholed, or do you think she finds comfort in her role in the family?

8. How does Zoe try to protect her own daughters from sibling rivalry? How much impact do you think a parent can have on the relationships among their children? Is there something Margaret could have done to help Katherine feel more included in the family?

9. Reread page 122, where Zoe talks with her friend Suzanne about her mother's desire to die. She attributes her mother's determination to "Fear of the unknown. Fear of losing control." Do you agree? What other reasons does Margaret give for wanting to end her life?

10. Why does Margaret keep pushing back the date of her death? Is she really as determined to die as she seems? At any point do you believe her death wish is "a weird bid for attention," as Jack says (p. 146)?

11. Discuss the different ways characters exert control over one another, both passively and actively.

12. Margaret markedly lacks emotions in her book, *The Sky's the Limit*. Why does she choose to leave out her own feelings, and relate only events and facts? Does this reveal something important about her character?

13. It seems everyone in this memoir hides behind a façade to disguise true feelings. Dress, social status and appearance are all very important. Discuss the ways in which the Drapers hide things from outsiders, each other, and themselves.

14. Were you surprised at the ending? Was there ever a point when you thought Margaret might choose life?

# Enhance Your Book Club

1. Margaret, Zoe and Suzanne talk about Margaret becoming a bird and dropping feathers for them. Have you ever received a sign from a friend or relative who has passed on? If not, would you want to? Do you believe in such things? What do you think the feather and the bird represent? If you could be reincarnated as an animal, what would you be?

2. Margaret is a member of the Hemlock Society. If you have any questions or want to learn more about the beliefs and work of the Society, visit http://www.compassionandchoices .org/hemlock. The "Student Kit" outlines the basics of the Society.

3. Research the cases of right-to-die activist Jack Kevorkian, also known as "Dr. Death," who was imprisoned for eight years for assisting suicide. Do you believe doctors should be able to help patients die? If physician assisted suicide was legal would this have made Margaret's death easier for her and her family?

4. Zoe uses running as a means to relieve stress and feel alive. Is there some physical activity that helps you feel less stressed out? Go for a jog or a hike with your book club and notice if moving your body helps you feel more relaxed and positive.

# Author Q&A

**This is an extremely personal story with intimate details of your relationships and your mother's death. Was it hard to open yourself up through publishing this book? Do you feel at all vulnerable?**

Yes, I do! I was actually a little alarmed when I sold the book. Putting it out there does feel exposing. But my goal when writing it was to be as honest as I could—even when it made me look bad. And whenever I'd talk to people about the book, they would share their own stories and memories and it felt like there was this hunger to have these kinds of discussions.

I try to focus on the universal aspects of my story. While most people's parents don't end their own life, many of us deal with our parents getting older, getting sick and—eventually—dying. By writing about my own experience, "imperfect" as it was, I hoped to provide some perspective and maybe even solace to those facing these difficult end-of-life situations with loved ones. Going through this can feel very isolating.

**Have your sisters read this book? If so, what did they think? What did your husband think?**

It's kind of funny, no one grows up thinking that someone in their family is going to put them in a book some day and, under the circumstances, both my sisters have been remarkably generous. They have both respected my right to tell my story—and include them in the telling. My husband has also been remarkably supportive, not just of the book itself, but of the time and energy it took to write it.

**How has your life changed since your mother's death? Have you been able to regain more stability in your life?**

I am happy to report that the year leading up to my mother's death was a uniquely stressful time in my life. Things have been much simpler and easier since then. My husband and I are doing well, my two daughters are growing into strong, joyful, independent young women, and I am blessed with a number of close and loving friends. In addition to my writing, I find time to sing, go on long bike rides in the Berkeley Hills and spend time on the rugged Northern California beaches with my family. Life is good.

**How is your relationship with your sisters? How has it changed since your mother's death?**

I am still very close to my middle sister, Hannah. We are in constant touch by phone and e-mail and spend part of every summer together. Her children are still very close to mine. But there is no longer the same urgency to "process" everything together the way we did during the last months of my mother's life. My older sister, Katherine, and I are also friendly. I think, by writing the book, I came to better understand her choices at the end of my mother's life, and this has brought us closer.

**Did you ever finish the murder mystery you were working on at one point in your memoir?**

Yes, I did, and I got an agent for it right away—and then it didn't sell. After being turned down by five or six major publishing houses, the book lingered at a smaller press for over a year and a half before being rejected. But I don't regret it. I learned a lot about writing in the process and if it had sold I'm pretty sure I never would have written the memoir. I'd still be writing mysteries.

**Are there any plans to publish either of your mother's books, *The Sky's the Limit* or *The Goslings Visit Grandpa Gander and Nana Goose*?**

No. The children's book is beautiful but it's very specific to our family. I think the novel is publishable but I haven't had the heart to try and get it published—it really doesn't feel like mine. A friend suggested that it would make an excellent screenplay, so we'll see.

**If you had been in your mother's situation, what would you have done?**

Well, it's impossible to know what you would do until you are there. But I like to think that with love and good drugs I could stick it out until death made its way naturally. That said, I would never rule out some form of "hastened death." I would only hope that I could make the burden on my family and friends as light as possible.

**Before your experience with your mother, did you support a person's right to choose death on their own terms? How do you feel now? Do you believe that physician-assisted suicide should be legal?**

I did support the right to "choose" death, but I hadn't thought that deeply about it before my mother started talking about it. And then, because I loved my mother and didn't want her to die, I spent months trying to talk her out of it.

I still believe assisted suicide—especially physician-assisted suicide—should be legal but I don't think we can underestimate the moral and emotional burden involved in participating in someone's death.

That said, I've often wondered if my mother would have stayed alive longer if physician assisted suicide had been legal in Washington, D.C., in 2001. I think if she'd known she could count on a trusted doctor to come to her house, *at a time of her choosing,* and help her die in a quick and compassionate way, she might have relaxed a bit more about it, let nature takes it course.

I also know that if my sister and I hadn't been worrying about the legal risks, we would have been more willing to help her. Having a doctor or hospice nurse there also would have allowed us to focus more on the meaning—instead of the means—of her death.

**Your mother passed away about nine years ago. What have you been up to since that time?**

I've been raising my children, playing music with my band, and—of course—writing. I am currently at work on a novel.

**What advice would you give to someone who is in a similar situation as yourself, caring for a loved one who wishes to die?**

I'm reluctant to give advice. Every situation is unique, so it's dangerous to generalize. I would only suggest that people listen deeply to what their family members are asking for and be honest about what they can and can't do for them.

**What advice would you give to aspiring writers?**

Find a good writing group, make a serious commitment to your writing—and don't give up!

Dear Reader,

Thank you so much for your interest in *Imperfect Endings*. One of the really great things about publishing this book has been the opportunity to meet and talk to so many of you, whether at readings or conferences or while visiting book clubs. I have also been thrilled at how many of you have contacted me through my website http://www.zoefitzgeraldcarter.com. I keep every one of these e-mails and have tried to respond to all of them. My sincerest thanks go out to each and every one of you who wrote.

I'd like to invite any new readers who are interested in sharing their story, giving feedback or discussing any of the issues raised in the book to get in touch with me. I am available to talk to book clubs either by phone or by Skype, and if your book club is in the greater Bay Area, I am happy to come in person.

I can be reached through the "book groups" page of my website or at zfccomm@mac.com.

I look forward to hearing from you!

With love and good wishes,
*Zoe*